ROOTLESS

ROOTLESS

KATE OWENS

NEW DEGREE PRESS

COPYRIGHT © 2019 KATE OWENS

All rights reserved.

ROOTLESS

ISBN   978-1-64137-226-8 *Paperback*

          978-1-64137-227-5 *Ebook*

For my mother, Lisa.

Thank you for opening up the world so I may touch the sky.

CONTENTS

DEAR READER

Dear Reader,

"Who is your target audience?"

That was the very first question I was asked in my very first interview for this book.

A former professor of mine asked a similar question when discussing my book early on:

"Who exactly are you speaking to?"

These questions stumped me.

Today, I'm less stumped, but I've realized there's no single answer that is sufficient.

All I knew when I started is that I wanted to write about supporting people in making long-term behavior changes.

I felt this great urge, this longing, to explore and address the apparent gap in the healthcare field when it came to addressing behavioral shifts. More importantly, I wanted to find a solution and uncover ways to help people make these important lifestyle changes in the long term so they may lead long, healthy, fulfilling lives.

I figured I'd take this chance to explore the world of behavior change in the medical field and see where it leads me—and hopefully others. So whether you are my grandma, someone trying to change a health habit, an idealist millennial like me, or the surgeon general himself, I hope to awaken you to a future in which patients given behavioral recommendations address them in a different manner so there may be hope for improving this nation's health and well-being.

Happy reading,

Kate

INTRODUCTION

———

"Have you ever had a stress test before?" I turned to Tom and asked.

"No," Tom grunted.

Tom was young, much younger than the average patient we typically saw. He was 5′11″ and 47 years old, and he weighed close to 300 pounds.

Skimming his medical records, I saw the typical clinical indications of DM (diabetes mellitus), HLD (hyperlipidemia), CAD (coronary artery disease), PAD (peripheral artery disease), +Smoking, CP (chest pain) and Palps (palpitations).

Tom is not a real person. And his clinical indications I referenced are also not real. This patient data is fictional in accordance with HIPAA.

While the specific patient and his health complications are *not* real, the problem absolutely is. You see, Tom was typical of many patients I saw on a daily basis.

And, perhaps more unfortunately, experts say there are as many as 150 million "Toms" in the United States.

**

As Tom got ready for his test with me, I looked up and saw a shirtless, nervous, overweight man being forced to walk on a treadmill until fully exhausted.

As I began explaining the test, I longed to ask him about his life, his family, to uncover how he got to the state he was in today. Placing the ten electrode stickers on his chest, I so badly wanted to help him find ways to enjoy physical activity and to teach him easy, quick techniques for making healthy meals. With each clip of hooking him up to the EKG, I held myself back from inserting myself into his life and his health.

Perhaps reaching conclusions based merely on my own biases and assumptions, I at least wanted to dig a little deeper and find a way to support his health rather than leaving him to his own devices. Instead, I asked mundane questions about his weekend plans, watched him last only a few minutes walking on the treadmill, and never saw him again.

**

Preventative interventions from medical physicians have undeniably become a necessity for the people of the United States.

While the obesity epidemic has been widely established for over a few decades, it has begun to take over quite drastically in the last few years.

The U.S. Department of Health and Human Services (HHS) now projects that by 2030 (only a mere ten years from now), half of all adults in the United States will be obese.[1]

Half.

This is a marked difference from the 1970s, when only around 13 percent of adults were considered obese.[2]

A study published in JAMA Internal Medicine in 2015 found that there are more obese than overweight people in this country.[3] Some comorbidities (concurring diseases) of obesity are hypertension, elevated blood sugar, type 2 diabetes, cardiovascular disease, elevated total cholesterol, low HDL cholesterol, pulmonary dysfunction (sleep apnea or asthma), psychiatric problems, and gastrointestinal disorders. While the actual physiological mechanism linking an

---

1   "Facts & Statistics". 2019. HHS.Gov. https://www.hhs.gov/fitness/resource-center/facts-and-statistics/index.html.

2   American Psychological Association. Accessed June 16, 2019. https://www.apa.org/pi/families/resources/newsletter/2012/07/childhood-obesity.

3   Yang, Lin, and Graham A. Colditz. 2015. "Prevalence Of Overweight And Obesity In The United States, 2007-2012". JAMA Internal Medicine 175 (8): 1412. doi:10.1001/jamainternmed.2015.2405.

increased fat content to these diseases is still largely unknown, we do know that it is preventable.

Obesity was also the second leading cause of preventable death in the United States following tobacco use—until recently. Research from the Cleveland Clinic and the New York University School of Medicine suggests that obesity has surpassed tobacco as America's leading cause of preventable death and that 47 percent more life-years are lost from obesity than tobacco.[4] We can only imagine how the numbers will continue to rise as the overweight and obese numbers increase.

**

Last summer I worked as an exercise physiologist at Premier Cardiovascular Specialists. It was concurrently the most instructive and most frustrating experience of my life. I learned a great deal. Not only was I taught how to take a patient's past medical history and blood pressure and converse with a physician, I was also trained to read EKG reports and monitor Loop recorders to identify arrhythmias.

Yet with every stress report I made, every Nuclear test I filed, the number of medications I found myself typing out for each individual patient began to weigh me down.

---

4   Cleveland Clinic. "Obesity is top cause of preventable life-years lost, study shows." ScienceDaily. www.sciencedaily.com/releases/2017/04/170422101614.htm (accessed June 12, 2019).

Checking the electronic boxes of "Continue present medical therapy," "Increase physical activity," and "Modify diet" under the physician's recommendations on the stress report tugged at my heart every single time.

The experience very quickly began to burden me. Was this the best we as individuals, as a society, and as a medical profession could do?

It was not that the doctors didn't address these necessary behavior modifications. No, the doctors I worked with were an incredible group of hard-working, kind, and successful cardiologists and surgeons. They'd fit as many patients into their schedule as they could, working well into the evening hours. They made sure to give each patient their full attention. And yet when it came time to talk about changing diet and increasing physical activity to improve the patients' health, it was just a simple conversation of telling them it was something they needed to do.

This is not uncommon.

Most physicians know to advise their patients about making lifestyle changes. Yet I am of the belief that not nearly enough time is spent supporting people in actually making these changes, let alone helping them keep it consistent.

We have failed to create lasting behavior changes in our patients.

And as we continue to fail, so too does the crisis grow.

**

The President's Council on Sports, Fitness & Nutrition has found that only one in every three adults get the recommended physical activity each week, with less than 5 percent participating in thirty minutes every day[5], and that a whopping 28 percent of Americans are considered physically inactive.[6] Physical inactivity is currently defined as "not engag[ing] in physical activity or exercise during the previous 30 days other than for their regular job" by the Behavioral Risk Factor Surveillance System.[7]

Say, for example, someone is a truck driver. Aside from walking to and from the bathroom and the truck in between drives, this person is not moving.

Let us consider the even more common scenario of someone who holds an office job: often the mere walks between the commute and around the home and office are all the moving they engage in.

Similarly, the landscape of our nation's food culture has shifted dramatically. Coupled with this decline in physical activity, America's relationship with food has shifted to increased consumption of quick and convenient processed foods as well as increased portion sizes.

---

5   "Facts & Statistics". 2019. HHS.Gov. https://www.hhs.gov/fitness/resource-center/facts-and-statistics/index.html.

6   "Physical Inactivity In The United States". 2019. The State Of Obesity. https://www.stateofobesity.org/physical-inactivity/.

7   2019. Cdc.Gov. https://www.cdc.gov/physicalactivity/downloads/pa_state_indicator_report_2014.pdf.

North Ohio Heart, a leading cardiac and primary care medical group in Ohio, posted numerous fast-food statistics on its "Partners for Your Health" website, two of which say Americans spend $200 billion on fast food annually and 24 percent of adults eat three or more fast-food meals per week.[8]

An article on the National Institute of Health's National Heart, Lung, and Blood Institute's page compared the drastic change in portion sizes from even the early 1990s to now.

One graphic depicts:

- a bagel's diameter growing from 3 to 6 inches,
- a typical cheeseburger from 4.5 to 8 ounces,
- a medium bag of popcorn from 5 to 11 cups, and
- a glass of soda from 8 to 20 ounces.

After laying out a sample meal with today's portion sizes, the article pointed out, "In one day, you would consume 1,595 more calories than if you had the same foods at typical portions served 20 years ago."[9]

This small depiction of the rise of the fast-food industry and the hidden increase in portion sizes are certainly significant contributors to this epidemic, ones often seamlessly and involuntarily woven into our society.

---

8   University Hospitals/North Ohio Heart/Ohio Medical Group. "Fast Food Statistics Infographic." North Ohio Heart. Accessed June 16, 2019. https://www.partnersforyourhealth.com/fast-food-statistics#slide0.

9   "Portion Sizes And Obesity, News & Events, NHLBI, NIH". 2013. National Heart, Lung, And Blood Institue. https://www.nhlbi.nih.gov/health/educational/wecan/news-events/matte1.htm.

In addition to the adverse physical effects, there is also a large medical cost associated with our nation's health crisis. Ultimately, the consequences are not just limited to an individual or family. There exist many economical and societal repercussions as well. The CDC reported that the estimated annual medical cost from obesity-related illnesses in 2008 was $147 billion and in just four years had increased by over $40 billion to $190.2 billion in 2012.[10] Conversely, in attempts to battle overweight on their own, Americans spend over $20 billion annually on weight loss efforts, such as pills, programs, books and surgeries.[11] Obesity has even been found to cost employers as much as $8.65 billion a year due to employee obesity-related absenteeism.[12]

I could continue to throw out statistics, as sadly, there are many to choose from, but all seemingly point to the same conclusion. A conclusion that most know: Americans are increasingly overweight, and it is largely (but not completely) owed to poor diet and lack of physical activity.

10 "Adult Obesity Facts | Overweight & Obesity | CDC". 2018. Cdc.Gov. https://www.cdc.gov/obesity/data/adult.html

11 Writers, Staff. 2019. "Why Are Americans Obese? | Publichealth.Org". Publichealth.Org. https://www.publichealth.org/public-awareness/obesity/.

12 Andreyeva, Tatiana, Joerg Luedicke, and Y. Claire Wang. 2014. "State-Level Estimates Of Obesity-Attributable Costs Of Absenteeism". Journal Of Occupational And Environmental Medicine 56 (11): 1120-1127. doi:10.1097/jom.0000000000000298.

To sum it up nicely, the CDC states that obesity is "common, serious, and costly."[13]

**

What prevents the medical profession from taking a more hands-on approach to health behavior change?

Kimberly Yarnall, M.D., and a group of researchers at Duke University Medical Center in Durham, North Carolina, sought to determine the amount of time a physician would need to spend addressing preventative services at routine primary care visits. They looked at the average time needed for a variety of preventative services in health care to determine the total time required to address all recommendations from the U.S. Preventive Services Task Force (USPSTF).

For example, using blood pressure as a screening tool took 0.25 minutes, whereas counseling for limiting fat and cholesterol in a patient's diet took 8.2 minutes. Yarnall and colleagues concluded that a total of 7.4 hours per working day per physician (1,773 hours annually) is needed for total adherence to USPSTF's preventive service recommendations.[14]

---

13 "Adult Obesity Facts | Overweight & Obesity | CDC". 2018. Cdc.Gov. https://www.cdc.gov/obesity/data/adult.html

14 Yarnall, Kimberly S. H., Kathryn I. Pollak, Truls Østbye, Katrina M. Krause, and J. Lloyd Michener. 2003. "Primary Care: Is There

This research suggests that within the current system—especially based on guidelines set for insurance reimbursements, patient turnover times, and the number of hours our doctors have available to them—time is the limiting factor.

Frankly, it is no wonder doctors tend to limit the discussion on preventative health care mechanisms.

There just isn't time.

Similar studies have also looked at why delivery of preventative services is low. The most common constraints are:

- lack of time during the office visit,
- inadequate insurance reimbursement,
- patient refusal to discuss or comply with recommendations, and
- lack of physician expertise in counseling techniques.[15]

In my dozens and dozens of conversations with medical professionals—nearly all of whom are incredibly conflicted about this tension—it's a clear reality that this is a problem for our society.

Thanks to the many contributions and efforts of physicians, public health and government officials, and health advocacies who have raised awareness about the magnitude of this problem (for example, Michelle Obama's valiant effort to address childhood obesity with the Let's Move

Enough Time For Prevention?". American Journal Of Public Health 93 (4): 635-641. doi:10.2105/ajph.93.4.635.

15 Kottke, Thomas E., Milo L. Brekke, and Leif I. Solberg. 1993. "Making "Time" For Preventive Services". Mayo Clinic Proceedings 68 (8): 785-791. doi:10.1016/s0025-6196(12)60638-7.

movement), a wide array of citizens have learned the negative effects obesity and physical inactivity can have on an individual's health. Understanding that the largest portion of preventable and premature deaths stem from obesity-related conditions such as heart disease, stroke, type 2 diabetes, and some cancers,[16] and knowing that people who are physically active generally live longer and have a lower risk for all of those diseases[17] is now information that has thankfully become more understood. The disconnect, however, lies after the delivery.

We have indeed come a long way in terms of awareness, but now is the time to take that next step to maintain this gained knowledge as well as fully immerse our country and saturate our society with tangible actions for health improvement. We must now not only "talk the talk," as they say, but also take much-needed action. I believe the current medical system needs to address the large gap of overweight and obese patients frequently left to their own devices in improving their diets and increasing physical activity and to provide them with proper help to make these necessary changes.

**

---

16 "Adult Obesity Facts | Overweight & Obesity | CDC". 2018. Cdc.Gov. https://www.cdc.gov/obesity/data/adult.html.

17 Centers for Disease Control and Prevention. State Indicator Report on Physical Activity, 2014. Atlanta, GA: U.S. Department of Health and Human Services, 2014.

My hope in writing this book is to shed light on a gap many have observed in our medical system:

A systematic approach to deliver efficient, successful interventions for preventative, chronic diseases resulting from overweight and obesity.

It's a crisis that can be solved, but not by doing what we've always done. How could we use principles of behavior change to combat the obesity epidemic. Said simply:

Applying the emerging science of behavior change to create a holistic intervention program

for overweight and obese patients and individuals looking to change health habits.

Throughout this book, I aim to offer a unique look at what we know and what we don't through the lens of this statement.

The book is broken up into four parts to further explore these themes and determine what exactly is required for successful preventative interventions. To simplify the approach, I've organized it into a simple-to-remember acronym: ROOT.

ROOT consists of:

Reflection

One thing at a time

Others

Tailoring

The phrase "rootless" represents the quick-fix nature of existing solutions that seek to assist people with increasing physical activity and changing diet. While techniques like fad diets and fitness trend followings can be helpful for some, the majority of Americans fade out on their personal health efforts just as quickly as their fascination with gluten-free foods and SoulCycle.

Or take medical offices, for example: there are just not enough resources for anything beyond than acknowledgment of the health issue, unless you are wealthy and can afford to see a dietician and counselor.

I call this rootless because our current model for addressing the paramount need for healthier lifestyles is lacking. The continuously rising number of people in the United States who are overweight and obese necessitates a systemic call for a more deep-rooted and widespread approach. The toxic and cyclical nature of band-aid fixes will eventually permeate our culture, building upon itself for generations, overtime compounding until we have gone too far to be saved.

But I also think within our problem we can find an answer.

During my research and interviews, I repeatedly uncovered similar themes, common mantras in the realm of behavior change. I have found there are four key components to an effective intervention for managing health habits throughout the course of a lifetime. We do, in fact, have ways we can reverse this rootless attitude and in turn establish roots that can nourish our country for decades.

Through stories and research, this book explores how and why these are critical factors when supporting someone in making a health behavior change. All these themes featured in every interview I conducted, often with all four concepts in one interview. For this reason, you will see a lot of overlap among the stories and the different experts. I have separated the parts I felt were the strongest depictions of each theme.

Reflection — In Part 1, I explore how the act of guided reflection can assist someone when making a lifestyle change. Reflection calls for working one-on-one with a patient to understand how their past experiences and environment have prevented attainment of certain behaviors. Uncovering what exactly is acting as a barrier in their life allows them to overcome the hurdle.

One thing at a time — Part 2 demonstrates the importance of taking things one at a time. Breaking up tasks into smaller chunks allows the change to feel more manageable. Slowly introducing shifts in behavior makes the process of changing health habits less overwhelming and is more likely to lead to long-term success.

Others — Part 3 touches on the incredible power of the presence of others, and how peer and community support can go such a long way.

Tailoring — Part 4's focus lies in tailoring treatment and the intervention to the individual, as each person works well under different approaches.

**

I believe the word "root" can also serve as multiple reminders for health professionals when working with patients to enable change:

1. To always explore the roots of the patient's past.
2. To provide constant motivation and support, consistently rooting for them to tackle these health changes.
3. To remember the roots of our ancestors and how they solely grew their own food, free of processed goods, only eating vegetables and fruits and nourishment that stems from the ground that is Mother Nature.
4. To maintain an attitude of mindfulness, both for the health promotion specialist and the patient, to always root yourself in the present moment and ground yourself to what is in front of you.

All of these should guide the treatment of establishing and rooting new patterns into their lives for the long term. These are further ideas I explore throughout the book.

I believe our bodies hold power that most of us have long forgotten. I believe we and nature in its simplest form have the answers we all seek, especially in finding (or re-finding) the path to health. It is with this in mind that I set out to discover ways to guide people that establish ROOTs for the long term in hopes of shedding light on a direction forward.

Here we go.

FOUNDATIONS OF BEHAVIOR CHANGE

———

At the ROOT of this book is a simple premise applied to a well-understood problem:

Applying the Emerging Science of Behavior Change

To Create a Holistic Intervention Program

For Overweight and Obese Patients and Individuals Looking to Change Health Habits

It's a simple idea—but also, of course, remarkably complex.

Before we go much further, we should understand more about overweight obesity as well as the emerging science of behavior change.

**

Much of my own discovery about the field of medical behavior change was that it's not as direct or organized as I'd hoped.

So, to find an effective and potentially feasible solution, I turned to many leading experts in this field by conducting personal interviews, reading academic teachings, and examining research into some of the emerging studies from PubMed, the leading research database run by the U.S. National Library and Medicine.

Throughout my research journey, I had the chance to learn from doctors and psychiatrists from the Henry Ford Health System and the University of Michigan Medical Center, academic and research professors, public health officials, nurses, and many authors to attempt to tackle this problem.

My personal passions further fueled this work—seemingly as long as I can remember, I have been passionate about eating healthy and exercising. Incredibly luckily, growing up I had a father, a former collegiate athlete, who encouraged joining sports teams, and a mother keen on teaching me and my sisters the lessons of balanced meals and a sound diet she learned from nutrition classes she took at the local hospital. From the time I was in kindergarten, I played on basketball and soccer teams, took dance and gymnastic lessons, and watched my mom weigh meat portions on a scale and frequent the local farmer's market. I will forever be grateful for my upbringing, for its effects have been incredibly and positively impactful.

Somewhere along the way, my childhood influences began to take on a life of their own.

Having found my niche in running competitively at the mere age of eleven, I began traveling the country to race in AAU (Amateur Athletic Union) national meets. On road trips, I refused to eat fast food like the rest of my family, firmly declaring it would destroy my body. Experiencing the wonders of physical activity and the benefits of healthy meals at such a young age greatly molded me for the future. Running outside became one of my greatest passions. There is something about the way my feet hit the pavement, the wood chips, the rocks, the grass, that grounded me. The way my body felt, for lack of a better word, *cleaner* when eating a snack of almonds and apples or fully satisfied for hours after eating a single piece of homemade bread and nut butter. Gliding through the very breath of Mother Nature is a wonderful experience I longed to share with others.

Running took me on some amazing journeys, gave me some of my best friends, and quite honestly opened the door to a beautiful world full of possibilities, including attending the amazing university that is the University of Michigan in Ann Arbor as a member of the women's track and field and cross-country team. Eating meals like a "football player," my aunts claimed at family parties, having plates piled high with fruits and vegetables and whole grains, is what supported me in getting there. But I quickly realized not everyone had the same opportunities as me.

Thus I became passionate about sharing this happy, fulfilling world with others.

I went so far as to become a movement science major from the School of Kinesiology and minoring in public health. Learning the science invigorated me and instilled in me a passion unmatched by any other. I was finally learning theories and putting names to concepts on how and why proper nutrition and exercise are so important to the functioning of the human body.

It seemed, however, that the more I learned, the more complicated this goal of helping people live healthier lives became. Chronic diseases, lack of resources, lack of knowledge, limited access to good food or a safe environment for activity, obesity, neonatal exposures, genetic predispositions, physician overworking, lack of motivation—every class I took brought to light a new complication, making the goal of wellness for all feel almost impossible to achieve.

Yet I have since realized it is only through acknowledgment of these barriers that true solutions can be found.

Understanding Obesity

The problem of obesity is often boiled down to overeating and under-exercising.

A common model used to explain the regulation of body weight for years is the Energy Balance Equation. Based on the first law of thermodynamics, this conceptualized approach to weight loss says intake must equal expenditure to maintain a stable weight. That is, total daily food calories must not exceed the daily caloric expenditure or else the excess calories will accumulate in adipose tissue as fat. On the flip side, if energy expenditure exceeds the amount of intake from food, body weight will decrease.

From this model, there are three ways to re-balance the scale and have weight loss. One is reducing caloric intake below the daily energy requirements. Two, maintain daily caloric intake and increase daily energy requirements. And three, decrease daily caloric intake and increase daily energy expenditure. While scientifically correct, this model from the 1970s is an incredible oversimplification. For energy input, the composition of the food—protein, lipid, or carbohydrate—must also be considered. Is the hundred-calorie snack a large apple or a candy bar? A calorie is not exactly just a calorie.

Similarly, on the energy output side, the type of energy expenditure matters. Your daily expenditure consists of not just your resting metabolic rate, but also physical activity and the thermic effect of food (the amount of energy required to breakdown food, typically 10 percent of TDEE). Not to mention, there's no consideration of hunger, satiety, anxiety, depression, boredom, or mindlessness: all important physiological factors that affect those scales. Additionally, there are so many situational and environmental factors also at play here, such as residency, occupation, family dynamics. Simply put, weight regulation is not as easy as in = out; it takes more than just dietary discipline and physical activity. Herein lies the challenge.

Because of the complex nature of a human being, it is crucial to take into consideration how much of overweight and obesity is driven by physiological mechanisms and how much is behaviorally driven. Human eating behavior relies on both external (environmental) and internal (physiological) cues.

For example, when I was a child, a common cry would be, "Mooom, I'm hungry. Can I have something to eat?" Upon my begging, she would first inquire if I was bored. If after following her suggestion of reading a book or going to play outside I still asked for a snack, she would then ask if I wanted something to drink, whether it be water or juice. Only after encouraging both an activity and a glass of fluid or upon answering no to both questions would she give me a snack, most often an apple and peanut butter or some crackers and cheese. While this may sound excessive, I firmly believe (and appreciate) this lesson in developing a sense of my own internal and external hunger cues. By slowing me down from immediately eating the second I decided I was hungry, my mom taught me the incredibly important lesson at a young age of listening to my body.

Even today, at twenty-one years old, I find myself checking in with my body before gorging myself on a big snack with my roommates or ordering out at a restaurant to determine what exactly my stomach is in the mood for. Disclaimer: my mom wasn't a complete stickler for sole consumption of whole foods. She also highly encouraged treats and was known for taking me and my sisters to the cider mill for donuts every Friday after school during the fall or out to get ice cream in the summer (another reason I think her approach was successful, for she never restricted but simply guided, but more on this later).

A fuller understanding of human eating behavior offers the chance to make better choices, specifically when it comes to the quantity, frequency, and type of food intake. In a world stacked against us—large portion sizes, fast-food restaurants, and both sugary foods and beverages everywhere—minimizing the subconscious control of hunger cues makes the task of eating healthy a little less challenging.

Luckily, I had someone to teach me. I will forever be grateful to have been raised by two parents who encouraged me and my sisters to engage in physical activity and join team sports and who alerted us to the importance of properly fueling our bodies with healthy foods. Yet, oftentimes, certain areas, particularly those of lower socioeconomic status, lack nutritional education, finances, or resources. Having a method or system in place to address some of these barriers, then, is necessary if we hope to address our nation's rising obesity and physical inactivity epidemic.

When it comes to weight loss, exercise alone is not sufficient. A common misconception is that all you need to do is increase physical activity and you'll be well on your way to shedding those pounds. While exercise is important for weight maintenance (as well as for numerous health benefits!), it often leads to excess eating. People often end up staying the same weight or perhaps even gaining some pounds, which can breed frustration and confusion when attempting to shift a lifestyle. At the end of the day, as simple as we want to make losing weight and eating well, it is a sufficiently complex process that requires acknowledgement from multiple disciplines.

Another common scenario is when people lose a lot of weight and then gain most of it back in the months and years immediately following. This roadblock can be understood through the set point theory. This theory proposes that regardless of weight (thin or heavy), each person has a well-regulated internal control mechanism (in the hypothalamus) that closely maintains a preset level of body weight and fat. The struggle arises when, upon a person decreasing their body fat below the pre established set point, internal adjustments resist the change and attempt to conserve or replace the body fat that became out of balance.

In an interview with the docuseries *Explained* on Netflix, Marion Nestle, Ph.D., M.P.H., a Paulette Goddard professor of Nutrition, Food Studies, and Public Health at New York University and author, commented on this theory. "Human physiology is set up to make sure that we maintain our weight," she described, "and physiology doesn't like being fought."[18]

---

18 Klein, Ezra, and Joe Posner. 2018. *Explained*. Netflix. Vox.

It is important to appreciate that there is not a predetermined set point at birth, but that your body largely establishes one once it has obtained an average mass throughout your life that is registered by the hypothalamus as normal, regardless of whether it's too heavy.

At the end of the day, as daunting and complex a process as losing weight and eating well seems, consideration of these intertwined bodily and mental processes is all it needs. Acknowledgement from multiple disciplines can contribute to a successful approach. Succinctly put, Nestle concluded in her interview, "Dietary advice is really simple: You eat fruits and vegetables, you don't eat too much junk food, and you balance caloric intake with the kind of activity level that you have. You try to eat unprocessed foods to the extent that you can."

"It really isn't any more complicated than that."[19]

It is here that we must create a solution—by discovering a way to support patients in finding that "easy" balance between the complications and difficulties that constitute their lives.

The Evolving Science of Behavior Change

This begs the question: what is already known in the realm of behavior change?

Despite the difficulty of measuring behavior change, researchers have conducted different meta-analyses on

---

19   Ibid.

programs and techniques to examine change techniques. One article published in the *Public Health Journal* written by Kelly and Barker from 2016 titled "Why is changing health-related behaviour so difficult?" looked at the six common errors found in medicine and policymaking when it comes to the discussion of behavior changes. They discuss the reasons why current efforts have not been successful in alcohol-, dietary-, and physical inactivity-related disease prevention models and suggest a possible replacement for ways of advancement in this field.

The first assumption is that the change is just common sense. This stems from the perspective that human behavior is so obvious it requires little to no explanation. Many professionals feel it is obvious what needs to be done, so they proceed in the most straightforward way possible. However, "Change is difficult and requires sustained motivation and support," Kelly and Barker explained.[20] Human behavior is not simple. Conscious choices result from years of habits, responses to their environment, and complex social cultures. This must be kept in mind as we approach ways to assist patients or write legislature. The authors suggested the use of current psychological, sociological, and anthropological research to save effort and money.

---

20 Kelly, Michael P., and Mary Barker. "Why Is Changing Health-related Behaviour so Difficult?" Public Health 136 (2016): 109-16. doi:10.1016/j.puhe.2016.03.030.

The second error is the belief that the point is solely to get the message across. Kelly and Barker used the analogy of commercial advertisements on television. While these commercials raise awareness to a product and act as a quick influencer, these efforts are not enough to enact long-term change. The repeated messages may serve as a continual reminder to consistently buy the product but do little to ensure the viewer actually goes out and buys the product.

The third misconception made by policymakers and medical professionals when it comes to supporting patients with health behavior changes is that knowledge and information are the primary drivers of behavior. When practitioners provide information or when school districts spend large sums of money on a nutrition education program, they follow the model of acute conditions in which expertise accounts for a large portion of adherence. Conversely, however, behavior change is almost always in response to chronic conditions. It has been found that changing behavior from information alone rarely occurs, especially when the information is already widely known. In most cases, we have reached a point at which a large majority of people understand that eating fruits and vegetables and engaging in physical activity is important for health.

A fourth error commonly made is the belief that people act rationally. Rather than intangible future-based benefits like good health or productivity, the main driving force behind human behavior is maximizing pleasure, gain, and comfort, in combination with minimizing the costs, pain, and losses. It is important to keep in mind that knowledge and rational thought alone do not influence actions. Rather, future programs need to acknowledge the emotions, feelings, and environment of the people to find ways to connect on an individual basis. Changes in smoking, eating, and alcohol consumption are largely embedded in a patient's social makeup. Because of this close tie to identity, it is ultimately not information and reasoning that will enact change. Kelly and Barker further raised the idea that in actuality "unconscious food choices and mindless eating involve little rational thought" 3. Misunderstandings like these stand in the way of true solutions for struggling patients.

The idea that people act irrationally is the fifth error found in health promotion efforts. "It is extremely arrogant to assume that people consume alcohol or cake because they are stupid or irrational," the authors stated matter of factly. Instead, the behaviors that persist across differing lives are functional. Everyone has their own reasons for doing things. And, quite often, these learned behaviors, whether healthy or not, in whatever capacity, are those that have served a beneficial purpose.

The final complication is that it is not possible to accurately predict how individuals will act. There exists a great deal of variance across people. So while population-level outcomes of health inequalities and behaviors can be observed, these models are difficult to apply on a smaller scale.

After evaluating the common problematic assumptions that accompany attempts to change health behaviors, Kelly and Barker surmised that "the way forward" lies in reasoning backward with behaviors. If interventions can target common antecedents for why someone acts the way they do, there would be a better chance of getting them to actually shift their harmful behavior. For example, Kelly and Barker presented the many scenarios in which someone could be consuming alcohol. Whether it is on a cruise, in a bar, or at a dinner party, the time, place, and people present will differ. All circumstances offer different expressions of where the health behavior occurred and therefore had different preceding conditions. Guidance for the intervention must then stem from elements in the meanings and competencies of the action so as to determine where the links are disconnected to find where and when they become problematic.

When it comes to the creation of a health promotion program, the model must base itself on understanding the complexities of the existing behavior and allow room to acknowledge the individual. Successful programs will thus not derive their efforts from overarching universal theories but instead hone in on the unique pieces that make up each person.

"All this is to say that predicting behaviour and supporting behaviour change is neither obvious nor common sense," Kelly and Barker concluded. "It requires careful, thoughtful work that leads to a deep understanding of the nature of what motivates people and the pressures that act upon them."

Another review study published by the *American Journal of Lifestyle Medicine* by Middleton, Anton, and Perri in 2013 looked at the current difficulties of long-term adherence and maintenance of health behavior changes. After exploring the reasons why, the authors offered different strategies and solutions for providers to combat this struggle.

The primary findings show that the success of health promotion and lifestyle change interventions is dependent on participant adherence. This makes logical sense: for a program to be truly effective, there needs to be full engagement. Poor adherence is sadly widespread across all realms of medicinal prescriptions. Currently, the high rate of chronic diseases does not necessarily result from lack of education and knowledge. Rather, the problem lies in getting people to take the given knowledge and apply it into their life. The issue is with *action.*

Following this reasoning, Middleton and colleagues looked directly at adherence as the basis of their research. Using the social cognitive theory as a framework, they took into account how a person's emotional, social, and physical environment influence behavior. Health behavior changes rely on health knowledge, self-efficacy, self-regulation, and barriers to change. Thus, interventions should target all four of these constructs.

They determined six ways to sustain these factors to enable the best circumstance for change. The first is extended care, because long-term contact allows for the continual reminder of the health behavior that needs changing. Whether this occurs through individual meetings, peer support groups, or via the phone or internet, repeated exposure to the message reminds patients of the change. The second necessity is skills training: providing people with relapse-prevention and problem-solving skills allows them the repeated chance to get things right when the changes get tough. The researchers' third found way to sustain change is through social support—whether from peers or with family members or friends post training, the role of social support is critical in this process. The fourth is tailoring the treatment to the individual; something as simple as acknowledging the patient's hectic schedule can change the direction of the treatment. The final two components consist of self-monitoring records—for example, a food log—and multicomponent strategies that take combinations of the five previously mentioned tactics.[21]

According to their website, the U.S. Preventive Services Task Force is an "independent, volunteer panel of national experts in disease prevention and evidence-based medicine." It aims to improve all of America's health by presenting

---

21 Middleton, Kathryn R., Stephen D. Anton, and Michal G. Perri. "Long-Term Adherence to Health Behavior Change." American Journal of Lifestyle Medicine 7, no. 6 (2013): 395-404. doi:10.1177/1559827613488867.

evidence-based recommendations about clinical preventive services by reviewing numerous scientific studies, meta-analyses, and systematic reviews. In 2014, it published its systematic evidence review on behavioral counseling for promoting healthy lifestyles in people with cardiovascular risk factors. After initially reviewing over 7,000 abstracts and 553 articles, it narrowed down to seventy-one trials that provided the exact subject pool, criterion measures, and data that it was looking for. Its conclusion is as follows:

Medium – and high-intensity diet and physical activity behavioral counseling in overweight or obese persons with CVD risk factors resulted in consistent improvements across a variety of important cardiovascular intermediate health outcomes up to 2 years. High-intensity combined lifestyle counseling reduced diabetes incidence in the longer term. The applicability of these findings depends largely on the availability of intensive counseling in practice and real-world fidelity and adherence to these interventions.[22]

In summary, the presence of diet and physical activity behavioral counseling in populations that need it led to cardiovascular health improvements and reduced diabetes.

---

22 Final Recommendation Statement: Weight Loss to Prevent Obesity-Related Morbidity and Mortality in Adults: Behavioral Interventions. U.S. Preventive Services Task Force. September 2018. https://www.uspreventiveservicestaskforce.org/Page/Document/RecommendationStatementFinal/obesity-in-adults-interventions1

These positive results are largely dependent on the presence of counseling and intervention adherence.

Additionally, the USPSTF published a review in September 2018 looking at the effectiveness of behavioral and pharmacotherapeutic weight-loss interventions in preventing obesity-related morbidity and mortality in adults. In both reviews, the counseling and interventions were primarily group- or individual-based, while some were technological or in print. The interventions were, however, vastly variable across the mode of delivery, the number of sessions, and the interventionist. This review also concluded that behavior-based weight-loss interventions with or without the presence of medications resulted in more weight loss than usual care conditions. These interventions also demonstrated a decreased rate of developing diabetes, especially with those who had prediabetes.

While both studies state further research must be done, specifically with different population subgroups (older adults, people of color, etc.), this research shows that health promotion programs for behavior change are effective. So why are more of them not implemented?

Another study conducted in London in 2018 (I know, I know, *another* study) recruited general practitioners, nurses, health care assistants, and practice managers as participants for a research study that sought to explain why there were so few health behavior change interventions being implemented in the primary care setting. While the study found the general consensus of health care professionals to be the belief that health behavior change programs for CVD risk reduction were important, the researchers were skeptical about the successful implementation for three primary reasons:

- Difficulty of sustained behavior change for the patients,
- Lack of evidence for effective interventions, and
- Limited access to appropriate resources for PCP (mainly time).

Alageel and his colleagues discovered that discussing the change of health behaviors was overwhelming for the patients and that there was very limited time to fully complete the program. The researchers thus concluded, "Advancing the prevention agenda will require strategies to support the delivery of behavior change interventions in primary care and greater emphasis needs to be given to promoting behavior change through supportive environmental context".[23]

**

Let's return to the fundamental aim of this book:
Applying the Emerging Science of Behavior Change
To Create a Holistic Intervention Program

---

23 Alageel, Samah, Martin C. Gulliford, Lisa Mcdermott, and Alison J. Wright. "Implementing Multiple Health Behaviour Change Interventions for Cardiovascular Risk Reduction in Primary Care: A Qualitative Study." BMC Family Practice 19, no. 1 (2018). doi:10.1186/s12875-018-0860-0.

For Overweight and Obese Patients and Individuals Looking to Change Health Habits

As I have said—and will continue to say—it's a simple idea, but it's of course remarkably complex.

Just how would we apply these principles to craft an effective program for individuals needing support?

That's what lies ahead in this book.

PART 1

Reflection

O

O

T

Life can only be understood backwards, but it must be lived forwards.

—SOREN KIERKEGAARD, DANISH PHILOSOPHER

In Part 1, I explore how reflection has successfully worked for those making a health behavior change and how the research that supports it is in fact beneficial for long-term engagement of activities.

Let's begin.

10/16/2018

Running was, is, and always will be my first love. It has given me so much, yet now I feel my body resisting. As much as I cherish the act of gliding through the air, the very breath of Mother Nature, it seems my feet are tired. It is confusing, trying to balance both taking care of my body through physical activity and rest. All I've ever known is an intensity that has taken me very far but has also left pieces of me shattered. I always want to consider myself and to be a runner, but I feel if there is any hope for our future relationship, I must set it aside for now and uncover new ways to move, for only if I do this will I be able to continue having it in my daily life. It's difficult but crucial I acknowledge my resistance to letting go in the ties running has to my identity. My ego must be silenced in order to fully honor the voice of my legs, my feet, my arms, the vehicle that is my body, for my mind, body, and spirit are more connected than I once thought. It's time to take care of them in different ways to sustain them all.

This was a journal entry I wrote after deciding to medically retire from the top-ranked University of Michigan women's cross-country and track and field team. It was an incredibly difficult decision, yet following four stress fractures and a foot surgery in two years, an almost obvious one to make. After months of agonizing over the pros and cons of continuing to run collegiately or not, I was ultimately left with a returned uniform and my senior year wide open in front of me.

At first, I felt free. I saw the time 4:27 p.m. on the clock for the first time since fifth grade (my practices were always, always, for eleven years between the hours of 3 and 5 p.m.). I could stay up late, because I no longer concerned myself with getting the proper amount of sleep in order to train well. No more alarms going off at 6:30 a.m. for morning lift. I even had the chance to say yes to getting coffee with a new friend. All these things were quite exhilarating!

Yet, sometime during the first few weeks, I began to struggle. Something that constituted a huge, defining part of my life for over a decade had come to an end. I felt lost. Finding new friends, no longer having the free breakfast and dinner that was provided to athletes every day, figuring out new ways to spend my time—these were all giving me trouble.

The most difficult thing, though? Ironically, it proved to be finding time to work out.

It was incredibly frustrating, if not mind-boggling. *I love working out,* I thought. *Running 50+ miles a week on top of strength training is my norm. I now have twenty extra hours in my week. How in the world can I be struggling to maintain fitness?*

As the semester went on, frustration gave way to despondence. Gone were the days of structured physical activity and in their place were ones of wandering, of hoping yet failing to make it to the gym. Another day of wishful thinking with plans to run gone.

It may be difficult to predict or understand how someone who competed athletically at a high level could also have problems with remaining active. You may scoff and say it's not the same, that I had it much easier, that it wasn't a true struggle, etc. And you're probably right. I am most definitely lucky that my default is and was running and exercising and eating well(ish). Did that give me an advantage when I began to stumble? Of course. But was it still a difficult and arduous process? Yes, it really was.

It was similarly hard in the sense that I too had to change a habit so ingrained into my daily life that had become too detrimental to continue. When running more than my body could physically handle started to affect my health, just in the way that not moving enough or eating poorly has negative consequences, I was forced to make an emotionally draining decision and set out on the arduous journey of change. And I too had to uncover ways to adjust to my new normal.

And then just as quickly as I struggled, things started to change. Slowly, I began to rebuild a routine and rediscover my passion for exercise. While a difficult adjustment, I believe I found success for a few reasons.

First and foremost, I took the time to think deeply about my past experiences with running. Even though diving into your past can be scary and quite honestly painful, it can also serve as a wonderful tool to help you move forward. This reflection can take many forms: whether through talking with a trained specialist, listening to others share similar stories, or working through it on your own, self-introspection is incredibly powerful. Personally, I found refuge in journaling.

Forever has writing been a huge part of my life. It is only as of late, however, that I realize to what extent it has helped me. Having kept a journal since I was around seven years old and been an avid reader my whole life, I am as familiar with the act of writing as I would be comforted by an old friend. The written language—the physical act of my hand gliding across a page—has allowed me to capture wisps of thoughts, mere figments of ideas floating in my mind, and make them tangible. This palpability allows for a transition from subconscious worries to an awareness that radiates inner peace, a rebalance of sorts that leaves me with a clearer mind and deeper understanding as to why I do what I do and think what I think.

I believe any sort of introspection allows you to unbury deeper roots that can be incredibly helpful when you are asked to make a change in your life. A nuanced understanding of yourself and the situation at hand, uncovering how you got to be in a particular position, gives way to a smoother transition of whatever it is you are trying to change. Admitting to myself that part of the reason I was having difficulty working out on my own had to do with my frustration at no longer being a Division I athlete allowed me to begin to move on toward a different approach.

It can also serve as a reminder later down the line if you ever find yourself getting stuck. When I get upset about not being able to represent the Wolverines in a race anymore, it is helpful for me to reread my journal entries to reground myself in my decision of medically retiring. Reminding myself how frustrated I was completing months and months of rehab years in a row and thinking a little bit farther into the future to understand I wanted to be able to be active as I got older were key components of solidifying the new direction I found myself headed in.

While coming from a different end of the physical activity engagement spectrum, I believe this approach can work for anyone starting at any place. For example, let's say there is a woman named Susie.

Susie is thirty-five years old, works a job with long hours, and has two kids. She is currently considered obese and has hypertension. Recently, her doctor has advised her to increase her level of physical activity and change her diet in order to lose weight. Despite understanding why it's important to exercise, Susie struggles to stick with it.

One of the many varying factors limiting Susie from reaching her goal could be an insecurity buried under years of living. In fact, part of the reason Susie is struggling ties into her fear of being judged, as she was made fun of for years in middle and high school during gym class for being uncoordinated.

It is only through writing or a conversation with a trained health behavior specialist that this is ultimately realized. Even though such an approach won't change her situation overnight, acknowledgment of this personal barrier brings out a power in Susie that is no longer quite as limiting. She can now take the next steps to eliminate this personal belief and get one step closer to long-term engagement in physical activity.

It is here in Part 1 that I will explore how and why reflecting can help people manage health behavior changes.

CHAPTER 1

THE ART OF INTROSPECTION

———

"I was always a fat little Jewish boy," Robert* (*name changed for anonymity*) laughed.

An executive producer at a television company in his mid-sixties, Robert said his unhealthy relationship with food began when he was very young.

Growing up on Long Island, his dad was a huge meat eater and his mom would have three cookies and a glass of milk laid out for him as an after-school snack every day. His family was also not super athletic. Consequently, he never participated in any school sports or extracurricular physical activities.

Ultimately, Robert believes his past played a large role in the development of his health behaviors. The repeated messages and habits he learned at a young age are what primarily drove his subsequent years of negative health choices.

It was dedicated, albeit painful, introspection that opened Robert's eyes to the personal barriers preventing him from living a life full of wellness.

Robert's story will demonstrate how important it is to consider past experiences when seeking to create a tangible plan for any health behavior change.

De-rootment

By age twelve, Robert was well over 200 pounds.

When his mom sent him to a weight watchers camp and began restricting his food, it just made him want to eat more. In retrospect, he believes the excessive restriction fueled him to do the opposite, simply feeding his inclination and longing to eat.

WebMD supports this notion, stating in an article targeting parents of overweight and obese children, "Diets may teach your child that certain items are 'bad' or off-limits, which can change how he or she sees food later in life."[24]

In fact, much research has been done suggesting restrictive diets actually lead to an overeat-binge cycle, further perpetuating weight gain.[25] Additionally, remember the set point

---

24 Liao, Sharon. "Safe Weight Loss for Overweight Kids." WebMD. Accessed June 13, 2019. https://www.webmd.com/parenting/ raising-fit-kids/weight/features/safe-weight-loss.

25 "Why Diets Don't Work...And What Does." Psychology Today. Accessed June 15, 2019. https://www.psychologytoday.com/us/blog/

theory? Since our bodies are wired to not let us starve, they respond to overly restrictive diets by slowing down metabolism, which of course makes weight loss harder.

"When you eat fewer calories, the body becomes more efficient and burns fewer calories, even as your desire for extra calories heightens," Dr. David Ludwig, an endocrinologist at the Boston Children's Hospital and Harvard Medical School, nutrition researcher, and #1 *New York Times* best-selling author of *Always Hungry* wrote in a blog post. "This combination of rising hunger and slowing metabolism is a recipe for failure."[26]

As a child, Robert's body was fighting to maintain his heavy weight, while he was also being taught eating was a negative thing. This combination of conflicting feelings largely impacted the remainder of his childhood, affecting him into adulthood.

At his heaviest, Robert weighed 455 pounds in his mid-thirties. Standing at only 5'11", this left him with a Body Mass Index (BMI) of 63.5. While sometimes a controversial measurement due to its lack of regard for body composition, BMI is still a quick and informative indicator for overweight or obesity; 63.5 is well above the obese criterion of 30.

changepower/201010/why-diets-dont-workand-what-does.

26 Ludwig, David. "Why Calorie Restricted Diets Don't Work." Dr. David Ludwig. February 09, 2017. Accessed June 13, 2019. https://www.drdavidludwig.com/why-calorie-restricted-diets-dont-work/.

"There was a lot going on in my head at that point," he sighed. "I knew I needed a shift."

When asked what finally motivated him to make this shift, Robert replied matter-of-factly, "when I was in enough pain."

Only when walking more than a few steps became painful and taking the stairs was no longer an option for Robert did he fully commit to taking the leap of changing his behaviors.

With someone like Robert, who had the initial drive and self-awareness required to reverse a lifetime of habits, this shift was successful.

So, how exactly did he do it? While his initial longing to live without pain was enough to get him out the door, this arduous journey of losing hundreds of pounds of weight and reversing lifelong habits was going to require much more than the distant reward of a pain-free life.

Cue reflection.

Recently recovering from alcoholism at the time (he proudly informed me he has remained sober for over thirty years now—an incredible, difficult feat), Robert found in the program Alcoholics Anonymous a great resource as he started the attempt to lose the weight.

It was through this recovery from alcoholism that he came to realize he was addicted to not only alcohol but food as well. By translating the approach he learned in AA, Robert turned to his past for a firmer grasp on the beginnings of his eating habits, which ultimately allowed him to uncover strategies and learn ways to overwrite age-old habits.

Dr. Vera Tarman, M.D., M.S., ABAM (American Board of Addiction Medicine), a physician, author, and medical director at the largest drug and alcohol treatment center in Canada, is a firm believer that obesity stems from food addictions. With years of medical experience and research devoted to conducting workshops on the science of food addiction and "comfort food" abuse, she believes the solution to beating obesity or overweight calls for a twelve-step fellowship.

Seems to me Robert knew what he was doing.

The food-related Twelve Step groups that exist today see food addiction as a physical, emotional, and spiritual problem, as well as a biochemical one. Because of this, a wider approach is taken for accomplishing "food sobriety." Rather than simply requiring adherence to a food plan, the treatment also consists of numerous group meetings, readings, and daily phone check-ins with other members to report food consumption.[27]

Though certainly not everyone who meets the obese threshold is addicted to food, Dr. Tarman raises an important point. The reason current weight-loss programs and medical assistance aren't working is not because the patient is lazy, unmotivated, or hopeless, but merely because healthy eating and weight loss involve so many variables. The idea,

---

27   Tarman, Vera. "Part I: 12 Steps To Beat The Odds, Abstinent Food Plans." Addictions Unplugged. Accessed June 13, 2019. https://addictionsunplugged.com/2015/10/13/part-i-12-steps-to-beat-the-odds/.

then, is that there are multiple underlying causes that must addressed for change to occur.

Dr. Tarman and Robert both agree the line of action required is introspection coupled with community support. Programs for changing health behaviors must target long-term results rather than quick fixes. This can be done by taking the time to explore the deeper roots of an individual's behavior.

The weekly group meetings, peer support, and most importantly the accountability that the AA program requires of its members were hugely important in unlocking the self-knowledge that Robert needed to change his diet and relationship with food.

After a few years, Robert was successful in losing a significant amount of weight. Even without having bariatric surgery, he was able to drop over 200 pounds. To this day, he has kept the weight off and now goes to the gym three or four times a week, despite his self-declared "aversion" to exercise.

The Power of Introspection

Robert was wildly successful for two reasons: not only did he want to change his situation, but he took on the intimidating task of uncovering the root of his unhealthy relationship with food and physical activity and sought to address it on a deeper level.

Robert's introspection was evident throughout our interview. Telling a widely mindful narrative, he included many formative details that explained and solved problems he had faced with food. This depth is what enabled him to make these health changes last.

While initially having started this journey in response to a desire to lose weight, Robert uncovered core parts of his personality and past that led to a firmer understanding of who he was, is, and wants to be. This knowledge proved useful in many aspects of his life.

For example, as Robert reflected on the influence of his childhood, I asked him what he would do differently with his kids. Perhaps with such restrictive diets at a young age in mind, he said the biggest thing you can do for someone struggling is to make them feel like they have a choice.

"There's a definite power in handing a kid a bunch of vegetables and saying, 'Which one do you want?'" Robert explained.

Giving children an active role in their diet early on, especially with the current challenge of video games and screen time, is key, Robert believes. The concept of choice is useful for teenagers and adults too. At the end of the day, each individual's body is their own.

Whether a physician, a healthcare professional, partner, or friend, when it comes to supporting someone making a drastic lifestyle change, allowing them to retain autonomy in their health decisions can go a long way. This realization is what enabled Robert to understand that he himself likes having a say. Specifically, this comes into play in his current life with limiting the eating restrictions he puts on himself. And it is as simple as purposefully leaving room for himself to make decisions about what foods he will eat each day.

Another element Robert unearthed was his preferred learning style. In addition to attending AA meetings, he met with several different health care professionals during his lifestyle change journey ranging from dietitians and counselors to surgeons. While helpful for receiving diets and meal plans, by his third or fourth meeting with his nutritionist, hearing the amount of cholesterol in a piece of meat was just not helpful. Being inundated with facts he could easily find online was not beneficial to him and instead rather discouraging, further cementing a perceived wedge of despair. The one thing that really stuck with Robert in these meetings, however, was a visual demonstration of the number of spoonfuls of fat found in a large handful of M&M's.

While some patients might prefer to receive loads of information and statistics, others, like Robert, may want educational visualizations. This was a crucial realization for Robert to determine how his mind works best and what he can do to support himself with that knowledge. It showed him a way to process and retain information and provided him a tool to use going forward when having to make challenging diet decisions daily.

It is also important for health care providers working with patients to consider individual preferences and differences. Robert wishes more dietitians would give people information in a way they are willing to absorb it. At the end of the day, their primary focus should be patient's health and well-being. If an information overload is not working, health care professionals have a duty to reevaluate and provide the best care for each patient.

This is a simple explanation for why reflecting on what has worked well in the past is beneficial. That one tactic the dietitian used stuck with Robert for years and assisted him with his success in losing over 200 pounds. Any little bit counts when the intervention meets the patient where they are at and can provide a personalized approach.

The After

Despite this hard work, Robert still struggles. During our conversation, he shared with me a decision he had to make just before meeting with me. He was in the store buying lunch and could not decide between a bagel or a whole-food dense granola bar. He knew he should pick the bar, but the bagel was incredibly enticing. In the end he chose the granola bar, but it was still a tough decision.

He also admits there have been periods when his weight has fluctuated by up to 50 pounds, generally due to his mindset he deems the "f**k-its"—the only remedy being the need for vigilance and the notion of never giving up.

Just as the common AA mantra of living one day at a time reminds members, Robert often needs to acknowledge that there will be difficult moments throughout his continual recovery of a healthy life.

So, what keeps him going, knowing it can and will be difficult?

For Robert: thinking about the future consequences of his food choices. Reminding himself how bad he felt physically at his heaviest and focusing on the mental image of how much fat and sugar are in that pop, candy, chips ultimately guides him through these relapse-able moments.

Note that only through honest introspection could Robert derive these tools of empowerment and use them as personal fuel.

"You can't forget the past," Robert reflected. "You can only change the future and do the next right thing in front of you going forward."

It is with this that Robert demonstrates a critical mentality to have when setting out to reverse negative patterns you've had your whole life—one of self-love and forgiveness. With these at your disposal, you can effectively brave the uncovering of your past and continue onward.

Takeaways

Interventions should contain a reflection component for three primary reasons:

- To uncover barriers (personal, physical, or mental),
- To identify strengths, and
- To target personal preferences.

Below are some guided discussion questions that can be implemented in a program to spark reflection in a client. They also can be used as a written exercise for someone attempting to make a change by themselves. These questions are simply examples; they can (and should!) be modified depending on the patient, the target health behavior, and the context of the intervention.

Some example questions to ask yourself and/or to include in a health promotion program for sustainability are as follows:

- When was a time you positively engaged in physical activity?
- How did it make you feel?
- What was so enjoyable about it?
- What do you feel has prevented you from exercising/walking/eating well in the past?
- Have you ever experienced something negative as a result of exercising?
- How did it make you feel? Why?
- What have you been taught in the past about eating?
- Do you notice a pattern of when you eat more than you would like?
- Do you feel supported by the people in your life?
- If so, what do they do that works well for you? If not, what do you wish they would do?

CHAPTER 2

THE POWER OF MEANING

———

Identifying Intent

When I first began research for this book, I struggled with where to start.

Much in the same way people find it difficult to begin to make a habit change, I felt overwhelmed. I knew I wanted to write about supporting patients in making health changes, but there seemed to be tons of information to sift through, multiple different approaches I could take, and countless reasons to stop.

Lacking confidence in my ability to narrow in, I was tempted to quit before I had truly even started.

It was only by reminding myself of the reason I wanted to write this book in the first place—calling to mind the utter frustration and despondency I felt working with my cardiac patients—that I was able to get back on track and begin the descent into research and interviews.

I vividly remember setting an intention one Saturday morning I was feeling particularly motivated asking the universe for some guidance:

Help me find the person I'm most meant to research so I can help the most amount of people.

Lo and behold, after reaffirming my passion (plus a little help from Google), I stumbled upon the work of Dr. Michelle Segar, a leading expert and pioneer researcher on behavioral sustainability later that day, while biking at the gym, ironically enough.

I had found my first step.

This chapter explores how the act of reflecting can tie meaning to your health behavior change and why that ensures long-term adherence.

Locating Your MAP

Author of the #1 book in diet/exercise in 2015 by the USA Best Book Awards, frequently featured in the *New York Times* and a National Institute of Health (NIH) funded researcher, Dr. Segar has dedicated over twenty-five years to improving adherence to fitness within the health care, private-practice, and corporate well-being industries. Her Ph.D. in psychology, master's in health behavior and health education, and master's in kinesiology, in addition to her marketing background, have given her a multidisciplinary perspective that allows for continual success in writing and administering lasting-motivation programs.

It was only after looking through her website, completely in awe, that I came across the best part. She lived in Ann Arbor and was a *professor* at the University of Michigan, as well as the director of the university's Sport, Health, and Activity Research and Policy Center.

How I had never heard of her before, who knows, but I was thoroughly and utterly impressed and instilled with a passion I had not felt before.

After reading her book, I had the chance to interview Michelle and sit in on one of her classes. From these interactions alone, I learned a great deal about the core of health behavior change and what is necessary for true success. Most everything I went on to discover throughout this writing exploration, whether from other professionals I interviewed, scientific studies, or different books, circled back to concepts Michelle had uncovered in her work. And though her book, *No Sweat*, primarily focuses on physical activity and how to prioritize self-care more generally, she trains health professionals and clinicians around the country to help patients adopt other health behaviors, like dietary change, in ways they can sustain. A majority of my explorations in this book are based on her framework.

Michelle's innovative framework to help individuals cultivate sustainable health behavior is called MAPS. Her method of sustainable behavior change, while simple to use with patients, is extremely comprehensive. It draws from self-determination theory, among other theories. SDT is a theory of human motivation that looks at the basic psychological influences, both external and internal, composing an individual's choices.

The three needs that must be met for motivational development are competence, relatedness, and autonomy. Thought to be universal and innate, if these needs are met, the theory argues that people will reach their full potential for growth and functioning. Competence refers to your effectiveness in accomplishing a task, relatedness states the need to feel you belong to a group, and autonomy is feeling independent and in control of making personal decisions.

To ensure an effective health and wellness intervention, Michelle developed a comprehensive program that incorporates three core concepts based on self-determination theory. Competency is required in the sense that the individual must feel comfortable and capable of engaging in whatever health activity they are choosing to focus on. Relatedness can be met through feeling in touch with the surrounding environment and being a part of a group. Autonomy is when the person attempting to eat better or work out more feels like it is *their* choice. I personally like to think of ensuring a wellness program fulfills the SDT theory by making sure it meets what I call the 3 C's.

Building **confidence** → competency

Creating a **community** → relatedness

Ensuring **collaboration** → autonomy

Feeling confident in whatever behavior you are targeting will yield a sense of competency. Community can help build that sense of relatedness by initiating feelings of connection. And collaboration is essential to ensuring both the intervention is effective but meets the needs of each individual. Efforts for building the three C's can help guide any intervention program meet the needs of the Self-Determination Theory and should be prioritized.

Today, Michelle is a firm believer that the current health and fitness message isn't working. While many people begin a regimented exercise guide or start a robust eating plan, their ability to continue that effort after a few weeks is often diminished. Life gets in the way, they lose motivation, it is just too hard to keep up—whatever the reason, their hard work has come to a halt, and they are right back where they started.

A typical example is that of the New Year's Resolution Maker. At the beginning of the year, there are loads of people convinced this is *it*: this is the time they will actually commit and achieve their goals. The problem with this scenario, and with most efforts to change a health habit, is that they view it as a separate entity from their ordinary lives. Health and wellness are approached as something outside of daily activities and viewed as something one *must* or *should* do.

The first step in overcoming this viewpoint is demonstrated in the M of Michelle's MAPS guideline. M stands for meaning and is related to how one feels about exercise. Because meaning is the underlying root of motivation, the key to changing someone's relationship with exercise is to change the associated meaning.

Just like in the New Year's example, the abstract motivator of "should," which is largely acquired unconsciously through socialization and past experiences, will not be enough to sustain a long-term goal. Instead, the intervention should target reversal of that should.

"The reason why people can have important epiphanies, I believe, is because of the angle in switching exercise from chore to gift," Michelle explained to me. The shift of exercise from chore to gift is a central concept in her book. Offering a variety of written activities to do while reading her book, she helps guide readers to make this switch on their own.

"The people who are really able to run with it and make real changes," she told me, "are people who have actually had positive experiences before with exercise."

With her observations in mind, an intervention, then, must seek to pull out these positive experiences. Arguably even more important, is to uncover someone's negative experiences with exercise or eating. If associations and experiences act as large drivers behind actions, reflection is critical for either a) finding a source for continual motivation or b) uncovering a barrier someone may subconsciously be facing.

Acknowledgment of the past is critical for finding the right meaning to sustain engagement in a health behavior. As seen with Robert in the first chapter, the power of reflection enabled him to uncover his food addiction, which ultimately allowed him to find success.

In her second part, Awareness, Michelle explained how to become more aware of your preferences, the realities of exercise, and specifically how to change exercise from a chore to a gift. Again, sprinkled throughout the book the reader can find written activities to complete that call for tangible reflection. The primary aim of these exercises is to help establish the *why*: why the person is choosing to lose weight, why they want to eat better—all reasoning that lies at the foundation of sustainable behavior change.

One study Michelle wrote about I found particularly fascinating. A group of researchers set out to determine how different reasons for walking influenced both the experience in general and how much the participant ate after. Both groups of overweight women were asked to walk for thirty minutes before receiving lunch. One group was told they were walking strictly for exercise, whereas, the other group was told they were walking to have fun. The fun group was allowed to listen to music to further their enjoyment.

Though the mileage and calories burned were similar, the women instructed to enjoy themselves felt less tired and grumpy than the other group. Further, when given the option at the lunch to have either water or soda to drink and either applesauce or pudding for dessert, the majority of participants who chose soda and pudding were—you guessed it—in the walking for exercise group. To ensure reliability and exclude the potential effect of music, the researchers replicated the study without music and found similar results.

This suggests that the *why* matters. Ultimately, how you feel about the call for increased exercise or nutrition change will determine the outcome.

Further, many studies have shown that having intrinsic goals and reasons, such as how it makes one feel, as opposed to external ones like "looking better" or losing ten pounds, were more successful in supporting long-term engagement.

In fact, having more than one "why" is thought to dilute motivation. "The best determinant of sustainability is not how much weight you hope to lose but how *participating in physical activities makes you feel* in the moment," Michelle described in her book.[28]

At the end of the day, in humans, feelings often trump logic. Especially when it comes to an unfamiliar behavior, the action with the fewest negative emotions attached to it will supersede the more hurtful ones. Only with proper

---

28 Segar, Michelle L. No Sweat: How the Simple Science of Motivation Can Bring You a Lifetime of Fitness. New York: AMACOM--American Management Association, 2015.

reflection of both past experiences and current goals can someone rewrite positive associations.

Call for Action

Because decisions made moment to moment are often dictated by emotions, a targeted approach to help people associate positive memories with these new health changes is critical. People need personally compelling reasons to choose movements that feel good to increase their likelihood of continuing.

A health behavior intervention program or medical professional who works closely on reframing the overall attitude of obligation to one of opportunity is necessary to help patients adhere to behavioral prescriptions.

Like me, Michelle thinks more effort should be put into assisting patients in making these health behavior changes. Upon asking her if she thought it would be feasible to implement a program in the healthcare field to support patients in this realm, she readily agreed. Having similar views, she explained to me that she has developed a "Train-the-Trainer" framework called the Behavioral Blueprints to teach health and medical professionals her way of approaching behavior change.

The Behavioral Blueprints guides health professionals to shift the dialogue about physical activity and diet from a "medical prescription" to a lifetime of daily bouts of vitality and joy. Her website states, "The essence of what

I've discovered is that when we rebrand health behaviors as a source of immediate happiness and well-being, individuals become engaged with taking care of themselves in a way 'disease prevention,' 'weight control,' and 'body-sculpting' motivators just can't accomplish."

And her efforts have proven wildly successful. Now asked to travel the world to speak at conferences and consult with a variety of both physicians and employee wellness programs, Michelle is happy to have reached the medical world.

"It is gratifying in a different realm because the reach is so much bigger," she told me, her passion evident.

Not just helping an individual, she is teaching a doctor how to help all their patients, multiplying her effect. This program has allowed her impact to be widely felt. In addition to being rewarding, the results of this program demonstrate the importance of training physicians. If there were to exist a whole new position to guide patients to reframe their health change journey in a new direction, it would minimize the responsibilities of the doctors and allow for more in-depth work.

Currently, Michelle is in the process of writing a checklist of sorts to help clinicians address these issues in a more straightforward manner. "In my own personal coaching, the sessions are an hour, but in health care you can't do that," she said. Ultimately, she wants to create a system to teach physicians who don't have the time to effectively get at the root of these issues to increase success with their patients.

In the medical system today, the existing understanding of behavior change stems from the Theoretical Model or Stages of Change Model, which describes five states of readiness a patient can exist at.

This is the model I have been taught and one most frequently used in textbooks. The five stages are precontemplation, contemplation, preparation, action, and maintenance. Wherever the patient is at, the physician is expected to meet them there. This is largely associated with honoring the patient's autonomy, part of the Hippocratic Oath. Later in this book I will discuss the already existing interventions in the healthcare field that target enhancing patient autonomy, one of which is called Motivational Interviewing.

While Michelle frames autonomous motivation at the heart of sustainable behavior change, she also thinks that the stages of change model don't go as deep as they could.

"The readiness to change framework has been very popular, and may be relevant for some, but I don't believe it cultivates the deeper reflection that many people need in order to change their meaning, and ultimately their MAP to sustainable behavior change," Michelle told me matter-of-factly. "This framework categorizes people as not being 'ready' to change. In my private coaching practice I've seen people who weren't ready to change because in fact they'd been simply turned off of exercise. They'd done it plenty of times! So while they might score as being 'not ready' to exercise, in fact, this answer might really be a smokescreen to having negative experiences from being active or having what I call the Wrong Why. There's a more efficient way to get right to that issue directly and address their meaning for a behavior like exercise first thing," she finished.

Thus calling for more guided reflection.

Addressing these patients' concerns directly and allowing them a space to reflect with a health professional would increase the chance of adherence to new health habits. Michelle's use of the word "we" signifies the call for the medical system at large to assist patients in this process.

Michelle is a highly sought-after expert on sustainable motivation for behavior change. Her mantra "What sustains us, we sustain" is the battle cry for her efforts. Her expertise is used across many platforms, including fitness and health promotion, employee wellness, professional and provider training, health app and software developers, and traveling the world to give speeches.

Takeaways

I was extremely lucky to have gotten the chance to speak with Dr. Michelle Segar.

What enabled me to learn from her came *after* I set my intention that Saturday morning. It was by taking the time to reflect and narrow in not only on my goal focus of health behaviors but also *why* I wanted to write about them in the first place that gave me the power to get through. Identifying the reason I was so compelled to write this book in the first place—my longing to help people achieve a life of wellness—was the fuel I used when the process became difficult.

I, in other words, had found my meaning.

Much in the same way a patient looks for continual motivation to assist them on their health journey, an intervention that both assesses initial goals and also delves deeper to help patients attach meaning to their health plan is necessary to carry them forward to a lifetime of good health.

A health promotion program should contain exercises that seek to uncover the subject's purpose to then guide their actions in the long run.

Some techniques to support someone after they have set the intention to increase physical activity or change their diet are as follows:

- Implement a physician check-list or guidebook like Segar's Behavioral Blueprints, a time effective solution in PCP offices.
- Have a staff member on board at medical office to have a brief conversation with each patient to assess goals and uncover personal meaning for exercise or diet change.
- Provide interactive opportunities such as worksheets to engage individual in a tangible plan.
- Make sure a program meets the 3 C's (confidence, community, collaboration)!

CHAPTER 3

UNCOVERING YOUR WHY

"If I feel better, people will respect me more."

Brian Sipotz was coaching one of his clients to help them unveil why they wanted to get in better shape, when he discovered their reason to lose weight was not quite what either one of them expected.

Finding a deeper meaning, an awareness of your inner workings, allows you to be more successful when approaching goals.

"This is the stuff that will keep you from eating chips at 9 p.m., not the ten-pound reminder," Brian shared.

And it's central to changing behaviors.

Determining Purpose

It was not always Brian Sipotz's goal to join the health and wellness movement. A retired American professional ice hockey athlete, he initially set out on the most logical next path in his career trajectory: coaching. "I felt like that was my world, what I knew best and so that was where I could help the most," he explained.

When he first opened Advantage Strength and Conditioning, his intent was to train young elite athletes both physically and mentally to compete at higher levels of competition. Conveniently located above the premier Ann Arbor Ice Cube, a local ice arena, his idea was that teams could be trained before or after practice. Brian successfully began working with young hockey players and figure skaters and for a year helped them improve balance, coordination, and strength to better their performance. It was then, however, that Brian started noticing a trend.

Parents started to ask him if he ever worked with adults. One wanted to be able to walk up the stairs without pain, another had hopes of recovering fitness they once had when they were young, others merely wanted to be able to keep up with their kids. However different these requests were, all were seemingly asking for the same thing: support in becoming more active.

Brian had stumbled upon a demand for guidance in adult functional movement—a hidden plea often masked by the need to adhere to society's image of wellness. This sparked a shift in his practice and thus began the transition to adding adult training to the Advantage community.

The Science of Why

"How Great Leaders Inspire Action," a TedTalk by Simon Sinek, author of multiple best-selling books, including the global bestseller *Start With Why,* has over 43 million views and is subtitled in 47 languages. He is best known for popularizing the concept of *why.*

In the opening of his TedTalk in September 2009, he explored what makes certain leaders—whether a company, person, or movement—more successful when there are several equivalent counterparts with access to same the tools, connections, and experiences. Sinek determined there must be something else at play.

"As it turns out, there's a pattern. As it turns out, all the great inspiring leaders and organizations in the world whether it's Apple or Martin Luther King or the Wright Brothers, they all think, act, and communicate the exact same way. And it's the complete opposite to everyone else," he explained.[29]

Sinek dubbed his discovery of this common denominator among the world's powerful leaders "the world's simplest idea" and called it the golden circle.

He then drew this on the board.

---

29 Sinek, Simon. TED. September 2009. Accessed June 13, 2019. https://www.ted.com/talks/simon_sinek_how_great_leaders_inspire_action?language=en.

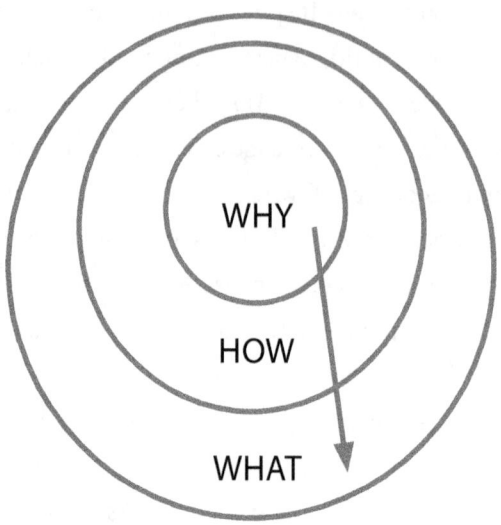

"Every person on the planet knows what they do, some know how they do it, but very, very few people or organizations know why they do what they do," he engagingly stated.[30]

The way we communicate and typically act is from the outside in. That's what most everyone does. People skim the surface, say what they do, some explain how they are different or better—but most of the time they don't do anything further and yet still expect results.

The goal must become thinking, acting, and communicating from the inside out. Starting with the why instead of leaving it unexplored. Uncovering a deeper purpose, he claimed, is what drives results.

---

30 Ibid.

He used a marketing example from Apple.

Their marketing message is not "*We make great computers* (what) *by making them user-friendly, simple to use, and with a beautiful design* (how). ... Want to buy one?"

They instead start with their *why*: "*Everything we do, we believe in challenging the status quo. We believe in thinking differently*" and then follow up with the how, "*the way we challenge the status quo is by making products beautifully designed, simple to use, and user friendly*," and the what, "*we just happen to make great computers.*"

"People don't buy what you do, but people buy *why* you do it," Sinek concluded.[31]

A *why* must not be results-oriented but rather tied to your purpose. What is your belief, your cause—why does your organization exist?

Sinek's model can be easily translated to the health behavior realm: why do you believe you want to get healthy? What is a reason that can get you out of bed in the morning to eat breakfast, a healthy one? What can you tie your existence of a health goal to that can drive your action towards it?

Doctors and physicians often fall prey to this line of thinking.

- *What* the patient needs to do: lose weight, change diet, increase PA.

---

31 Ibid.

- *How* they try and "sell" it: good for your health, you have high blood pressure, lose weight
- *Why*? Because I, the research, society … say so?

This *why* is often missing in our medical model! Why should the patient truly, really engage in these lifestyle changes? What's in it for them besides the proposed health benefits that are more often than not going to be felt in the distant future?

Using Sinek's model, this missing link of *why* must be established to increase the likelihood of success, i.e. engagement in proper health behaviors. Without a purpose, that conversation between provider and patient is uninspiring.

The goal then must be to reverse the direction of the conversation. A healthcare professional needs to firmly establish a *why* for the patient before then telling them what they need to do and how to do it.

Saving A Life

Brian Sipotz tells his clients to think of their *why* in terms of saving their own life. A critical doctrine of Advantage is to keep people engaged in working out and coming back.

And that comes because health and fitness tie into your *why*—something critical to your own life's purpose.

Sometimes it's difficult for humans to contemplate long-term consequences; health implications decades from now are difficult to conceptualize.

But what about in a natural disaster such as a fire that strikes your home? An earthquake that hits while you are at the office? Or a tidal wave coming to the shore when you're on vacation.

As Brian shared, in natural disasters, many people sadly perish because they can't run fast enough, hop from car to car, etc. Could being in better shape help you avoid death in a natural disaster? How would you change your behavior to prepare for that?

Or perhaps, in less dramatic terms, are you able to play soccer with your son in the yard? Can you carry your heavy suitcase or groceries up the stairs?

What do you care about?

Every person has different motivators. A program must seek to pull out these differences to help every individual find success.

Rather than following the trends of high-intensity interval training or dramatic fat-loss programs, Brian has personally decided to focus on functional movements when creating individualized strength programs. "I believe the fitness industry, these intense calorie-burning sessions, is so one-dimensional," he explained. "This idea of burning extra calories, of sweating super hard during the day to have that glass of wine or beer at night is not very authentic." Brain sought to combat this sale of fitness by sharing with others his passion for functional movement.

Functional movement stems from the belief that we should all move in ways the human body was meant to. For example, exercise should enhance the ranges of motion and activities your genes and biology agree with. Instead of emphasizing fast weight loss or toned physiques, Advantage focuses on strength and resistance training for improved mobility, heart health, and bone density.

This approach pairs nicely with finding a deeper purpose to your health goals. Instead of focusing on physical appearances, a program should guide people to reflect on the things they deeply care about. And if that means looking better, great, but Brian has found that's not always the case once you dive a little deeper and reflect.

When joining Advantage Strength and Conditioning, you get dedication and commitment from the team to get you strong to move well so you can keep doing the things you love, whatever those activities may be.

Making health behavior changes sustainable, Brian believes, is hard work. "It needs to be more than conscious, more than just willpower," he reflected.

The Five Whys

Getting to the deeper root behind someone's goals allows for creating greater accountability.

Brian offers a nutrition class to his strength training members to teach a more balanced approach to well-being. He takes each client through an exercise he calls the 5 Whys.

First, he asks what their goal is to learn their reason behind taking the nutrition class or joining the gym. Next, he asks the person five times why it is important to them.

To demonstrate, Brian used the following example.

Question: Why do you want to learn about your nutrition habits?

Client: Because I want to lose weight.

Q: Why is losing weight important to you?

C: To lose ten pounds for my daughter's wedding.

Q: Why is losing weight for the wedding important to you?

C: To fit in my tux better.

Q: Why is fitting into your tux important to you?

C: I will look better.

Q: Why is looking better important to you?

C: If I look better, I feel more confident.

Q: Why is feeling confident important to you?

C: If I feel better, people will respect me more.

All of a sudden it goes from losing weight to wanting to be respected.

Finding a deeper meaning, an awareness of your inner workings, allows one to be more successful when approaching goals.

"This is the stuff that will keep you from eating chips at 9 p.m., not the ten-pound reminder," Brian agreed.

The personal nature of this reflection is very influential. Uncovering and then assigning a deep-rooted purpose gives people a more innate and natural incentive to continue pursuing their goals.

System Implementation

Exercise Is Medicine is a national health initiative backed by the American College of Sports Medicine and American Medical Association that seeks to make physical activity assessment and promotion a standard in clinical care. Its website states, "The scientifically proven benefits of physical activity remain indisputable, and they can be as powerful as any pharmaceutical in preventing and treating a range of chronic diseases and medical conditions."

EIM's vision of PA promotion consists of achieving four primary goals:

1. Have health care providers assess every patient's level of physical activity at every clinic visit.
2. Determine if patient is meeting the U.S. National PA recommendation.
3. Provide patient with brief counseling advice to help meet guidelines.
4. Refer patient to either health care or community-based resources for further PA counseling and guidance.[32]

In its 2014 global initiative update, seven years after EIM's creation, researchers determined the global spread of EIM to thirty-nine other countries; the initiative has formally

---

32 "Exercise Is Medicine." Exercise Is Medicine. Accessed June 13, 2019. https://www.exerciseismedicine.org/.

moved on from its initial phase of building infrastructure and awareness and begun the transition to implementation. Broad PA counseling interventions and referral systems improve PA at the population level and have strong potential to contribute to achieving global goals of reducing inactivity and related morbidity and mortality.[33]

As a member of the University of Michigan's Exercise Is Medicine campus chapter, I am part of the student group seeking to promote exercise and physical activity in general to all individuals at the university. One such effort has been our goal of helping physicians recognize exercise as a vital sign of health and having them distribute personal exercise prescriptions to students and faculty as necessary.

Recently, our group has made major strides in implementing this initiative into our University Health System. In partnership with the chief of the sports medicine department, Dr. Corrigan, and the UHS Physical Therapy supervisor, we have compiled a list of local Ann Arbor gyms with trained exercise professionals on site who are willing to accept patient referrals from UHS.

Our next step is processing through the healthy system to get the exercise prescriptions rolling with university members, such as students and faculty. If we find success, we

---

33 Lobelo, Felipe, Mark Stoutenberg, and Adrian Hutber. "The Exercise Is Medicine Global Health Initiative: A 2014 Update." British Journal of Sports Medicine 48, no. 22 (2014): 1627-633. doi:10.1136/bjsports-2013-093080.

would begin to implement the prescriptions throughout the whole hospital system.

This is one such way of incorporating wellness programs that focus on reflection into the medical system. Finding facilities and groups that already have existing programs to be used as a referral site is one way to tie health behavior initiatives into the current system.

The Epiphany

"Why were you able to lose a hundred pounds *this time*?"

In a conversation I had with a mentor after she lost a hundred pounds, she mentioned the kickstart required for anyone looking to lose weight or improve a diet calls for an epiphany moment.

Without that initial, internal drive, there will be no fuel to use as support throughout the difficult journey of making those life changes. For her, this moment came when all of a sudden one night she had the thought that she didn't want to be the "fat mom" at her child's functions.

Ultimately, she told me, this is what enabled her to lose the weight. Regardless of why or how this idea is sparked, people need both the personal inspiration and understanding to guide them.

This epiphany, though, is not always easy to come by.

Often, it only occurs when the situation becomes too unbearable to live with or someone in the person's life has gone through much effort and nagging to persuade them to consider a shift.

Even then, it is not a true epiphany, for it does not stem from the individuals themselves, but an outside entity. For a lifestyle change to stay afloat among the continual waves of hardship, the reason for doing so must come from the person directly and, even further, must involve deep reflection.

To make this jump and have the efforts not fizzle out, to avoid just skimming the surface of what is expected, one needs to actively reflect on the recesses of their minds.

Four Crazy Questions

Another written exercise Brian has people do is Four Crazy Questions. He asks them to draw out a box (shown below) and jot down the good and bad aspects of making and not making a specific change.

Cut out all dessert	CHANGE	NO CHANGE
GOOD	Lessen sugar intake	Dessert is delicious
BAD	I won't have a way to satisfy my sweet tooth	Gain weight and feel unhealthy

Despite being a simple exercise, it gets a mind churning to help a coach or provider with an understanding of what a person's mental barriers might be. It also can help unearth what can be used as fuel going forward. This method helps people understand why they do the things they do and points out any fears they may have that could hold them back; it also offers the chance to find solutions!

In the example above, I filled out the chart with my personal goal of eating no desserts. I'm here to tell you that this is an incredibly hard goal for me, as just last night I had three cookies after dinner and helped finish off my friend's lemon bar. Ideally, I would start by limiting myself to only having one dessert three times a week, and then changing it to twice a week, and then once per week until I could comfortably get to zero times in a week, but more will be covered on that in the next section.

If you look at my responses, you should notice a few patterns. Both when answering why it would be good for me to continue eating desserts and why it was bad for me if I didn't stop, I mentioned enjoying the taste of dessert. In one, I stated I have a sweet tooth—suggesting I crave sweets often and it is hard for me to control. From the other response, we can gather that I think desserts taste very good. Similarly, looking at the other boxes, we can glean that the way my body looks and feels is important to me and that I believe sugar is unhealthy.

Even just from looking at two of these boxes, we can 1) expose a deeper reason why it's difficult to change (I enjoy the taste too much), 2) identify a motivator (I think too much sugar is bad for my body and I like feeling healthy, therefore

I should try to align my beliefs), and 3) highlight a solution (find healthy dessert alternatives that are satisfying but good for me, ex. yogurt with chocolate granola).

Considerations

How do these insights change the way we implement behavior change with obese patients?

It will certainly require more research and testing, but the idea is to find ways to balance effective reflection and coaching of a patient with time constraints for medical professionals. Perhaps Sipotz benefits from selection bias—patients who want to change seek him out where others do not—but at the end of the day, there should be tools that unlock the *why* side of this problem.

Exercises like these are not necessarily difficult to administer: these mental exercises could be explained to a patient in less than five minutes and prove beneficial in helping them adhere to the task of changing their behaviors. But perhaps just as important is implementing the changes thereafter.

Much like Michelle, Sipotz pointed out ways to help people find deeper meanings and create a sense of awareness to help guide the process.

Brian has found that his success with his diverse array of clients lies in his approach; he's switched the focus from losing weight to becoming an active participant in your own life, which is key to the longevity of these health changes.

The other large component is Brian's humble creation of a community, which will be explored later in Part 3. Engagement from the trainers, peer support, and a sense of commitment all contribute to his members wanting to stick with working out consistently.

Takeaways

This chapter highlights the importance of helping an individual discover the right reason to make changes in their life. Because most people want to remain comfortable in life, coupled with the fact that change is scary, individuals often need help finding a compelling reason to change. Providing them with a program that has exercises embedded in it to help them overcome the initial inertia of change is a necessary component. Reflection is what will determine that magic key.

Below are some ideas to include in a program to cue reflection of a deeper reason to ensure sustainability:

- Include diagram of what/how/why, and ask patients to fill it out.
- Use the 5 Whys Exercise.
- Try Four Crazy Questions.
- Provide patients with a list of local gyms in the area.
- Create a partnership between the doctor's office and fitness centers to serve as "pharmacy" for their exercise prescriptions.
- Consider having an exercise event at the doctor's office to promote.

CHAPTER 4

CULTURO-SPECTION

———

"I would lose maybe five or ten pounds, and then I would just put it right back on," Amanda*, a teacher in her early thirties shared with me.

After struggling with weight loss on and off for five years, Amanda found herself feeling hopeless and deeply frustrated with her diet attempts. "You don't feel so great about yourself—you start to feel like a failure," she admitted.

This chapter will explain why Amanda and so many other Americans struggle with diets, and what exactly we can do about it.

Quick Fixes

Every day there seems to be a new diet book, a new exercise fad, ground-breaking evidence on a macronutrient—all seemingly claiming the same thing: this is life-changing!

This is all you need to lose weight, be healthy, find happiness, be successful, and solve all your life problems!

Especially in this technological day and age, communication and spread of information are at their peak. While it's difficult to sift through all this data and navigate the minefield that is quality sources, I believe this cyclic trend inherently speaks to an even larger issue. People are constantly writing and researching and sharing all these ideas not because they have all been successful in improving our nation's health, but because of exactly the opposite.

They've *failed.*

The reason, I believe, that the presence of countless diets and fitness trends hasn't ceased sweeping our country is because they aren't sending home the right message. And, more importantly, they aren't sustainable.

Amanda is a prime example. After graduating college and starting a new job as a teacher, she began putting on the pounds. Attempting to navigate her new life off campus, she started making the more convenient choices of quick, easy meals and couldn't seem to find the time to go to the gym.

Desperate to see results, eventually she turned to different diets, began counting calories, and started using apps like MyFitnessPal.

These trends result in a continuous loop of never-ending, oftentimes misleading information. A cyclical culture of sorts, this perpetual seeking of an answer for weight loss, better eating habits, or a healthier lifestyle often leads to failure, which further discourages people from making a change. People who find success through these fad diets and exercise regimes typically have some sort of X-factor—usually time, resources, or a mentor—that more easily allows them to make the leap and stick with it.

In the case of Amanda, she was juggling a new job, moving into a new house, and an upcoming wedding she had to plan. She also suffered from lifelong depression, which added a further layer of difficulty to making these lifestyle changes. This was a lot to manage in addition to trying to lose weight. Like many others, she turned to the "easy" solutions our society has deemed the answers—low-carb, low-fat, high-protein, gluten-free, vegan, ketogenic, or paleo diets (the list goes on and on)—and found no success. It is not, however, the fault of the dieter, but rather the essence of the diet itself.

We must acknowledge this unhealthy approach of restricting foods and crash exercise regimes and instead seek ways to achieve success for the long term. Our focus must be on establishing healthy habits rather than limiting or burning calories, for only following this shift will people see sustainable results.

Amanda shared with me her exasperation. "It's definitely frustrating with social media and with what's broadcasted on TV; it's always in your everyday life. So much emphasis is placed on expectations and how people should look as opposed to being healthy."

Sophie Egan, director of health and sustainability leadership and the editorial director for the Strategic Initiatives Group at the Culinary Institute of America, explored this unstable, and often unhealthy, U.S. food culture in her book *Devoured.* In the chapter "Diet Evangelism" specifically, she rather satirically examined the "Modern Diet Landscape" and how this diet culture can impact an individual.

Personal reflection, in combination with environmental and societal introspection, is required to find a solution to lifestyle changes.

Deep-Rooted History

Starting with the history of diets that date back to the 1400s, Egan worked her way to the present "semi-cultish fitness and hobby subgroup" through exploration of paleo diets, CrossFit, and the fashion trend of women wearing yoga pants and running outfits while doing everything but yoga and running.

Aside from being appalled that our country has enough diets to rank thirty-five of them on the *U.S. News* Best Diets list, Egan further explained that the ever-popular paleo diet was, in fact, ranked last by a panel of America's leading nutritionists and public health professionals. This ranking was based on ease of adherence; how nutritious, safe, and effective it was in helping people lose weight; and evidence on reducing the risk of diabetes and heart disease.

Thirty-fifth place out of thirty-five! These diets aren't even beneficial!

Further, Brian Wansink and colleagues at the Cornell Food and Brand Lab research center found that 75 percent of people who try diets don't make it past a month.[34]

According to the Boston Medical Center's Nutrition and Weight Management Program, an estimated 45 million Americans go on a diet each year.[35] This means that, on average, 33 million Americans who choose to go on a diet will fail and fade out their efforts.

Additionally, 36 percent will only last one week, and the smallest percentage—only 8 percent, or roughly 3.6 million people—will sustain a diet for more than three months.

Amanda is definitely not alone in her struggles!

Wansink's research greatly stresses the need for more long-lasting solutions. Americans are desperately trying anything and everything to shed pounds, and their odds of being successful are slim to none.

Egan then went on to write about a common diet brand "formula" (mockingly, in a Mad-Lib manner), marketing and sales techniques, and the religious-like followings most diets

---

34 DiGregorio, Jaclyn. "The CUSP Method: Your Guide to Balanced Portions & a Healthy Life EBook: Jaclyn DiGregorio: Kindle Store." Amazon. Accessed June 14, 2019. https://www.amazon.com/CUSP-Method-Balanced-Portions-Healthy-ebook/dp/B06Y5LXN6G.

35 "Weight Management." Boston Medical Center. September 07, 2017. Accessed June 15, 2019. https://www.bmc.org/nutrition-and-weight-management/weight-management.

receive and how these things grouped together make for an influential marketplace succeeding in hooking of individuals.

Egan, Sophie. *Devoured: How What We Eat Defines Who We Are.* New York, NY: William Morrow, 2017. So, why does this matter in the realm of long-term health habit change? Aside from reflecting on an individual's history, it is also incredibly important to observe the role a nation's surrounding culture plays in human behavior.

Societal Influences

An article from PublicHealth.org suggested that the bigger portion sizes and mixed consumer messages permeating U.S. culture are primarily to blame.

According to the U.S. Department of Agriculture, Americans ate almost 20 percent more calories on average in 2000 than in 1983[36] and another paper by researchers in 2016 revealed that the sugar industry has spent decades manipulating, molding, and guiding nutritional research to downplay the effects of sugar and instead blame saturated fats.[37] These are only two brief examples of the latent messages that lay hidden in American culture.

---

36 Writers, Staff. "Why Are Americans Obese?" PublicHealth.org. Accessed June 13, 2019. https://www.publichealth.org/public-awareness/obesity/.

37 "How Big Sugar Hid the Dangers of Sugar." Mercola.com. Accessed June 13, 2019. https://articles.mercola.com/sites/articles/archive/2017/12/06/industry-buried-evidence-hiding-sugar-harms.aspx.

Sophie Egan summed it up best by describing the reality of being on a diet rather than focusing on an individual's eating habits across a lifetime. "Some people might feel that an extreme fad diet is what it takes to jump-start their shift to a set of more sensible habits that actually feel doable over the long run." Yet she went on to devalue diets, concluding, "A lot of them don't work, overall they're difficult to sustain, and in many cases a person is actually better off never dieting in the first place."[38]

If dieting and monitoring food intake can be a negative thing, what should you do? She too pondered: "The nagging question for most people still: What should we eat?"[39]

Her consensus aligns with that of Michael Pollan, an incredibly successful and well-established U.S. author, journalist, and activist, when he said, "Eat food. Not too much. Mostly plants,"[40] but Egan more deeply believes the key lies in reasonable suggestions. Rather than limiting food intake through extremes that are difficult to maintain, a softer approach to eating can lead to a more holistic diet over time.

Amanda also found success once she strayed from the societal expectations of an ideal image and a culture saturated with quick-fix diets. "Reminding myself that making

38 Egan, Sophie. Devoured: How What We Eat Defines Who We Are. New York, NY: William Morrow, 2017.

39 Egan, Sophie. Devoured: How What We Eat Defines Who We Are. New York, NY: William Morrow, 2017.

40 Pollan, Michael. The Omnivores Dilemma: A Natural History of Four Meals. New York, NY: Penguin Books, 2016.

healthy choices and achieving small term goals *will* have an impact was so important," she shared with me. "You know, habits take a while to develop, it's not something you can change overnight, but is something you must keep building on."

It was this critical shift in attitude—from one of fast results to a humble acceptance of slow progress—that enabled our friend Amanda to lose over fifty pounds.

Amanda's Way

Amanda outlined to me four key pieces that enabled her to increase her confidence, have more energy, and overall feel better both mentally and physically. Eventually she found success with changing her lifestyle, and it was *not* through dieting.

One was portion control. Rather than following a strict diet, Amanda focused on limiting the amount of food she ate. She believes it is very important to not only watch *what* you eat, but also how much.

An easy guideline to follow is the visual aid of USDA's MyPlate recommendations, which depicts a colorful plate sectioned off into the recommended portion sizes for each meal.

Your plate should consist of ½ fruits and vegetables, ¼ whole grains, ¼ protein, and 1 serving of dairy.[41]

---

41 "What Is MyPlate?" Choose MyPlate. March 13, 2019. Accessed June 17, 2019. https://www.choosemyplate.gov/WhatIsMyPlate.

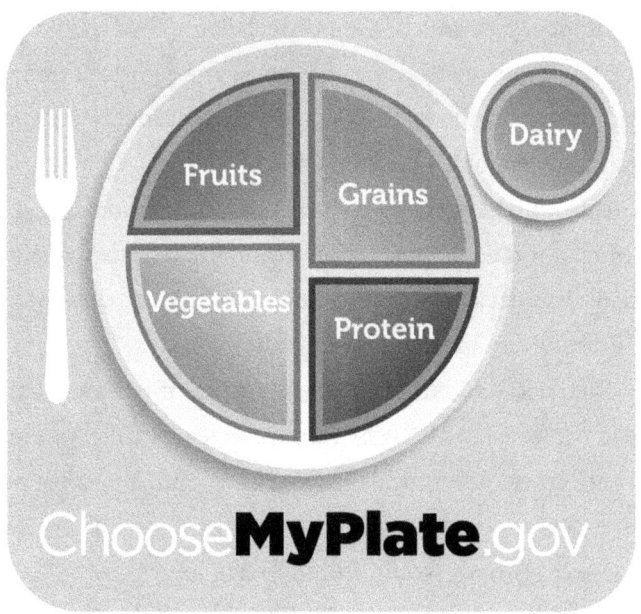

Amanda also found it important to be mindful of all the "empty calories" hidden in her foods and drinks throughout the day. For her, this was as simple as buying a water bottle to ensure she drank more water throughout the day and limited her beverage intake of things like Starbucks drinks, beer, wine, and soda.

A similar approach is the Whole Diet Approach for American Adults. Using the MyPlate federal guidelines mentioned above, this model suggests that if you are unable to adhere to the strict dietary guidelines at every meal (I mean, hello, no one is perfect), eating a variety of foods from each food group each day is sufficient.

In theory, if you choose nutrient-dense foods, limit portion sizes, minimize processed foods, and caloric beverages, over time you will meet all the individual nutrient needs and maintain adequate nutritional health.

When first learning about this in my nutrition course at UMich, I was equal parts relieved and excited. This meant if I had a bad day and had eaten too many cookies or went out to eat for every meal, it was … okay.

Even if it were a difficult week—let's say finals week—and I had neglected my body by eating at irregular intervals and having quick, easy "meals" (if you can count a piece of peanut butter toast and soy crackers a meal), I wasn't entirely screwed! My body would still support me!

This approach also excited me for a couple of reasons—the biggest being room for flexibility. As long as I kept up my end of the deal (engaging in physical activity, drinking water, and minimizing my processed food intake), I could enjoy eating whatever sounded good to me in the moment, which includes getting a greasy burger, french fries, and a Batido milkshake from my favorite restaurant Frita Batidos in downtown Ann Arbor.

Invigorated by this newfound trust in the whole total of my diet, my belief in how the nature of eating should be was solidified. It was all about small goals and balance.

This inherently makes sense. In order for a goal to seem doable in the long run, it can't be out of reach. Small changes consistently done are eventually what become a habit. Later in this book I will offer a wonderful tool to approach eating both healthily and positively through manageable chunks called the CUSP Method, created by Jaclyn Digregorio.

Amanda's second piece of advice for long-term success was also the notion of taking small steps.

"Don't focus on a number you have for losing weight and instead set attainable and actionable goals," she advised me.

For her, this was beginning to go to the gym just once a week and eventually working her way up to the four day a week regimen she now regularly attends. Breaking things up helped make Amanda's goal of losing weight feel more manageable. What she didn't know was that it also set her up nicely for a lifetime of healthy choices as opposed to crashing on her efforts after a few months like people typically do on diets.

This concept of breaking things up will be covered more in depth in Part 3.

The third piece of advice Amanda had was to find a deeper reason to keep you going when the best choices continue to be the most difficult to make.

This is where reflection can be so powerful.

Amanda's deeper reason to eat healthier and engage in physical activity was becoming a mom. Her drive shifted from external and image-focused to the internal one of providing for her beautiful young daughter. Currently, it is maintaining a sound diet to ensure the healthy transfer of nutrients with breastfeeding. In the coming years, it will be by modeling healthy behaviors as well as ensuring Amanda herself will remain in good health to stay on top of her mothering game.

Additionally, she uses the reminder of how bad she felt physically when she was overweight as further inspiration. "I don't want to go back to the heaviest I've ever been, I want to be more aware of the choices that I'm making," Amanda relayed to me adamantly. Reflection, whether personal or through prompted efforts, also helped Amanda identify reasons to keep up her habit changes of eating less and working out more.

Using the written exercises outlined in the previous chapters—like Brian's 5 Whys, Michelle Segar's book *No Sweat*, or answering some of the personal reflection questions—will help you get a better handle on why you want to make these changes. It also will be what assists you when your efforts become difficult and feel like hard work.

Amanda's fourth and final piece of advice to others looking to change their lifestyle was, to me, not only the most overlooked, but also one of the most important pieces people need to remember:

Be gentle with yourself.

"I think it's important to be kind to yourself and to recognize there will be bumps in the road," Amanda humbly shared.

Reversing years' worth of ingrained habits is no easy feat. As a loved one, health care provider, and society, we must stop treating eating better and increasing physical activity as such. Shows like *The Biggest Loser*, and the countless infomercials circulating television with *before* and *after* pictures all discount the demanding, hard work that must occur to change lifestyles and improve health outcomes.

When Amanda found herself discouraged, she consistently reminded herself she was doing the best she could. Remaining positive and not getting down on herself was critical in helping her continue her efforts to eventually find success.

In addition to outside sources of support remaining understanding and supportive, the person taking on the challenge of changing health behaviors must also stay positive.

The biggest source of this would be limiting that negative inner monologue that commonly plagues us all. You know the voice I'm talking about—the one that feels the need to comment on *anything and everything* over the course of your day. The harsh voice that judges actions and narrates happenings. The one that right now is either agreeing with me or saying, *No, I have no idea what she is talking about.* Yeah, that one.

Later in this book, I will touch on a very useful tool for overcoming this obstacle. This increasingly popular practice of mindfulness can be used in many aspects of your life. For now, I will set up a brief analogy to help begin the awareness that is necessary to shift negativity into powerful fuel for motivation.

I like to think of this in terms of a boss or a best friend. If your boss came to you with a project that was going to take months to complete, would you truly be able to thrive under constant comments of how terrible of a job you were doing, how long it was taking you, or how you probably couldn't even finish it anyway so why bother even trying? Probably not!

What if you asked a close friend to serve as your "motivator" as you set out to change your diet or begin physical activity? If they called you every morning and every night to remind you how tough this task of eating better or going to the gym was and how you're not equipped to handle this, wouldn't it be difficult to refrain from feeling the same way? And even harder to keep up the momentum of all the progress you have made?

I wouldn't feel like I could do it or even want to finish if I was constantly reminded of my failures. What kind of motivation is that? (If you're reading this and are one of the few people I have met who works well under this environment, to you I both say kudos and inquire if you want a hug?)

Like Amanda, I believe success can be had when individuals remain positive. Refraining from negative self-talk and instead highlighting personal strengths can prevent you from eating those two desserts at night or skipping your physical activity for the day.

I hope you reflect not only on what messages you are hearing in society, but also on who and what is surrounding you—including the messages you tell yourself. There exists within us all the power of resiliency to overcome hardship and the strength to change; sometimes we just need help finding it.

In the conclusion of *Devoured*, Egan shared with readers her simple wish for U.S. society in navigating the confounding marketing tactics of fad diets and the current trend of outsourcing our food.

Her vision of a perfect food culture to help maintain our country's food literacy and well-being looks a little something like this: "Work less and savor more. Make it real and stir the pot."[42]

Let's take a look at what she uncovered and dive a little deeper.

Work Less

Egan believes the reason so many people are no longer making home-cooked meals is overwork. "Feeling that there are just never enough hours in the day leads us to some troubling daily conclusions," she explained.[43] Making troubling decisions like choosing not to exercise, eating in the car on the way to work, and neglecting quality time with the family all make sense when we're faced with the harsh reality of time and never-ending to-do lists.

---

42 Egan, Sophie. Devoured: How What We Eat Defines Who We Are. New York, NY: William Morrow, 2017.

43 Ibid.

While Egan's proposed solutions lie in employer wages and federally mandated paid time off, there are other more accessible ways to manage this pressing reality of busyness.

Some band-aid, quick-fix methods are the new development of apps and services for meal-assembly kits and grocery delivery. They offer a smooth way to ensure availability of good food when extremely busy. However, with the use of these services, it is important to not let it be just another vise to do more work. Instead, an emphasis should be placed on allowing you to make time for more important matters, whether that be eating together as a family or going for a walk while the food cooks in the oven.

Another concept I briefly touched on before is mindfulness. This practice has surprisingly come up in many of my interviews with medical professionals. A quick check-in with yourself about where you are and what you're doing right in front of you can do wonders for the stressed air of rushing you may feel at all times of the day. Even simply the art of purposefully noticing your breath, the flowing of air in the nasal cavity, deep into your lungs, and then out again can reground you to the present.

There will be more on the concept of mindfulness and its intersection with health behavior changes in Chapter 20 of this book.

Savor More

The "savor more" mantra refers to indulging in the actual eating of food as well as the experience surrounding our food. Something as simple as focusing on the taste and texture of the apple you are eating, every juicy bite gliding over your tongue, or eating a meal with other people can remind us of the joys of eating.

Food is inherently a great thing! Associating positive experiences with the act of eating is a necessary bridge leading us back to a healthy relationship with food. Finding ways to enhance and encourage a sound attitude toward food will make the later shift in diet more bearable.

Human eating behavior is very closely tied to external (environmental) and internal (physiological) cues, both of which play a role in signaling a true need for food (Lippincott Williams & Wilkins 2013). Because of the effect your environment can have on eating behavior, it is important to look at the specific circumstances surrounding your food intake.

Lippincott, Williams, and Wilkins suggest that behavioral approaches can help someone be more cognizant of their typical eating habits. They propose asking the following eight questions to raise awareness of your environment around eating.

1. When were the meals eaten?
2. In what place were meals eaten?
3. What was the mood, feeling, or psychological state during the meal?

4. How much time was spent eating?
5. What activities were engaged in during the meal?
6. Who was present during the meal?
7. What food was eaten?
8. How much food was eaten?

Though answering and recording these questions after every meal is tedious, you can still find value in simply going over them in your head or aloud.

A meticulous food journal does not necessarily have to be kept (although if that is what works for you, wonderful). Even just acknowledging these questions and having them floating around your subconscious can keep you more aware of what food you're putting into your body and when and how you're doing it.

Say, for example, you have a family of four.

Dad consistently travels for work, which leaves Mom at home with the two kids on a regular basis. Because they are tight on money, Mom picks up extra shifts and often arrives home late from work with takeout from the diner down the street. Typically exhausted, she heads straight to the shower, while the son grabs his dinner to eat in front of the TV and the daughter eats while doing homework.

Remember, one key to longevity is one step at a time. Before Mom can begin to tackle the goal of cooking home-made meals for her family, the family should first aim to eat the takeout together at the table. Even if just for twenty minutes, eating together allows the time, however brief, for this family to connect both with each other and with the act of eating. Rather than focusing on a screen or assignment, face-to-face contact calls for acknowledgement of the task (eating) and situation (family time) at hand.

Additionally, this family can begin to ponder these questions. At the end of dinner, for example, they can each take turns asking each other the questions, even if it is just used as a reflection tool once a week. The first step in making any behavior change is awareness of the problem at hand.

It is important for this family to be gentle with themselves as they begin to notice and think about their food habits. Whether in their mind, aloud, or on paper, having these questions drifting around their subconscious is an accomplishment in and of itself, for they are one step closer to having food awareness become their norm. This awareness, over time, will foster better relationships with both food and the family, allowing healthier habits to take root.

Family Meal Times

There have been a number of studies conducted, articles written, and efforts made to encourage families to eat dinner together. Most findings suggest that an increased frequency of family dinner is associated with a greater consumption of fruits and vegetables, lower rates of overweight and obesity, lower likelihood of developing abnormal eating patterns, and even a decreased use of alcohol, drugs, and tobacco in teenagers who participate in family meals (Kit Broihier Wild

Blueberries article). It is no surprise that registered dieticians and public health officials are making a public effort to push for structured dinner time.

One such movement by the J.M. Smucker Company, the Mealtime Movement, coined the phrase, "*You are* who you eat with,"[44] implying that indeed the environment and people you surround yourself with ultimately permeate every aspect of your life.

For the daughter in the above example, even though she may think she is being productive and making the most of her time by eating with her homework instead of her brother and mother, she is actually ingraining in her psyche that food = work = to-do list = chore. Eating then becomes less of a pleasure and more of an inconvenience, allowing poorer decisions to be made more easily in the future—made about something you don't care much about.

Make It Real and Stir the Pot

The third part of Egan's wish for U.S. food culture is a pact to keep making it real. "Real food, grown responsibly, prepared in fresh, delicious ways, to be enjoyed together," she wrote longingly.[45]

---

44 "Join the Mealtime Movement." The Mealtime Movement. Accessed June 15, 2019. https://www.mealtimemovement.com/.

45 Egan, Sophie. Devoured: How What We Eat Defines Who We Are. New York, NY: William Morrow, 2017.

To combat the convenience of eating out, Egan called us all to look for hidden incentives to cook at home, the largest one being that we're losing our sense of control. This refers not simply to control over what we put in our bodies, but also the control we give to the growers and retailers at large. She argued that we are approaching a time in society when only food-service industry professionals will posses the basic culinary skills (I would like to add that we've well surpassed that time in terms of farming and basic gardening skills, with an overwhelming, terrifying dependence on grocery stores, however I digress—another problem exploration for another time).

Aside from the many health benefits home cooking yields, having the power and making the time to cook actively shapes a personal food culture, she explains. A personal food culture—much like eating habits—takes active exploration and fine-tuning to create.

Though she admits it is a difficult order, she believes a national cultural shift from focus on macronutrients to whole foods and eating patterns at large is ultimately the place to start. Recognition that there is no quick, easy fix to the problem we as a country have seemingly dug ourselves into can save a lot of time, money, and pain down the line— all of which are setbacks to long-term changes anyways. Until science can find that "secret elixir" as Egan put it, "It's safe to stick with the boring but timeless 'everything in moderation,'" she concluded.[46]

Balance, after all, seems to be the universal lesson hiding among every difficulty.

To sum up, creating an enjoyable environment around meals, whether through eating with another, slowing down to appreciate each bite, or finding more ways to cook for yourself, is necessary for a lifetime of eating well. In order for us to stick with a diet change for the long term, we must first ensure that the roots able to nourish sustainment of these habits are in place and that the efforts we make are rooted in reality, as our surrounding culture will always play a role.

Moving Forward

A majority of people in this country are not satisfied or successful with diets or trendy exercise classes, simply because they still struggle with their health goals. There has yet to be a seemingly universal method that works. While idealistic, I do believe we can reach a solution that targets the people struggling and provides them with structure and support when tackling the monstrous task of changing a health behavior. As the CDC stated, "Losing weight takes more than desire. It takes commitment and a well-thought-out plan."[47]

---

46 Egan, Sophie. Devoured: How What We Eat Defines Who We Are. New York, NY: William Morrow, 2017.

47 "Losing Weight: Getting Started | Healthy Weight | CDC." Centers for Disease Control and Prevention. Accessed June 13, 2019. https://www.cdc.gov/healthyweight/losing_weight/getting_started.html.

Amanda had both that commitment and a detailed plan to help her with her weight loss—and she feels better than ever. "Since I've made more health-conscious choices, I feel better about myself overall. I had a weight lifted off me both figuratively and literally," she laughed.

Health behavior promotion programs must consist of cultural reflection, both on the macro- and micro-levels. We also need to leave room for patience and kindness to permit growth. We must find ways to support more patients and individuals to find the success Amanda had on her own.

Regardless of how long it takes or what barriers the medical system might face, I believe even slow change is good change and that as a nation we have the potential to reduce the obesity and chronic disease rates. We must use the already existing momentum to eat better, to move, to live well, and translate it into a more effective and widespread effort that yields results.

Takeaways

Questions or programs for health behavior changes should highlight ways for the patient or individual to remain positive. It is important to keep in mind that this journey is a long one, and though people want to see fast results, it is ultimately the slow and steady efforts that will lead to longevity of behaviors. A greater emphasis should be placed on long-term lifestyle changes as opposed to the mentality of strict, restrictive, and quick diets.

Below are some questions to integrate into the intervention; whether it be by survey, written exercises, or in conversation, calling for reflection of the surrounding culture is important to identify why things are the way they are and more importantly how to get past them.

Cues and Questions:

- Reflect on culture surrounding you, whether it be our society at large, your hometown, the workplace, your family, or the environment within your own head.
- What are some pros of these environments?
- What are some cons?
- List five of your greatest strengths.
- What are some barriers you face in achieving your health goal?
- Why are these holding you back?
- What are some potential ways to overcome these barriers?
- Do you have access to healthy food options?
- Refer to the questions by Lippincott, Williams, and Wilkins to assess eating behaviors.

For healthcare providers:

- If you have a typical patient population, gather a list of resources for them to find local healthy food banks.
- Create a map that highlights where they can access fresh fruits and vegetables.
- Consider hiring a clinical social worker that can meet with patients either individually or in a group setting to assess cultural setbacks and ways to overcome these barriers.

PART 2

R

One Thing at a Time

O

T

When eating an elephant, take one bite at a time.

—CREIGHTON ABRAMS, U.S. ARMY GENERAL

Part 2 explores how successfully rooting healthful habits for the long term requires us to slow down and tackle things one at a time.

Upon entering my senior year, having left behind the only college life I knew as an athlete, I was quite honestly terrified of what lay ahead.

The past three years had been filled with morning lifts, running workouts in the afternoon, races and long runs on the weekends, and the little time in between packed with school, studying, and the occasional team bonding activity.

By taking my place on the team out of the equation, the only familiar thing left was my class schedule. Even the majority of my friends and social life revolved around the team, as spending close to all hours of the day together understandably lends quite nicely to close relationships.

I would like to add that at this time I was also struggling greatly with a personal tragedy. My mom, at only fifty-one years old, passed away unexpectedly from liver failure a few months before my senior year of college. I say this not for pity, but to merely expound on my understanding of life's difficulties getting in the way.

Even on the most daunting of days, taking the next right step kept me grounded. Even if it was as simple as putting on clothes and leaving the house only once that day, knowing I at least did something left me feeling satisfied and accomplished. Approaching all aspects of my life with manageable tasks and gentle care was what ultimately allowed me to continue engagement in living. It arguably saved my life.

One way I specifically translated this approach to continuing physical activity without a structured exercise routine was making realistic goals.

Changing my goals was a difficult concept to implement during my transition after sport. Acknowledging that my expectations as a Division I collegiate runner differed greatly from those of someone simply trying to maintain health took me awhile to fully do. I'll admit, I do occasionally still go to the track and run intervals just to see if I can still hit certain times. I have, however, come a long way in terms of being realistic and honest with myself about what I should expect going forward. I have reached a point where I am comfortable only running three miles twice a week as opposed to eight miles a day. It is through tackling this change in personal goals that allowed me to consistently remain active.

Another key that helped me reengage in movement was changing my belief about running and exercising. Initially, the inner monologue that plagued my mind upon leaving the team was incredibly forceful and ultimately detrimental.

You need to run. Go lift. Go to the gym. Do something! Anything! What is wrong with you? Why haven't you exercised today? You're going to get out of shape!

I had fallen into the trap of feeling like it was something I *must* and *should* be doing. Because it was something I had done for as long as I could remember, I believed I was supposed to continue doing it without question. So, when I wasn't able to continue with what I had always known, I began to feel discouraged and frustrated. I became extremely negative toward myself, those inner thoughts turning increasingly degrading, which only further perpetuated my lack of involvement in working out.

It was only when I reminded myself why I loved to exercise that I began to reengage. After weeks of not running, when I finally had the courage to go for a single run, I was reminded of how calming it was for me.

Immediately upon returning I felt infinitely more grounded, the long list of things I needed to do feeling more manageable, my mind seemingly quiet. When I stopped thinking of it as a *should* and reframed it as something I *wanted* to do, I began to actively choose to work out again.

I also had to learn how to effectively include going to the gym in my new schedule. Before, attendance at practice was necessary to retain my position on the team. Skipping was a nonnegotiable: simply not an option. Having practice physically and mentally blocked into my schedule every day created a smooth, unquestioned sense of obligation. It was only after removing that scheduled requirement that I realized how difficult (and important!) finding and making the time to include physical activity in my everyday life was.

It took me a month or so to settle into a new, fresh routine, but eventually I found ways that worked for me. On the days I knew I was going to be extra busy with school and work and volunteering, I would not make going to the gym a priority but instead choose to bike or walk to class. Conversely, on the mornings I knew I had more time, I would purposefully lay out a workout outfit on my dresser so it was the first thing I saw and put on upon waking up. Similarly, to ensure I remained eating a healthy diet, I purposefully wouldn't buy junk food at the grocery store and only allowed purchase of one dessert per shopping trip. Packing lunches the night before was also an essential part of my health behavior maintenance.

Taking the time to evaluate the places where physical activity or eating well can smoothly be inserted into your life is critical.

Both the efforts of changing my goals, my attitude, and schedule toward working out were bolstered by lessening the to-do list in my mind.

If Susie, our fictional friend from the Reflection introduction, had never exercised before setting out to accomplish the goal of going to the gym five days a week, she would most likely be sorely disappointed. Before Susie focuses on going to the gym twice a week, or even once a week, she should attempt to add activity into her already existing daily life. For example, rather than always taking the escalator or elevator, she should opt to take the stairs and simply focus on that until it feels doable.

Emphasizing taking the smallest next step can lead to a smoother transition into her living a life full of activity.

More solutions on how and why taking things one at a time is helpful for behavior change will be explored in this section.

CHAPTER 5

IDEAL-LESS

———

If Melissa Antal, MPH/MBA, were to sum up her views on behavior change, she would boil it down to one thing: letting go of the ideal.

Often, when someone is told they need to change a specific behavior, they are inundated with facts and guidelines of what and how much they should be doing that which they currently aren't. It can be incredibly discouraging to be immediately told what is wrong and then given an unrealistic standard to meet.

Melissa explained to me not only the importance of setting realistic expectations, but also the amount of systemic support that needs to be in place for effective change.

Great Expectations

Melissa offered herself up as an example. She understands that she needs to work out at least five times a week for X number of hours, but she finds that incredibly overwhelming. Instead, if you tell her she could walk the long way to work—which would take her thirty minutes as opposed to ten—it feels much more manageable. Melissa otherwise finds these intense expectations of physical activity to be too much, which can often lead to a freeze-up; this is entirely the opposite of what health professionals and patients themselves are looking for.

A way to combat this "freeze-up" is to start with smaller bouts, whether of healthy foods or exercise. Melissa explained to me, "What's important is identifying what the person's perfect practice is and then unpacking it to figure out how people can make the small changes to get to the ideal."

When trying to make a health change, if you start by demanding excellence immediately, of yourself or as a health-care professional, it is typically very discouraging. Just like Melissa, when people are told to lose weight, they immediately think of having to join a gym, participate in an intense exercise class, or go on long cardio bouts.

But this doesn't have to and shouldn't be the case!

This common misconception of having to jump right from zero to a hundred is a primary cause of the lack of physical activity in this country. Ideally, the guidelines call for two and a half hours a week of moderate aerobic activity a week, paired with any type of muscle-strengthening exercises at least two days a week. But if you have not done any physical activity for years, the expectation should in no way immediately be five days a week.

According to the most recent Behavioral Risk Factor Surveillance System (BRFSS) data, 48.3 percent of adults in the United States do not meet the national Physical Activity Guidelines for aerobic activity.[48] Another study by the CDC's National Center for Health Statistics found that only 23.5 percent of Americans are meeting the federal standards set in 2008 for time spent exercising, both aerobic and muscle-strengthening activity.[49] While staggering, these statistics show just how much room for improvement there actually is.

The U.S. Department of Health and Human Services has done a relatively good job making the physical activity recommendations known. Like for Melissa and many others, there is a wide understanding that a certain amount of exercise is required for good health and that not enough Americans are reaching that goal. The disconnect lies, however, in the expectation that this recommendation should automatically be the norm when making the initial shift from sedentary to active.

---

48 "Physical Inactivity in the United States." The State of Obesity. Accessed June 13, 2019. https://www.stateofobesity.org/physical-inactivity/.

49 "FastStats - Exercise or Physical Activity." Centers for Disease Control and Prevention. Accessed June 13, 2019. https://www.cdc.gov/nchs/fastats/exercise.htm.

For the four-fifths of the American adult population who don't meet the PA requirement, the emphasis should be on small gains, which will limit discouragement, ultimately increasing the likelihood of long-term adherence.

Melissa has taken this approach with her launch of foublie, a telehealth coaching platform that empowers families with food allergies to eat healthily and safely. Setting out to apply what she's learned from successful international public health development, she built foublie on three foundational elements: the spread of evidence-based, judgment-free, and real information for all her patients.

Melissa believes the "real" element is crucial. Acknowledging the struggles families face when having to adjust to a new allergy and change their dietary habits permits you to emphasize smaller changes as opposed to drastic ones, thus making the transition a smooth one.

She even believes that something as simple as the way she portrays her weekly newsletters can influence the engagement of families to developing new habits. A perfect example of this approach can be found in one of foublie's blog posts that looks at the necessary amount of exercise a child really needs. Below is a list Melissa and her co-founder Dr. Maria Rivera, M.D., MPH, included in the post:

What could moving more look like for your family?

We rounded up our favorite ideas. Remember you know your child, so keep it age appropriate.

- *Try a family activity, like a weekly walk or ball game.*
- *Go to the mall instead of online shopping.*
- *Park your car at the back of the lot and walk.*
- *Take the stairs instead of the elevator or escalator.*
- *Get an active job as a dog walker, rake the leaves, shovel snow, etc.*
- *Start a garden.*
- *Do sit ups or push ups during TV commercials.*
- *Sign up for a community walk. We love the Food Allergy Heroes walk!*
- *Active chores: unload the dishwasher, take the trash out, fold laundry*
- *Dance party in the living room*

So get out there and move! Remember you don't need to make the change in one day. Start small and have fun. Every movement counts.[50]

This is a great depiction of presenting information in an easy-to-read manner that demonstrates the accessibility of ways to increase movement.

Simply put, making realistic and manageable goals rather than jumping to the ideal behavior is a critical first step in the sustainment of new behaviors.

---

50 Antal, Melissa, and Maria Rivera. "Foublie's Blog: What You Must Know about Hot Topics in Child & Family Food." Foublie. Accessed June 14, 2019. http://foublie.com/blog.

Team Approach

Melissa also believes that sustainable behavior change takes multiple levels of clinical support. It is not just one doctor or one conversation that will make the difference, but rather a whole team with repeated exposure and guidance.

"The way I see behavior change," she informed me, "is that everyone has a role to play. It's not one partner alone, but a whole ecosystem around one person that is required."

Having a team of clinical support for a person combating chronic disease would offer a wider perspective of resources. If the current medical system shifted and allowed for a new program to be developed, it would prove beneficial to have a wide array of knowledge from multiple health care professional backgrounds. Helping people replace habits that have been ingrained for years is bigger than just fixing one part of the problem. Therefore, help should come from more than just one area of expertise.

"Nutritionists might not know as much about behavior to recognize that you actually have to suggest something that is not ideal in order to work with them long enough to get to that ideal behavior," Melissa clarified.

She raised a good point. While each health care provider, whether a primary care physician, cardiologist, or nutritionist, is more than qualified to treat any number of chronic diseases, their time constraints and specific specialties only offer a narrow scope of treatment.

A typical public health concept is ensuring as many people as possible are vaccinated for certain communicable diseases. The public health ideal in this scenario would be everyone being vaccinated to fully eradicate and eliminate a pathogen in a certain region.

Let us consider the necessary roles needed to achieve the highest possible number of vaccinated patients.

A community health care worker's job might be to get as many people to go to the doctor's office to get the vaccine, but this can only go so far in achieving the goal. Once the person gets to the clinic, it is up to the doctors and nurses to be friendly, and the office must be run smoothly to ensure the clinicians have the correct supplies and the wait isn't too long. Transportation must also be considered. Are these patients expected to walk ten hours to get to the vaccination site or is there public transit to assist them in travel? There are many factors requiring efforts from many different domains to achieve the ideal.

Using the above example as a model, let's say the public health ideal is either making a diet change or increasing physical activity. Similarly, for the physician recommendation or individual effort to be successful, the proper support across all health care domains must exist. Proper modes of delivery, treatment locations, health professional intercommunication—all necessary components to ensure patient susceptibility to a public health message is considered and fully functioning.

The collaboration between health care professionals that Melissa spoke of has increasingly become a priority at many health professional schools across the country. Known as Interprofessional Education (IPE), this approach recognizes the importance of multiple medical perspectives when seeking to improve health outcomes in patients. Beginning in 2009, six national education associations of health professional schools formed this collaborative to promote efforts meant to advance and foster team-based care for patients. IPE fosters learning among students of health to optimize patient care and improve population health outcomes.

I was excited to receive the opportunity to attend a workshop conference at the University of Michigan Health System's Interprofessional Education conference. Being the only undergraduate student, I learned a great deal from working with medical students, dental students, pharmacy students, public health students, social workers, and nurses when creating health plans.

The World Health Organization stated, "Once students understand how to work interprofessionally, they are ready to enter the workplace as a member of the collaborative practice team. This is a key step in moving health systems from fragmentation to a position of strength" (World Health Organization 2010). Coming together for a more holistic approach is of the utmost necessity if we hope to completely address the wide array of health problems facing our country. If we take a closer look, diseases are more intertwined than we could ever have imagined.

As an example, I will share one of the patient scenarios that was provided at the conference.

Marty is a 43-year-old male. He has type 2 diabetes and has been prescribed Januvia 50 mg twice daily, hydrochlorothiazide 25 mg daily, and Repatha 140 mg injected every two weeks. His doctor has also recommended that he try to lose 50 lbs through diet changes and by incorporating an exercise regimen. Marty's diabetes is uncontrolled and quite severe (HbA1c is 10). Marty does not see a health care provider regularly. He was not diagnosed until he had gone to the emergency room for a wound he had developed while at work in his seasonal construction job. When he was diagnosed nearly a year ago, he was provided with information about the long-term consequences of poor blood sugar control through pamphlets. Sifting through this information was overwhelming since he did not understand much of the terminology used in these reading materials.

Regarding his social history, Marty obtained his GED 10 years ago. Marty has three children and a wife who works a 9–5 job at a local business providing administrative support. Marty has been attending Alcoholics Anonymous groups at his local church and has struggled with alcohol use for most of his life. He and his family recently enrolled in the Healthy Michigan Plan since neither Marty nor his wife have affordable insurance through their employer. They have also accumulated a lot of debt because of periods of unemployment, investments that made their financial situation worse, and trying to help other ill family members pay for medical expenses. They have also had increasing health care expenses within their own family due to a recent emergency tooth extraction for Marty as a result of his chronic periodontitis that resulted from his uncontrolled diabetes. Marty had avoided preventive dental care because he could not afford it and did not see a need for it. Due to the cost of assisted living, his mother-in-law has recently moved into their small home. Marty, his wife, and oldest child are the primary caretakers with limited additional support because of the expense associated with home nursing care.

The family lives in a rural area where there isn't much light at night or sidewalks. Further, his home is on a dirt road with numerous potholes. Marty's wife does all the cooking and grocery shopping and does not understand why she has to change old family recipes to meet Marty's new dietary needs. Marty also loves his wife's cooking and is not interested in modifying his diet.

His wife, oldest daughter, and mother-in-law are
critical of his lifestyle choices and are constantly mak-
ing negative comments about his weight and lack of
motivation to lose weight. They are also "always on
him" about getting another job in the winter to provide
additional income for the family.

Marty has been diagnosed with diabetes for eleven
months now, but his doctor has not seen many changes
from Marty regarding implementation of diabetes
management recommendations. Marty presents to
the clinic today with concerns related to tingling in
his feet and feeling unsteady.

How overwhelming! Where do you even begin?

Sadly, Marty's case is not uncommon. In fact, hundreds of thousands of patients share stories just like Marty's. Lives are messy, as are health conditions. In our medical system today, often only a small piece of that story is gleaned from the patient-doctor interaction that lasts a few minutes, and that sliver always depends on which medical professional is assessing the case.

A doctor might focus on ensuring Marty's adherence to his diabetes medications through a verbal reminder. A social worker might look at underlying reasons he struggles to take them. A pharmacist would suggest other drug options that are cheaper and/or easier to administer, whereas a nurse practitioner might enlist the help of his family to provide support. Regardless of the profession, each approach is equally feasible and technically correct. Yet a more powerful method might be one that incorporates parts of all ideas.

My team for this exercise consisted of one medical student, one nurse, one pharmacy student, one MSW student, and myself, a kinesiology major and public health minor. It amazed me how unique each of our perspectives were when talking about Marty's care. While we all agreed the primary concern was managing his diabetes and the secondary concern was advising weight loss, our approaches were all incredibly different.

Marty's case speaks to the importance of understanding the many complexities that contribute to a patient's health profile. The conference solidified the wide array of knowledge each medical professional brings to the table that in turn supports Marty's multifaceted case.

From Melissa, we learn the great importance of not only setting manageable goals, but also the benefits that can come from a multi-pronged approach to changing behaviors. Consideration for these qualities in an intervention program is critical for helping patients navigate lifestyle changes.

Takeaways

Going forward, I believe there needs to be a trained health professional who can take on the blended roles of a physician, public health specialist, dietitian, and social worker when it comes to addressing behavior health concerns, specifically surrounding weight loss. I imagine this profession could be branded a health promotion specialist, health behavior educator, or wellness counselor, (whichever title fits) and act as a liaison between the other medical providers and the patients to ensure a quality intervention.

Some ideas for a program would be:

- Guiding patient to small wins,
- Setting manageable goals,
- Making programs and information accessible to patients/ easily digestible, and
- Fostering collaboration among a wide range of medical providers for a complete, holistic treatment plan.

CHAPTER 6

JUST CUSPIT

———

"Intuitive eating and a nonrestrictive diet is key to consistency with nutrition," Jaclyn DiGregorio, professional speaker, best-selling author, and entrepreneur, shared with me.

Only after an intense personal struggle with an eating disorder and low confidence did Jaclyn challenge one of the main concepts of a diet and find astonishing results.

This chapter will explore why Jaclyn's method of focusing on your body's wants and needs is effective for sustainability of a healthy lifestyle.

The "CUSP Moment"

Jaclyn first struggled with nutrition during her transition to college. Away from home-cooked meals and structured athletic teams, Jaclyn found it difficult to adjust to this new environment where decisions surrounding diet and exercise lay entirely in her hands.

Especially being constantly surrounded by other girls who were extremely concerned with their weight, Jaclyn found herself slipping into a pattern of restrictive diets followed by binge-eating episodes. Not only did she gain close to thirty pounds, but she began to lose friends, drop grades, and become depressed.

Initially turning to fad diets to help her regain control, Jaclyn became obsessed with diet plans and excessive exercise during her freshman year. What ensued was confusion and pain—and no results.

"I honestly didn't realize that I had an eating disorder until I stepped off the merry-go-round to realize the cycle I put my body and mind through," she admitted in an interview with a local Pennsylvania newspaper. "I figured, if I had this issue, most of the other excessive dieters and exercisers around me must have it too and not even realize."

Incredibly overwhelmed in her struggles with losing the weight, Jaclyn felt helpless. Eventually, she turned to working with the on-campus nutritionist to help her begin the slow journey back to health.

And it was life-changing.

It was here she discovered she had binge-eating disorder, which causes people who feel out of control to consume large amounts of food in one sitting. Working with the dietitian also showed Jaclyn that her poor eating habits were linked to her feelings of low self-confidence.

"During my first two years of college, I dealt with an emotionally and physically vicious cycle of overly restrictive diets resulting in binge eating," DiGregorio said honestly in that same interview with the *Daily Local News.* "I gained weight, and I lost confidence, happiness, passion, and my sense of self-worth."[51]

Though the weekly nutrition meetings were incredibly helpful in providing her a space to talk through meal plans and resetting her body to its natural eating patterns, she still struggled with incorporating the knowledge she learned from them into everyday life.

Her seeking help, personal curiosity, and drive to live better enabled her to lose twenty-seven pounds, run a marathon, and start her own business, all while still in college.

What she found to be most helpful was something she felt not many people were talking about in the diet and wellness world. Rather than placing herself on a restrictive diet, she began to listen to her body and simply eat good food when hungry. And this translated into many other aspects of her life.

51 DeGrassa, Peg. "Delco Woman Recovers from College Eating Disorder and Launches Unique Wellness Business." Daily Local News. July 20, 2018. Accessed June 14, 2019. https://www.dailylocal.com/business/delco-woman-recovers-from-college-eating-disorder-and-launches-unique/article_266f4037-f5ef-52fb-afcb-dd6f850aecb2.html.

Highly encouraged after her success with this approach, she longed to share it with others who faced similar frustrations. Her book, *The CUSP Method: Your Guide to Balanced Portions and a Healthy Life*, became an Amazon bestseller, and she now gives speeches at college campuses such as the University of Pennsylvania, Villanova, Penn State, Bucknell, and others all over the United States.

The Movement

The CUSP method combines the psychology of eating behavior and cutting-edge nutritional research to deliver a simple, sustainable approach to a lifestyle of wellness.

CUSP is an acronym that stands for Concentrate, Understand, Supplement, and Portion.

Her book demonstrates the importance of Concentrating on what your body is in the mood for, Understanding what food groups make up this craving, Supplementing the missing food groups, and Portioning the correct amount of this food.[52] Jaclyn lays out these four simple yet incredibly helpful tools to guide eating habits without drastic calls for extreme diet changes.

Her research and emphasis show that restrictive diets can often lead to overeating and setbacks, thus necessitating

---

52 DiGregorio, Jaclyn. "The CUSP Method: Your Guide to Balanced Portions & a Healthy Life EBook: Jaclyn DiGregorio: Kindle Store." Amazon. Accessed June 14, 2019. https://www.amazon.com/CUSP-Method-Balanced-Portions-Healthy-ebook/dp/B06Y5LXN6G.

an approach that does the opposite. Through her method, she highlighted the importance of breaking things up into a simple, "pocketbook" approach that can be used anywhere and anytime.

In addition to focusing inward, all Jaclyn's method calls for is learning the different food groups and understanding the correct portion sizes based on your body's makeup, which she lays out simply for her readers.

I have found myself using the CUSP method quite a few times since reading her book. I love it both for its acknowledgement of reality as well as its ease of use. For example, I used it when going out to eat with my friends the other night for dinner. We chose to go to MANI Osteria, a local Ann Arbor Italian restaurant known for its delicious pizza. Because it was finals week, I was extremely busy with studying and work and had neglected to go grocery shopping for the week. Consequently, I had no fresh produce at my house and had been eating out more frequently than I liked for all meals of the day.

Come dinnertime, I was craving pizza, though silently my body was also begging for an apple and some greens. When perusing the menu with my friends, I heard Jaclyn's CUSP acronym chiming in my head. If we ordered pizza, that would handle the grains and calcium food group requirements for my meal. Recognizing that I was still missing protein and vegetables, I advocated for getting the pizza with both sausage and pepperoni as well as the green peppers and mushrooms. I even suggested splitting a salad, to which my roommate thankfully and readily agreed. It was after completing the C, U, and S that I remembered I needed to hone in on my portion control. To ensure I did not eat more than I was hungry for, I purposefully only took one piece at a time and made sure to drink water in between bites.

And that was it! I was able to enjoy the rest of dinner without constantly thinking about food and proper nutrition.

Despite my having neglected meal prep for the week, Jaclyn's method allowed me to smoothly get back on track with eating a sound diet. All it took was the mental reminder to CUSPit and check in with myself to ensure I both enjoyed a night out with my friends and properly fueled my body.

Listening Deeply

On top of her developed method, Jaclyn has noticed three crucial concepts when working with her clients in making nutritional changes. Listening deeply to people's stories, increasing confidence, and acknowledging differences in individual preferences are all key to long-term commitment.

"A really common thing I have found is that people really just want to confide in someone and just be able to say it; they want to be heard," she explained to me.

She went on to tell a story about the time a girl approached her at a restaurant two years after she had given a speech at the girl's campus. The girl asked Jaclyn if she was the "CUSPIt girl" and went on to say how moved she had been from Jaclyn's talk and began to tell her own story.

She had started to follow Jaclyn's CUSP process and was inspired to get professional help, which drastically changed the direction of her life. Despite presenting to a large audience, Jaclyn shares a kind of vulnerability when telling her story that touches people and in turn gives them the courage to acknowledge and divulge their own stories.

In the current medical system, there is neither the time nor the resources to offer this space for respectful, honest, and genuine conversations that ultimately allow for personal growth. Though there already exists professions in the healthcare field with these roles, such as social workers or therapists, I believe the people who really need these conversations are often not seen by these clinicians. Specifically, when it comes to the required nutrition and physical activity changes chronic disease patients need to make, there is not a robust medical support system in place to help guide them.

Increasing Confidence

To Jaclyn, confidence also holds a huge power. CUSPIt is foundationally a wellness community that focuses on the empowerment of young women in order to be healthy and find balance. The first step in the creation of this community? Increasing women's sense of self-worth.

For a young woman, this process centers on body image and her relationship with her own body. Jaclyn encourages her clients to stop following people on social media that make them feel negative about themselves. Instead of comparing yourself to others, focus internally on your own goals and shift the focus to feeling better and having more energy. While it's easy to say, Jaclyn feels one way you can shift the focus inward is truly understanding your own being.

"A key part of confidence is being kind to yourself and doing small things every day that make you feel good," Jaclyn emphasized.

For example, Jaclyn walked me through the transition a lot of women face when arriving to college. The NCAA typically reports that only 2 percent of high school athletes will continue to participate in athletics at the collegiate level. This results in many former athletes, both male and female, left to their own devices for fitness.

Jaclyn's research suggested that most of these teenagers never learned to work out on their own outside of a team environment. In particular, she found that many women had a fear of the weight section and working out in general in the college world for lack of comfortability and confidence with both the machines and the large presence of men.

Sadly enough, coupled with university students' lack of time, the most common response is to simply not work out at all. But when you take a deeper look, why would anyone engage in something they feel they are supposed to do in an environment that is not preferred doing something they don't feel confident in?

In fact, very few people would ever actively put themselves in a situation like that. Yet, not uncommonly, it is expected of patients and clients alike to do exactly that. If a program were to be created, targeting a way to boost someone's confidence could lend to increased engagement in an activity.

To combat this insecurity, Jaclyn encourages these young women to seek out activities they enjoy doing. There is no one correct way to add physical activity into your daily routine: whether yoga, cycling, resistance bands, or indeed weight-lifting at the gym, it is important to find what works for you.

In order for someone to truly want or merely tolerate engagement in physical activity, there needs to exist a feeling of competency. Partaking in activities that bring out confidence shifts it from feeling like a chore to something more enjoyable. Further, listening deeply to each individual about their struggles and finding what works best for them can go a long way in supporting people.

Realistic Expectations

Personally, Jaclyn became a huge runner. After she had made strides on her own nutrition work, she started to train for a marathon. She acknowledged, however, that running is not for everyone—just in the same way other forms of physical activity don't work for her.

Laughing, she told me about a time she set her alarm early to go to a local pool and swim laps and just could not get herself to do it.

"For exercise, it is important to focus on the internal benefits, not the external ones and specially to choose something you enjoy," Jaclyn affirmed.

And the best part? These exercises don't have to be high-intensity workouts that last an hour or more!

Jaclyn firmly believes any form of exercise is better than nothing and that a quick ten-minute workout is still worth doing.

Similarly, Michelle, from Part 1, also emphasized this notion of broken-up physical activities with a list of "Opportunities to Move" shared in her book. They range from taking the "Long Cut" by parking farther away from your destination and walking the extra steps to enjoying "Cleaning Calisthenics" through adding more trips to and from the laundry room up and down the stairs.

In fact, recent research supports a necessary shift from aggressive, super intense, and short-period weight-loss programs to ones more aligned with realistic health outcomes.

A study published in the American Journal of Clinical Nutrition by Tate and colleagues sought to answer the question of whether higher levels of physical activity were protective against weight regain.

The answer? Resoundingly, no.

Participants were broken up into two groups: high-intensity physical activity (HPA), defined as burning over 2,500 kCal/week from exercise, and a standard behavioral treatment group that burned only 1,000 kCal/week.

With monetary incentives and exercise partners of their choosing, the HPA group was able to keep up the energy expenditure target for up to eighteen months. In this period, as expected, the higher physical activity participants achieved greater weight losses than the standard behavioral treatment group. However, the HPA participants were unable to sustain the energy expenditure target once the treatment ended. In fact, at a two-and-a-half-year follow-up, there were no between-group differences in activity or weight loss for either group.[53]

In other words, greatly increasing physical activity only for a relatively short period of time does not lead to long-term weight loss.

This greatly suggests the need for more consideration by health care providers when prescribing large bouts of physical activity to people who may not be physically ready. Further, more modest goals should initially be set for individuals who need to increase their physical activity levels or improve their diet, as increasing intensity of physical activity goals was not found to affect long-term engagement.

Additionally, more communication between providers and their patients about what realistic goals actually look like is imperative. Consistent with previous research, a study that

---

53 Tate, Deborah F., Robert W. Jeffery, Nancy E. Sherwood, and Rena R. Wing. "Long-term Weight Losses Associated with Prescription of Higher Physical Activity Goals. Are Higher Levels of Physical Activity Protective against Weight Regain?" The American Journal of Clinical Nutrition 85, no. 4 (2007): 954-59. doi:10.1093/ajcn/85.4.954.

examined individuals seeking weight-loss treatment found large disparities between dream, happy, acceptable, and disappointed weight goals and the weights people ultimately achieved. Participants who had more frequent contact with their primary care physicians, however, frequently endorsed more realistic goals.[54]

Asking patients who already struggle with maintaining certain lifestyle behaviors to keep up with high standards of health practices won't lead to sustained achievement of these target behaviors and could instead encourage the opposite. Additional studies have indicated that setting unrealistic goals leads to discontinued efforts by the participant and that more weight loss has been noted when there are no specific goals set (Dawson, 2018).

Given the magnitude of the problem, it is easy to believe that setting smaller goals would not generate substantial changes. However, weight loss as low as 5 percent of body weight has been shown to reduce or eliminate disorders associated with obesity. Specifically, for obese patients with non-insulin-dependent diabetes mellitus (NIDDM), hypertension, or hyperlipidemia, modest weight reduction appeared to improve glycemic

54 Dutton, Gareth R., Michael G. Perri, Melissa Dancer-Brown, Mary Goble, and Nancy Van Vessem. "Weight Loss Goals of Patients in a Health Maintenance Organization." Eating Behaviors 11, no. 2 (2010): 74-78. doi:10.1016/j.eatbeh.2009.09.007.

control, reduce blood pressure, and reduce cholesterol levels, respectively.[55]

Guiding patients to making more realistic goals as well as encouraging smaller behavior changes is actually more beneficial to someone's health profile than commonly thought. Initial goals should be within a patient's reach to demonstrate competency and limit emotional distress and don't have to be drastic in order to experience improved health outcomes.

It is important to note that setting large goals can and does work for many individuals. In fact, there is a large body of evidence supporting the notion that setting high weight-loss goals can actually heavily motivate people and yield dramatic results. As I will discuss further in the next section, this is where consideration of the individual at hand is so critical to ensuring sustained improvement with health behaviors, as not everyone works well under the same conditions.

At the end of the day, the primary goal of all health care providers and wellness interventions should be guiding patients to a lifetime of movement and eating well. By breaking up the target behaviors into realistic goals, patients can feel empowered tackle wellness one step at a time.

---

55 Goldstein, DJ. "Beneficial health effects of modest weight loss." International Journal of Obesity Related Metabolic Disorders. 16, no. 6 (1992): 397-415.

Takeaways

While her focus is primarily on college-aged women with body image issues, Jaclyn touched on widely applicable and critical pieces of health behavior management. The first comes from her focus on restriction-free diets and emphasis on balanced portions rather than rules and limitations. The CUSP method's goal of honoring the body, understanding nutritional basics, supplementing the missing nutrients, and monitoring portion sizes provides a simple yet effective approach to eating well. Secondly, she commented on the need to increase people's sense of competency and confidence to ensure engagement in these behaviors necessary for a healthy lifestyle. Lastly, and most importantly, I believe the CUSP method is suggestive of the need for more simple recommendations and asks of patients when they first begin this journey of shifting health behaviors. It is only by breaking things up into manageable and digestible chunks that individuals may find the courage and confidence to uphold their efforts for the duration of their life.

Programs and interventions for wellness must:

- Seek to emphasize the patient's individual strengths,
- Teach methods with which people can be successful,
- Help patients set realistic goals, and
- Highlight the importance of movement and a well-rounded diet as opposed to intense physical activities and dieting (CUSP and Opportunities to Move).

CHAPTER 7

THE CLIMB

———

"In retrospect, I think it was focusing on one thing at a time that really helped me get back on track," Patrick, a Ford Marketing Executive in his mid-fifties, told me.

He was referring to his three bouts of large weight loss in the past two decades. Though he struggled with maintaining his gains across the years, he was successful each time because of his use of what Dr. Sean Young, a researcher at UCLA, deemed "incremental power."

This chapter looks at what exactly Patrick did and how he was successful. Ultimately, his journey demonstrates why breaking things up truly helps people manage their behaviors. And after our conversation, excitedly, he is ready to add the missing elements of ROOT to ensure he has sustained success this time around.

The SCIENCE of Behavior Change

Sean Young, Ph.D., believes the current approach to making personal life changes has it all wrong. The UCLA medical school professor, psychologist, and executive director of the UCLA Center for Digital Behavior and the University of California Institute for Prediction Technology thinks the current emphasis on simply developing good habits and changing who you are to uncover willpower and motivation doesn't quite address the whole picture of making a change.

"I think one of the biggest problems or disservice in behavior change is all this self-help and motivational stuff that says we have to be inspired to change," he said in an interview on the *Art of Manliness* podcast. "We think that motivation or willpower or something like that will be all that we need to change behavior ... but there are different forces that are acting on us all the time to be who we are and act the way we are. We need to be aware of those forces and then we can use the right forces to help us change."[56]

Rather, the key to success is to understand the science behind lasting change and create a process to fit the individual. From over fifteen years of research in a variety of fields (psychology, technology, health/medicine, and business),

---

56 "Podcast #329: Stick With It — The Science of Behavior Change." Interview. Art of Manliness (audio blog), August 10, 2017. Accessed June 12, 2019.

Young has put together seven of these key psychological forces that can be used as a strategy for lasting behavior change addressed in any context.

Based on the core belief that the underlying problem in all habit change scenarios is the same, "People have stopped doing something"[57], his framework SCIENCE can be adapted to meet the needs of any individual attacking any habit change. In his book *Stick With It*, Young explained how these necessary components can successfully help anyone achieve their habit goal, whether it is a struggling dieter or a failing business.

Similar to my frustration working as an exercise physiologist, Young's initial inspiration on behavior change was tied to the medical world. After a life-saving surgery to repair his burst intestines, Sean's cousin was prescribed daily medication and instructed to change both his diet and exercise routine to remain healthy and avoid future complications from his Crohn's disease. Despite being an incredibly health-conscious and motivated person, his cousin failed to adhere to these lifestyle changes. Sean became incredibly confused and unsatisfied with the insistent medical professional's suggestion that his cousin was simply not educated enough.

57 Young, Sean. Stick with It: A Scientifically Proven Process for Changing Your Life -- for Good. New York: Harper, 2018.

"The biggest misconception of behavior change is that education alone is enough," Sean said in the *Art of Manliness* interview.[58]

This story of his cousin coupled with the convergence of this topic in other aspects of his life began Young's research journey on lasting behavior change. Now able to say his SCIENCE method has consistently demonstrated a 300 percent increase in lasting change for individuals and groups—in other words, people using his method are three times more likely to be successful than a control group (Young 11)—he has discovered an approach that actually works in helping people "stick with" their goals for the long term.

Just as with Michelle Segar, explored in our first chapter, he combines personal stories, research, and interactive written exercises for readers to complete while reading to demonstrate ways to live a life of consistency. Though his current focus of SCIENCE in the medical field is on the opioid crisis, people suffering from chronic pain, HIV/AIDS patients, and patients at risk for suicide, in many podcasts and his book itself, Young fully acknowledged the importance this method can have for people who want to exercise more or eat better.

There exists a call to translate this method into the health and wellness sector. Young hopes people will use his validated and peer-reviewed framework to change themselves

---

58 "Podcast #329: Stick With It — The Science of Behavior Change." Interview. Art of Manliness(audio blog), August 10, 2017. Accessed June 12, 2019.

and others for social good—for example, public health officials or medical professionals.

By now you are probably wondering what exactly his process looks like. It is not too different from what I have discovered in my own and others' research and observations. Young further brings to the table years of self-conducted and peer-reviewed studies to back his discoveries all to satisfy one recurring question:

Does this stuff actually work?

Though it's extremely difficult to measure behavior change, Young and his colleagues have delivered a simple, trustworthy, and successful approach in seven principles that yield positive results in bringing the "want to" into an actual "do."

Young called these seven principles for change *forces* for a reason. "I deliberately use the word *forces* because psychological forces are constantly pushing and pulling people to make different choices. These forces determine what people do and how they feel. They create emotional, chemical, and neurological changes," he explained in the introduction.[59]

A more solid understanding of these inner workings, whether by a medical professional or the individual themselves, offers a greater chance of success when making health changes. It should be required for a health promotion professional to fully understand the science behind behavior

59   Young, Sean. Stick with It: A Scientifically Proven Process for Changing Your Life -- for Good. New York: Harper, 2018.

change in order to effectively address the complicated nature of each patient.

The first force of Young's research, Stepladders, will be discussed here in Part 2. The second force, Community, will be touched on in Part 3. The remaining forces of Important, Easy, Neurohacks, Captivating, and Engrained will be explored in Part 4. While the final four forces are all equally important, I felt most of them could all fall into the subcategory of tailoring to the individual.

Patrick's Battle

"The first time around, I lost fifty pounds," Patrick proudly told me.

His initial weight loss efforts started in 1994 in response to a corporatewide health initiative at Ford Motor Company, where teams signed up to see who could lose the most weight when put up against other teams in the company. He and his work buddies were excited to give it a try—because all had played sports in high school, there was a competitive, albeit friendly, nature to their challenge. No one wanted to be the one who lost.

Even though Ford offered health guides to help its employees, Patrick was set on doing it on his own.

"I didn't really want any help. I knew what I needed to do—change my diet and increase physical activity—and I didn't think it would be that hard." When pressed further, he said his unquestioning positivity and self-confidence ultimately drove him. "I just knew I could do it, I guess, so off I went."

When Patrick started the challenge, he was thirty years old and 237 pounds. Standing at 5'11", he had a Body Mass Index score of 33.1: clinically obese. Though I've mentioned before why I sometimes don't like using the BMI scale for its lack of consideration of body composition and build, it can be helpful as a loose guide, especially at the population level.

A man with a strong build, Patrick was very toned and muscular in his arms and legs. The excess fat, however, existed around his abdomen and stomach, largely increasing his risk for heart disease. Research depicts that any BMI score above 30 increases risk for heart disease, hypertension, diabetes, and other related illnesses.[60] Though he may not have appeared extremely overweight, shedding pounds was important to mitigate his health risks.

Before starting, Patrick made a loose plan for himself. He knew he wanted to lose weight, and he knew he needed to change his diet and increase physical activity to do it. He didn't, however, want to skimp on either part, so he decided to initially split them up.

"My first focus was on caloric intake and second was changing my workout from muscle-building to more cardio

---

60 "Diabetes, Heart Disease, and Stroke." National Institute of Diabetes and Digestive and Kidney Diseases. February 01, 2017. Accessed June 15, 2019. https://www.niddk.nih.gov/health-information/diabetes/overview/preventing-problems/heart-disease-stroke.

and total body conditioning," he explained. "I focused on the calories first to get my body used to the drop-in calories so when I changed my workout it had the maximum impact on my weight reduction."

During the first three weeks, his only focal point was changing his dietary habits. He didn't eat any bread or rice; turned to lean proteins like grilled skinless chicken breast, salmon, and tuna; and made sure to add raw veggies and fruits while limiting snack foods like chips or pretzels. An interesting tactic he employed was using absolutely no condiments. He completely cut out his use of mustard, mayo, ketchup, and even salad dressings.

He also turned to methods of measuring his food, actually reading food labels, eating the recommended serving sizes, and limiting his portion sizes. He limited himself to just 1,000 calories a day. Meal spacing was another incredibly helpful tool for Patrick. He made sure to eat breakfast every morning, a small snack at 10 a.m., lunch at 12 p.m., another snack at 2 p.m., and a small dinner after work.

Spacing out meals and keeping his eating times consistent allowed Patrick to eat on a schedule that suited his particular lifestyle. This is a common approach nutritionists recommend to patients to manage their food intake. Incorporating healthy snacks can help suppress appetites and curb excessive and mindless eating at and in between meals. It also allows the body to adjust to a regular eating schedule, which further limits overeating and enforces development of proper habits.

It was only after Patrick felt he had a comfortable handle on his diet changes that he began to change up his exercise routine. Once he thought his body's metabolism had adjusted, he was able to shift his focus to his next goal of changing his workout routine.

Jokingly, he said to me as he laughed, "Not quite sure if there is science behind this, but I didn't want my body to go into starvation mode. I felt if I reduced my calories and upped my physical activity at the same time, my body would go into shock, which would lead me to failed efforts. I didn't want to fail."

Though his reasoning may be a tad off from reality, there *was* science backing his method and success. It just wasn't what Patrick thought.

Patrick was unknowingly making use of a tactic Young called incremental power, or what I like to call taking things one at a time. Let's take a look at why this method works so well and how it helped Patrick lose fifty pounds.

Force 1: Stepladders

Sean Young's first force is called Stepladders, which explores how people have a better chance of succeeding if their goal is broken up into smaller chunks.

Though it may seem obvious, Young believes many people still fail with this step because they don't understand just how small the initial steps need to be and don't have a model to guide them.

Let's consider the more common, everyday example of creating a to-do list. I know I myself have used this technique quite often—especially when I notice I am feeling extra stressed and overwhelmed with all I have to do. Even the act of writing what I have to do on paper and simply *making* the to-do list makes me feel somewhat accomplished and more organized, let alone the amazing feeling of getting to cross things off.

Young explained what happens neurologically when people break up tasks and why even the act of writing a list calms my mind for the time being. According to his research, any time the brain accomplishes something it sets out to do, it releases a surge of dopamine. Dopamine is the neurotransmitter tied to rewards and is closely associated with feelings of euphoria, bliss, motivation, and concentration. Even when I simply write the to-do list, I feel rewarded because 1) I decided it was a goal of mine to create a list, and 2) once I finished writing one, my mind had completed its goal and released to neurotransmitters and I felt accomplished. As I begin to do my laundry, finish writing my paper, and go for a run, crossing more items off my life, it results in more dopamine being released.

This means when you and your brain set too-lofty goals and struggle to reach them, you don't get a rush of dopamine and are thus not rewarded for your efforts. Instead, it leaves you with a feeling of disappointment and failure. On the flip side, when you initially set a small, easier goal, you are more likely to feel accomplished and successful, leaving you with the feeling of wanting more and the confidence to know you can get there.

To combat this misunderstanding and address the inner workings of our subconscious decisions, Young built a step-ladder model to help people truly think small. This model is broken up into Steps, Goals (Short-Term and Long-Term), and Dreams.

Steps typically take less than one or two weeks to accomplish and can be seen as minuscule tasks to check off to begin the quest of accomplishing a habit change. Next come goals, which can take anywhere from one to three months and are considered the in-between objectives. Dreams, which are things you have never personally done before, focus on the long term and typically take longer than three months to achieve.

"People need to be reminded of their dreams to keep them motivated, but focusing entirely on dreams can lead people to give up," Young wrote (Young 28). It is only realism coupled with a hint of inspired imagination that keeps someone motivated for the long run.

Take, for example, a man named Robert. Robert finds himself wanting to cook homemade meals at least five nights a week. Imagining a world where he comes home from work every night to eat fresh vegetables and fruit with lean protein, he longs to lose weight.

Under Young's model, before he can even begin to reach this envisioned reality, Robert must first break down this dream into manageable steps and goals. An initial step, as an example, could be buying a cookbook. A short-term goal might be going to the grocery store to buy ingredients, with the long-term goal of using those ingredients to actually make a meal at least once a week. Only then can Robert's dream have a chance to become a consistent, sustainable reality, for he is making use of incremental power.

This approach is similar to that of the commonly used SMART goal structure. First coined in 1981 in a paper on management objectives by George Doran, a consultant and former director of corporate planning for a water power company in Washington, this acronym is used by countless business professionals, organizations, academics, and medical professionals all over. Even my high school cross-country coach was a fan!

SMART refers to making a goal specific, measurable, attainable, relevant, and timely. Yet Young's approach goes a little deeper, allowing room for both the realistic and the imagined realm of a habit to support engagement from all sides. This is not to say that SMART goals can't be helpful—the model has remained popular and widely used for a reason—but Young's approach covers a wider breadth of the goal setting process and gives a more tangible process.

Relating it back to our friend Patrick, he also broke up his health tasks into smaller chunks. He unknowingly used the model Young had laid out for long-term behavior success. Patrick's completion of Young's Stepladder would have looked a little something like this:

Step 1 (1–2 weeks):

- Increase lean protein and vegetable intake.
- Cut out condiments and grained carbs.
- Use portion control/limit serving sizes.

Step 2 (1–2 weeks):

- Add thirty minutes of cardio work to his gym lifting routine.

Short-Term Goal (1 month):

- Incorporate both nutritional changes and workout shifts into daily routine.

Long-Term Goal (2–3 months):

- Be physically active and capable in daily life.

Dream (3+ months):

- Win the challenge after nine months.
- Lose the most weight out of all his friends.
- Reach college graduation weight.

Despite wanting to achieve a lot of goals at once, Patrick was able to first make his nutrition changes, and then his exercise goals, because they were his sole focus those first few weeks. By breaking them into sections, he made his ideal behaviors more attainable. He didn't ask himself to go to the gym in addition to shifting his diet until he comfortably met his target behavior of eating better. Only then did he feel confident in moving on to his next goal of adding more cardio into his physical activity routine.

Depending on an person's capability, knowledge, and confidence, these small tiers can, and should, be adjusted accordingly. Because Patrick was already relatively active at the gym and seemed to know a lot about nutrition on his own, he was able to make his starting goals loftier than, say, his sixty-two-year-old neighbor, Helen, who is looking to increase her activity level and has been rather sedentary for years. A health promotion intervention or health care providers should help their patients set realistic and attainable goals while still breaking them up.

Jack Canfield, American author, motivational speaker, corporate trainer, and entrepreneur, most famous for co-authoring the best-selling *Chicken Soup for the Soul* series, outlined on his blog three additional ways to take small steps and make big changes.

The Rule of 5 is his idea that you must take action on five specific things per day that will move you closer to your goal.[61] The most important note is that nothing is too small. I have used this notion many times throughout the process of writing this book. It is incredibly overwhelming when I zoom

---

61 "How Small Steps Make Big Changes | Jack Canfield." America's Leading Authority On Creating Success And Personal Fulfillment - Jack Canfield. January 29, 2019. Accessed June 14, 2019. https://www. jackcanfield.com/blog/big-changes/.

out and think about the big picture of having a completed manuscript to publish. Especially on top of my other responsibilities of work, school, and volunteering, it was incredibly intimidating to ponder how I would ever get it done.

One of my professors shared with me a tip similar to the Rule of 5—one I will always carry with me. He said, "No matter what you do, make sure you do something, anything, every single day that helps you with the writing process."

To this day, I try to follow exactly that. Even if it was as small as reading an article about behavior change or listening to a podcast on my walk home from class and jotting down quick notes, doing something that brought me closer to my goal every day added up. Trusting the process and yourself is an incredibly important piece of accomplishing any goal. We must not forget that when taking on seemingly formidable tasks.

Canfield's second tip is to link a new habit to an already existing behavior. For example, I encourage my families at the ShapeDown program to do five squats every time they go to the bathroom or to do heel raises the whole time they are brushing their teeth. Pairing a goal activity with something you already do daily will help you solidify it as a mandatory part of your routine.

His third tip is to track your progress. Using a journal or an app to keep an updated list of what you've accomplished can visually show you how little tasks can add up to create big results. It is important to constantly check in with yourself to see where you stand to then help you look forward to where you're going. Canfield shared an ancient Chinese proverb in his blog: "A journey of a thousand miles begins with a single step." How true that is.

Interventions must seek to remind individuals that small progress is just as important as big gains. It is the missing ingredient that makes the whole dish taste a tad off. Without daily progress, we will never reach the goals we set.

Finding Balance

At the end of the nine-month challenge, Patrick had lost fifty pounds and weighed 187 pounds—exactly what he weighed at his college graduation nine years earlier. He ended up coming in second place, but only because his friends decided to adjust pounds lost to percentage of total body weight.

"I technically lost the most pounds," he laughed, explaining to me his friend only beat him relatively by the percentage. "He was just a smaller dude to begin with."

Unfortunately, a few years later, at age forty, Patrick found himself back where he started.

"After I achieved my weight loss goal, I slowly climbed back into the bad behaviors. Slowly though!" he was quick to add.

Slow or not, it is this transition back into old ways that constantly trips people up with weight loss. This common struggle results from using the wrong approach. Rather than focusing on creating a life of wellness and finding ways to incorporate new, healthier habits seamlessly into your daily routine, people seek quick fixes, target weights, and ideal images. It is this misconception that health and wellness exist separate from the rest of our lives that must be remedied in order to find lasting solutions.

"It grew back over time. I'd notice clothes that no longer fit, knowing exactly which ones in my closet I had to go back to wearing," he explained. "It just really bummed me out."

I could see his frustration with himself, even as he recounted this story to me now, years later. This frustration, sadly, is not uncommon. And it's part of the problem! When people feel discouraged, time and time again, they ultimately stop trying. It is necessary, then, to ensure patients feel successful and notice progress, to make sure they continue with their efforts. Whether that progress is feeling better physically, having more energy, minimizing symptoms of another disorder, or even looking a certain way, there must exist triumphs. No one likes fighting a losing battle. Setting up a program so that patients have wins is important.

"Once I went through the finish line of the weight-loss goal, I no longer had the discipline to focus as intently," Patrick reflected. "You know, life just happens."

He went on to lose forty more pounds at age forty when the frustration of gaining the weight back became too much to deal with mentally. He took on the challenge of losing weight for a second time. Using the same approach of breaking things up, he again found success and lost the weight. This time it lasted for fourteen years, which brings us to present day.

A few months ago, Patrick realized he's the heaviest he's ever been. At fifty-four, he understands it's time for his third go-around with the dieting and increase in exercise and that it may be the most important time. Part of the weight regain he knows has to do with his aging. He told me he can feel the difference this time and can't move as fast as he used to and gets achy more often. As a result, he thinks his transition to increasing cardio will be more difficult. He feels he will need to do more now to see similar results. As he begins his attempts again, he hopes to see the same changes. At the time of this interview, he was three weeks in and down ten pounds.

As he gears up for this next go-around, I asked him to reflect on what he thinks went wrong the last time.

"Maintaining a regimented diet is what usually falls off for me," Patrick concluded.

His confidence, however, doesn't waver. Just as he did when he was younger, he believes in himself to make it— which is exactly why I think he will.

I then asked why he thinks it was so hard for him the past two times to keep up the positive changes he made in his behavior and what he can do about it to ensure the changes stick. To buffer against future intermittent periods of slow weight gain, he believes his focus should be on building healthy habits rather than on an ideal body image.

"I suppose I should focus on the rewards of a healthy life-style as opposed to the specific weight-loss goals," he knowingly stated.

How right he is.

Since the previous two times he has lost the weight, Patrick has already successfully maintained an active lifestyle. He plays on a recreational basketball team with games every Monday night. In the spring and summer he typically rides his bike to and from the grocery store and likes to go on walks after dinner with his girlfriend or oldest daughter. He also continues to go to the gym a couple of days a week, though he loves lifting a lot more than doing cardio work.

Now, his long-term goal is to focus on weaving the nutritional changes into the fabric of his daily life, just like he did with the physical activity. A new international marketplace just opened near his house called Nino Salvaggio. Home to the freshest produce and quality food options, Nino Salvaggio's offers Patrick an exciting place to carry out his healthier choices.

It is my hope that people like Patrick who struggle on and off for years will eventually receive the support they deserve when making lifestyle shifts. My vision consists of a wellness program that incorporates the themes and ideas of ROOT so these people can find success that traverses a lifetime. Eating better and being active should exist within our lives—not as a separate entity we must battle our entire lives.

Takeaways

Through this book and my future career work, I want to help patients and individuals come to the realization that Patrick has throughout his journey. Shifting the focus from an ideal standard image of health to finding a lifestyle of wellness should be the goal of every health promotion program. I believe more support should be in place to help people across the country find ways to ensure their efforts last.

Below are things to consider when creating a new wellness program.

- Use stepladder framework like Young's model to help people set manageable goals.
- Consider the Power of 5 rule and encourage completing small acts every day.
- Tie new habits to already existing ones.
- Track progress via journal or app.
- Emphasize goal is achieving a lifestyle of wellness, not focusing on individual acts.

CHAPTER 8

#FATGIRLFEDUP

———

"I'm in if you are," Danny Reed turned to his wife, Lexi, and said in response to their friend's New Year's resolution healthy living challenge.[62]

Having struggled with her weight since she started Weight Watchers when she was just twelve years old, Lexi was hesitant to agree. Though skeptical and nervous, she eventually decided to join. The lack of rules, points, and plans from the challenge was enticing.

As such setups are notorious for leading to failure, this chapter will explore how and why Lexi and Danny Reed's initial thirty-day resolution of eating healthy, cooking at home,

———

62 Staff, Editorial. "From 'Fat Girl Fed Up' to Food-Tracking Pro: How Lexi Reed Lost 312 Pounds and Kept It Off." Woman's World. September 26, 2018. Accessed June 14, 2019. https://www.womansworld.com/posts/fatgirlfedup-myfitnesspal-success-story-166847.

and exercising for thirty minutes a day was accomplished and how it largely surpassed everyone's expectations.

"I focused on the single day ahead of me, not the 300 pounds I knew I had to lose, because that would have overwhelmed me," Lexi stated in an interview with *Trimmed and Toned,* a health and fitness platform. "It made me feel like I didn't have such a long way to go."[63]

Together they lost a collective 400 pounds in two years, with the sole support of MyFitnessPal, each other, and tackling things one at a time.

Here's why it worked.

#fatgirlfedup

Lexi and Danny Reed, a married couple from Terre Haute, Indiana, gained national media attention when they collectively lost 400 pounds in just two years after making a New Year's resolution together.

At her heaviest, Lexi, 28, at 5′6″ weighed 485 pounds; Danny weighed in at 281 pounds, standing only 5′8″ tall. After years of eating large amounts of fast and fried food and drinking soda at every meal, mindlessly watching TV and eating junk food, the Reeds were "fed up" and decided it was time to change their lifestyle habits.

---

63   TrimmedandToned. "Lexi Reed 'FatGirlFedUp' Lost 285 Pounds In 18 Months With These 2 Simple Steps!" TrimmedandToned. August 17, 2017. Accessed June 14, 2019. http://www.trimmedandtoned.com/lexi-reed-fatgirlfedup-lost-285-pounds-18-months-2-simple-steps/.

Similar to Richard from Chapter 1, it took the pain and regret of not being able to participate in the simple activities of life, like walking up the stairs or going seashell collecting on their honeymoon. After setting the initial resolution to lose weight, a friend then challenged the couple to a month with no alcohol, soda, cheat meals, or going out to eat.

They accepted and what followed was a reality the couple never dreamed possible.

No surgeries, no weight coach, no nutritionist—all pounds shed stemmed from diet and physical activity changes they made on their own. Though at first it wasn't easy, Lexi said on the *TODAY* show, "We started small ... we focused on small changes every single day and they added up to big results."

Some of those initial small steps included cutting out soda completely, slowly adding vegetables and lean protein to their diet in addition to solely cooking their own meals, and breaking up her thirty-minute cardio exercise goal.

Rather than going on a strict diet, Lexi chose healthy foods that appealed to her and simply logged them using the MyFitnessPal app. The food log allowed her to stick with the app's calculated total daily allowance of 1,800 kCal/day. She also found success making healthier versions of her favorite dishes, such as General Tso's chicken.

On the physical activity side, instead of jumping straight to high-intensity interval training, she started with walking on the treadmill and allowed herself to take breaks when tired.

Where she wasn't lenient? Both with the frequency and total time of her engagement in exercise.

No matter how she did it, she made sure to get a total of thirty minutes of cardio in four or five days a week. Even when it meant creeping to a very slow pace, she refused to stop until she hit her total of thirty minutes.

Eventually, she worked her way up to the elliptical and other forms of movement, always adjusting based on her body's needs for weight maintenance. "I have picked up the intensity of my workouts and adjusted my calories to continue losing consistently," she said in an interview with *TODAY*.[64]

Within two years Lexi dropped 312 pounds. Ultimately, it was finding that sweet spot of doing enough to see results, but not such an exorbitant amount that it overwhelmed her.

"It wasn't one moment that made everything click; it was that everything kind of added up. I was just so fed up with where I was and where I was going," she explained to *Trimmed and Toned*.[65]

Initially making small goals was touched on in the previous chapter with Dr. Young's research on Stepladders. Another best-selling author and speaker, James Clear, focused on habits, decision-making, and the importance of

---

64 TODAY. YouTube. May 24, 2018. Accessed June 14, 2019. https://www.youtube.com/watch?v=_qgtwz77hZM.

65 TrimmedandToned. "Lexi Reed 'FatGirlFedUp' Lost 285 Pounds In 18 Months With These 2 Simple Steps!" TrimmedandToned. August 17, 2017. Accessed June 14, 2019. http://www.trimmedandtoned.com/lexi-reed-fatgirlfedup-lost-285-pounds-18-months-2-simple-steps/.

continuous improvement in his *New York Times* bestseller, *Atomic Habits.*

Tiny Changes, Remarkable Results

James Clear is one of the world's leading experts on habit formation. Using concepts uncovered from a variety of fields of academia, such as biology, psychology, and neuroscience, he has explored in his book and many other articles the science of small habits and explained why they can lead to such success.

In one article titled "The Paradox of Behavior Change," Clear debunked the myth of radical change.

Remember the concept of having a set-point? Our bodies are hard-wired to maintain all senses of equilibrium, both physically with things like changes in blood pressure or weight, as well as mentally with things like actions and habits.

Clear contends that the idea of setting lofty goals and looking for large gains after placing high expectations actually disrupts our natural stability.

"What we fail to realize, however, is that any quest for rapid growth contradicts every stabilizing force in our lives," he wrote in a blog post on his website. "If you step too far outside the bounds of your normal performance, then nearly all of the forces in your life will be screaming to get you back to equilibrium."[66]

---

66   James Clear. James Clear. September 01, 2018. Accessed June 14, 2019. https://jamesclear.com/behavior-change-paradox.

This means if Lexi *had* initially set her weight loss goal at losing a hundred pounds as opposed to simply eating better and working out for thirty days, her efforts would have been thwarted, both by the pulls to her previous unhealthy lifestyle and by her own mind. It takes a lot of energy to go up against the forces of years' worth of behaviors and maintain that fight for change.

To avoid resistance and ensure the sustainability of health behaviors, the size and the rate at which you force these changes needs to be considered. Within a narrow window exists an optimal rate of growth.

Below is Clear's hand-drawn graph to demonstrate this need for small wins to establish sustainable change.

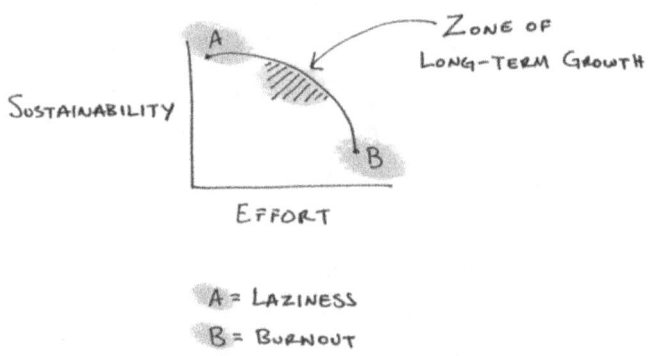

Clear likened this "sweet spot" to a quote by systems expert Peter Senge: "When growth becomes excessive—as it does in cancer—the system itself will seek to compensate by slowing down, perhaps putting the organization's survival at risk in the process."[67]

To simplify, if a sedentary individual with a poor diet is asked by a physician to immediately engage in exercise five days a week in addition to cutting out their processed sugar intake completely, everything in their being will attempt to halt those changes to remain as stable as possible.

To combat this constant force pushing people toward their already established norms and make change, they must not stray too far from the baseline. Instead, they should initiate action and focus on making more manageable shifts.

One way Clear suggested to do this is through the two-minute rule: each day or every couple of days, you should engage in something you want to change for *only* two minutes. If you want to run your first 5k, the first step should be putting on your shoes and walking around your driveway for two minutes. The next day, you add two minutes. And so forth. This may seem tedious, but we know 1) anything is better than nothing, and 2) slowly making small changes is more likely to lead to engaged, long-term success than burnout.

"The best way to achieve a new level of equilibrium is not with radical change, but through small wins each day," Clear concluded.[68]

---

67 Ibid.
68 Ibid.

Another set of research studies has established the finding that when people set tangible intentions by stating when, where, and how they intend to implement a particular behavior, the odds of achieving said target behavior increases.[69] The important caveat that Clear drilled home is the notion that developing a specific plan will only enhance your likelihood of success *if you focus on one thing at a time.*

Lexi and Danny's approach of taking small steps at a time is an incredibly crucial part of their lifestyle success. They managed it because they did not attempt to drastically change their life immediately and instead took it each day at a time, step by step.

Other Factors

Aside from taking the process one step at a time and setting small goals, there were three additional factors that the Reeds believe enabled them to both lose the weight and keep it off through sustainment of their new health habits.

One was making the daily ritual of going to the gym a nonnegotiable. "I just kind of try to set it up like a business meeting. I am my own boss and I can't cancel," Lexi explained.[70]

---

69 Ibid.
70 PEOPLE.com. Accessed June 14, 2019. https://people.com/health/this-couple-dropped-395-lbs-together-we-fell-in-love-with-taking-care-of-ourselves/.

By making it a priority, Lexi and her husband were able to consistently keep up their goal of working out. And on the days it was tough for them to continue with that "date"?

"I mean, I honestly think just having each other was the biggest key that helped us tremendously," Danny said as he looked to Lexi in the *TODAY* show interview.[71]

Lexi and Danny made perfect use of a buddy system, which brings us to the third factor. By taking turns encouraging and supporting one another, the Reeds were able to hold each other accountable on the days when one of them was not feeling up to it. "We would be tired and sore because our bodies weren't used to it," Lexi told *People Magazine*. "But we had a buddy system, so every step of the way, every pound, we were there to motivate each other."

Finding someone you not only trust and feel comfortable with but also enjoy being around can make the experience more bearable—and even fun. Lexi and Danny found themselves getting closer than ever before. Previously having spent a majority of their time together watching TV and not talking, they now found extra time spent together allowed them to reconnect.

Though they made it look easy, sticking with a difficult goal for over a year with benefits well down the line is tremendously tricky. There are bound to be days or quite honestly weeks where you're just not up to the task.

---

71 TODAY. YouTube. May 24, 2018. Accessed June 14, 2019. https://www.youtube.com/watch?v=_qgtwz77hZM.

Aside from having a companion to work alongside you, Lexi suggested finding a deeper motivation to keep you going. For her, it was family. She had always wanted to have kids and enjoy a long, full life with Danny. Her weight physically prevented her from bearing children and predicted fewer years of life, and she also didn't want to set an unhealthy example for her future kids.

Even activities such as biking, riding a rollercoaster, or walking came at no ease to Lexi. She longed to live a normal life rather than simply existing.

Visual Cues

On top of her long-term incentive, Lexi found a daily source of motivation to keep her engaged: Instagram. Hiding a smile, she told the *TODAY* audience, "It really kept me accountable because I knew that if I went to the gym, I could post a sweaty selfie or post what I was eating and knew that I was helping people."[72]

Having a way to monitor her progress on a smaller scale gave her little things to look forward to daily. Later, after receiving national attention, her tracking pictures also served as an inspiration to countless women and girls also looking to lose weight in hopes of changing their life. Now with a following of over 1.1 million users, Lexi has begun running weekend retreats to assist people in their own life-changing journey.

---

72 Ibid.

Clear wrote about this idea of using a visual trigger to help motivate consistent habit performance. He coined it "The Paper Clip Strategy" in honor of a young man named Trent Dyrsmid who quickly became a top salesman within his company by simply moving one paper clip from the full jar of 120 on his desk to the empty one sitting beside it, not stopping until he had completed all calls for the day.

"Making progress is satisfying, and visual measures provide clear evidence of your progress," Clear explained. "As a result, they reinforce your behavior and add a little bit of immediate satisfaction to any activity."[73]

Visual cues are convenient, easy to use, and a cost-effective method to keep track of progress. They can also serve as a reminder when the busyness of everyday life gets in the way.

Lexi and her husband demonstrate three of the critical factors necessary for long-term change. One, a support system. Whether from one training partner or a large group of twenty, having someone to hold you accountable and actually make it more enjoyable while you take on the difficult task that is rewriting age-old habits is essential. Two, uncovering a deeper reason for your change. Having personal goals as motivators gives you energy when making shifts becomes hard work. Finally, without the Reeds' mentality of taking things one step at a time, their buddy system and reflection efforts may not have taken them this far.

73   James Clear. James Clear. September 01, 2018. Accessed June 14, 2019. https://jamesclear.com/behavior-change-paradox.

"It's not about the weight we lost, but the life we gained," Lexi reflected.[74]

Takeaways

To gain the life you've always wanted or, as a medical professional, to help people find theirs, interventions must drill in the notion that taking baby steps will ultimately help people achieve longer-term success.

Programs should include:

- Small goal-setting sessions,
- Written, tangible plans of when, where, and how to accomplish goal,
- Visual cues—whether through pictures, paper clips, or even sticky notes to track progress, and
- Patients focusing on changing *one* health behavior at a time.

---

74 Astorino, Dominique Michelle. "Lexi Lost Over 300 Pounds in 2 Years With These (VERY) Small Changes." POPSUGAR Fitness. February 18, 2018. Accessed June 15, 2019. https://www.popsugar.com/fitness/Lexi-Reed-FatGirlFedUp-Weight-Loss-Before-After-44555157.

PART 3

R

O

*O*thers

T

Alone we can do so little. Together we can do so much.

—HELEN KELLER, AUTHOR AND POLITICAL ACTIVIST

Part 3 will explore the incredible power of others and how social support is essential when looking to make long-term habit changes.

"What do you think about when you run?"

I, like many runners, have been asked this question more times than I can count. What follows is always a scramble of an answer, as I attempt to grasp within my mind a coherent thought that accurately depicts the incredible beauty of the heightened, intense physical and mental awareness that stems from running. Of course, I could also include the many expletives that frequently would course through my thoughts when completing a hard track workout, as I pondered why I ever agreed to competitively run and subject myself to such pain in the first place. More or less, however, my resounding answer was never *what* I think about when running but rather *who* I am with on those runs.

Running is often seen as an individual sport, but I feel it is just as much a team sport as any other. While I agree there is an inherent difference when comparing the dynamic among a soccer team's field of eleven or a basketball court's five to a pack of milers rounding their last lap, this difference is primarily due to the perceived interplay among team members. There exists just as much communication and connection between running teammates; it just takes on a different form.

It is through my running teammates throughout the years that I have been taken to amazing places. Both physically—in terms of qualifying for relay races across the country and reaching varying training thresholds—and emotionally, overcoming mental barriers I did not know was possible.

We have consistently served as multiple roles in each others' lives, from best friends to training partners to "therapists"—and even at times fierce competitors and rivals. I often explain this closeness by asking, *what else are we to do when we find ourselves side by side for miles and days on end besides talk?* It is communication coupled with our shared experiences and goals that enables us to rely on each other for continual support.

We have seen each other at our worst, talked about our deepest fears, and competed on many levels with each other. From this, we have learned a great deal from one another as we simultaneously traversed the throes of exams, personal bests, time cuts, boyfriends, and family struggles together. Running allowed us to create a community that offered benefits more than just the physical and traversed more of our lives than simply our running careers.

As soon as a few days after being on campus upon retiring, I began craving the structured community my place on the Michigan track and cross-country team had offered me for the past three years. Never had I realized the strength it gave me until its absence was felt daily. Navigating my newfound struggles without the constant presence of my teammates to keep me engaged in running, I had to stumble my way into finding a new solution. Ironically enough, it was refinding what I already knew to be true:

I needed others.

I was lucky enough to be surrounded by many teammates at Michigan before me who had also quit the team, whether for medical reasons or otherwise. At the beginning of my senior year, I was thrust into this half-team world, where members no longer had the obligation to train but still possessed the somewhat obsessive longing to move. That fall, there was almost always someone looking for a workout buddy. As the weeks went on and people's schedules began to pick up, however, it became harder and harder to find a time that worked for everyone.

Despite the difficulties of lining up schedules, whenever I had a training partner my spirits lifted. The highest predictor of whether I would go on a run or take a yoga class or lift at the gym or not during my transition off the team was almost always the presence of someone else. When I made plans with my roommate Becca to wake up early before class and run, I was much more likely to actually run than if I had plans to do it on my own. Even growing up, I recalled having my little sisters ride their bikes next to me for miles on end as I got my training run in for the day, practically begging them if they so much as thought of saying no.

Aside from the deeper motivational and emotional benefits of working out with someone, having a friend join is also more enjoyable.

Imagine that! Working out and eating well can be … *fun.*

Physical activity can be an incredible way to socialize. On campus, working out together allowed me the space to hang out and catch up with my closest friends even when school and volunteering and research and theses took up our time. Similarly, it is not uncommon whenever I return to my hometown on school breaks that my high school teammates and I still meet up for a run on our old routes and proceed to get smoothies or brunch afterward. It is a great way to reconnect and catch up on each others' lives and stay connected with those you care about.

Rather than potentially dreading waking up early, pairing physical activity in my mind with people I enjoy being around helps me associate physical activity with positive emotions. Rather than dreading my alarm, I am eager to hop out of bed. The second it goes off, it is thoughts of *I can't wait to see Kaela this morning to hear about her date last night!* or *Better not snooze and be late for Natalie. Wouldn't want to disappoint her. She's counting on me!* that keep me from abandoning my plans of self-care I had so thoughtfully laid out the night before.

Let's take our friend Susie, for example. Say she has been meaning to catch up with an old high school friend for weeks now, but between work and her children she just has not found the time. Rather than trying to squeeze in a coffee date with her friend on Saturday morning, she could suggest they meet up for a walk at the local park. This not only allows them to spend time together but also motivates each of them to add some movement into their days. It is even likely that this will leave Susie and her friend in a better mood the rest of the day and allow them to accomplish even more than a cup of coffee could have.

There exists a definite power in numbers. Working alongside one another holds each individual accountable, fostering a connection that allows you to be the beacon of light when another is struggling and providing encouragement for strides of growth.

Taking on a difficult goal such as increasing physical activity or improving your diet is tough stuff! Having a partner, a peer, a group of supporters, or a community backing you and guiding you to overcome that initial inertia of change is huge and facilitates a smoother transition down the line. Friends and family also fulfill key psychological needs, such as the longing for trust, the feeling of fitting in, and empowerment.

It is through others you may find a strength within you didn'tt know was there.

We must capitalize on this innate piece of human wiring to get us moving and eating well! Whether enlisting a family member, friend, or coworker or joining an already existing wellness community, individuals seeking lifestyle changes must take advantage of the support surrounding them. Health providers and wellness interventions need to guide others in finding their own version of a personal support system.

Part 3 explores many communities that have been created around changing behaviors and seeks to determine why and how they are effective. It is my hopes to motivate you to find your own personal community that can help you engage in your wellness efforts.

CHAPTER 9

STRENGTH IN NUMBERS

"It was a great place of community," Dr. Anne Eshelman fondly recounted to me over breakfast at a local Coney Island.

Smiling, she reminisced over the first-ever peer support group she created at Henry Ford Hospital in Detroit, Michigan, for bariatric surgery patients.

Tapping into that sense of community is key to increasing adherence to behavioral changes.

This chapter will lay out why Dr. Eshelman's support group saw such positive results and what is required to start one on your own (spoiler: not nearly as much as you think). It also covers other techniques Dr. Eshelman has found effective from over three decades of working with patients on making behavioral modifications.

Alignment of Goals

Dr. Anne Eshelman Ph.D., a senior staff health psychologist at Henry Ford Health Hospital, is no stranger to the realm of behavioral health. Having worked with the Henry Ford Transplant Institute since 1985, she has over thirty-three years of experience helping her patients manage the medical stresses and behavioral side effects of lifesaving treatments that improve quality of life.

A six-time winner of the Henry Ford Health System Behavioral Health Teacher of the Year Award (1995, 1996, 2002, 2008, 2011, 2012), Dr. Eshelman believes autonomy and mutual respect between patients and their doctors is a critical piece to her care philosophy. Ultimately, it is this, as well as working with patients and their families to create support networks that help contribute to long-term success.

"I think the biggest thing is to help patients see that their goals are aligned with their health professional's goals," she began.

Say a doctor walks into their meeting and says, "I need you to do this, this, and this"—almost immediately, it feels like a chore. Often a patient will see this request from the doctor and this required task, say losing twenty pounds, as taking away time from things that are important to that patient.

"Helping patients see that their goals are aligned with the doctors is a real challenge but is a necessary first step. If they don't see or feel that, they start off on the wrong foot," Dr. Eshelman explained.

Once they set this tone, it is difficult to shift the rest of the interaction and subsequently the patient's mind. Typically, this then leads to the patient cheating on prescribed interventions and having a lack of desire to engage. What makes it even more difficult is that the doctor has no idea what goes on at home. To avoid these types of situations, and to have a successful health behavior promotion effort, a physician needs to talk with the patients and see where their goals lie.

Assessing where the patient hopes to be months, or even years, from now and finding a way to help them see that making these lifestyle changes can get them there is crucial. Patients need someone to help make this connection for them, to tie it all together for a cohesive effort.

Infinite Opportunities for Growth

Just as we covered in Part 2, Dr. Eshelman further believes that, when approaching the monstrous task of changing life-long habits, the reminder to think small is often overlooked. She explained, "Behavior and lifestyle change involves hundreds of small choices, not just one decision."

Though agreeing to that first big step in losing weight, beginning to exercise, or whatever health behavior you are asking to be changed is a large decision, the remaining path forward doesn't have to be. Keep in perspective that, despite these habits taking up to a few years to completely rewrite, all you can really do in each moment is tackle one thing at a time.

To demonstrate, Dr. Eshelman used the example of someone managing their weight and the decisions they have to make on their way home from work. Let's say this individual, Leah, consistently swings by McDonald's to get a nice, refreshing drink of pop to enjoy on her drive home.

First comes the decision of which route to take. There is the shorter one that has the McDonald's drive-thru, and then the one that is slightly longer where there is no temptation. If Leah does decide to drive by the McDonald's, there is the decision of whether to stop. If she chooses to stop, the decisions then become what food to buy, how much of it, how about a drink, what size?

If Leah is asked by her primary care physician to improve her diet and get more physical activity, she has many opportunities sprinkled throughout her daily routine where she can begin to make these changes. Even on the ten-, twenty-, thirty-minute drive home, there are chances for her to actively engage in her health and make healthy decisions. The physician should take the time to reiterate that they do not expect a perfect day of health, but rather small, beneficial choices at her own pace can limit feelings of being overwhelmed; reminding her that she has the power to make these choices is critical for preventing a freeze-up.

Our days are consistently filled with countless decisions to be made, both about health behaviors and other things.

While we are so easy to define ourselves by the average of decisions we make as individuals, is it not just as important to look at each single choice we make? For is it not a positive step to decide just for one day not to stop at the fast food joint? Or how about deciding to drink water with your chicken sandwich and fries instead of a soda?

While eventually it will become necessary to make further adjustments, at least in the beginning it should be about changing things one food (or exercise!) decision at a time—for awareness is the ultimate catalyst for change that must not be overlooked. We must start small to bring us home to big.

Bariatric Surgery

Dr. Eshelman typically works with patients who are either preparing for or recently had a transplant surgery because of a serious illness. In particular, she has worked with many patients preparing for bariatric surgery. Bariatric surgery is a general term for the collective group of weight-loss surgeries. Simply put, these surgeries change the digestive system to help a patient lose weight by limiting the amount they are able to either eat or absorb.

Gastric bypass (also known as Roux-en-Y) is largely considered the standard weight-loss option due to several decades of comprehensive studies and experience. This approach effectively shrinks the size of the stomach by creating a pouch and then bypassing a large portion of the patient's stomach and initial segment of the small intestine, physically limiting patients from eating large amounts of food.

A newer surgery, gastric sleeve (aka vertical sleeve gastrectomy), is slowly becoming the more popular option for sustained, long-term weight loss. During gastric sleeve surgery, 75 percent of the stomach is removed, leaving behind a narrow tube for digestion. It does not bypass parts of the intestine or decrease nutrient absorption like gastric bypass does. Because of this and many other reasons, it is deemed faster, less expensive, and more effective than other weight-loss procedures with lower complication rates. The only catch is that limited research exists on longer-term effects and there aren't decades' worth backing consistent results.

In addition to reducing stomach size, a study at Harvard Medical School found that weight-loss surgery also plays a role in suppressing satiety hormones, such as ghrelin, which stimulates appetite and resets leptin, the hormone that signals the body is full. It has even been observed to reset the patient's metabolism and reverse obesity-related health conditions like diabetes and high cholesterol.

Despite being the most successful treatment out there for severe obesity, a study by the Obesity Society found that out of the 20 million people who are eligible in the United States, fewer than 1 percent get bariatric surgery for weight loss.[75]

So why exactly is this?

An article posted on Advanced Surgical and Bariatrics of New Jersey and Pennsylvania lists misinformation, fear

---

75 Accessed June 14, 2019. https://www.vox.com/science-and-health/2017/12/7/16587316/bariatric-surgery-weight-loss-lap-band.

of surgery, false belief in diet and exercise, refusal of help, and misconception of malnutrition odds as the five primary reasons 99 percent of eligible patients don't choose bariatric surgery.[76]

Further, WebMD states that the typical cost of weight loss surgery runs from $20,000 to $25,000, though several other factors like type, surgeon, hospital, and insurance also affect the price. Most insurances, including Medicare and Medicaid, actually cover bariatric surgery.[77] It also may be cost-effective if it prevents comorbidities and the associated costs with managing other illnesses. It is important this is conveyed to patients so they can make the most informed decision.

Though bariatric surgery for people who are morbidly obese is largely the best option when compared to diet and exercise, finding ways to promote quality information and lessen the cost to make it more widely available remains the critical issue. Until then, promoting diet and exercise in a way that helps it become the norm in these patients' lives should be the primary focus.

For people who are overweight and not obese, diet and exercise maintenance are still the most important aspects for ensuring it does not progress into a more serious

---

76 "Why Only 1% of Eligible Patients Choose Bariatric Surgery." Advanced Surgical and Bariatrics of NJ, PA. June 21, 2018. Accessed June 14, 2019. https://www.bariatricsurgerynewjersey.com/why-only-1-percent-patients-choose-bariatric-surgery/.

77 "Financing Weight Loss Surgery." WebMD. Accessed June 14, 2019. https://www.webmd.com/diet/obesity/financing-weight-loss-surgery#1.

condition. The main goal should be finding ways to incorporate it into everyday life and support people in creating it a lifestyle habit as opposed to viewing it as hard work or mandatory.

The important thing to remember is that weight loss surgery is *in addition* to diet and exercise changes. Lifestyle becomes even more important after bariatric surgery, which is where Dr. Eshelman's work came in.

Support Groups

When asked to tell me more about her work with the bariatric surgery patients, Dr. Eshelman's face absolutely lit up. She then started to tell me about the support group she created for these patients.

Having counseled people individually on the required diet changes they would have to make once undergoing this surgery, she noticed a common theme. Though family support was helpful, a lot of patients asked Dr. Eshelman about other people who had gone through the surgery before, curious how others had gone about this drastic change.

Already fully appreciating the positive effect of support outside the immediate medical community, Dr. Eshelman created the first bariatric surgery peer support group at Henry Ford Hospital.

To allow for the attendance of anyone who wanted to go, she gave up her own personal time after hours to supervise these meetings at no cost. Despite the time commitment,

Dr. Eshelman felt incredibly rewarded by what she observed taking place at these meetings.

"It was a great place of community," she described. "People developed friendships that lasted long after the group meetings were over. The greatest moment," she recalled proudly, "was when a group of them traveled to Disney World together for a 5k!"

The families all came back wearing their t-shirts and compared racing prizes—the competitive nature both friendly and motivational. It was wonderful for Dr. Eshelman to see local walking or running groups form within the unit.

The best part? The patients did it all on their own. "I mostly just sat in the back and let everyone else do the talking. I was simply there to oversee the whole thing," she explained.

I believe this speaks volumes about the hidden longings of patients that often go unnoticed or unmentioned within doctor/patient interactions. All Dr. Eshelman had to do was provide them with the space and structure to seek out the peer support they so desperately craved. Her presence did play an important role, however. As a group leader, she prevented negative forces from interfering, by monitoring bullying and low attendance, ensuring everyone is heard, and making sure more serious problems get addressed and that people are referred to other professionals.

Much research has been conducted on using peer support groups for successful interventions and treatment across a wide array of illnesses including addiction and mental health disorders. In recent years it has transitioned to over-weight and obesity care for lifestyle modifications.

A meta-analysis published in Patient Preference and Adherence looked at factors that promote adherence with weight loss interventions and found that offering social support and having programs with supervised attendance had better adherence than interventions without those factor.[78]

Further, peer support is a proven strategy to motivate and sustain behavior change in general health care populations, as reported by many studies mentioned in an article in the journal of *Translational Behavioral Medicine.*[79]

One application of peer support groups in the academic world has been consideration of health coaching. Though popular, there exists limited empirical support for this practice.

One randomized controlled study tested three different types of health coaching for obesity treatment with professionals, peers, and mentors serving as the coaches. The professional was a trained interventionist, the peer was a fellow participant, and the mentor was someone who has

78 Lemstra, Mark, Yelena Bird, Chijioke Nwankwo, Marla Rogers, and John Moraros. "Weight Loss Intervention Adherence and Factors Promoting Adherence: A Meta-analysis." Patient Preference and Adherence. August 12, 2016. Accessed June 14, 2019. https://www.ncbi.nlm.nih.gov/pmc/articles/PMC4990387/.

79 Aschbrenner, Kelly A., John A. Naslund, and Stephen J. Bartels. "A Mixed Methods Study of Peer-to-peer Support in a Group-based Lifestyle Intervention for Adults with Serious Mental Illness." Psychiatric Rehabilitation Journal39, no. 4 (2016): 328-34. doi:10.1037/prj0000219.

successfully lost weight. All coaches were trained on appropriate coaching strategies and feedback delivery and sent feedback to the participants' progress emails. Perhaps surprisingly, 50 percent of participants lost 10 percent of their initial body weight when paired with a peer, as opposed to only 17 percent who lost weight with the mentor serving as their health coach.

The researchers concluded that combining a reduced intensity behavioral weight loss intervention with health coaching by peers (or health care professionals) holds significant promise as a cost-effective overweight and obesity treatment paradigm[80]; further trials are called for, however.

Another promising and cost-effective application of peer counseling is through online support groups. Imanaka and colleagues examined the effectiveness of web-based self-disclosure peer-peer support groups for weight loss and found that when peers had access to others' weight-loss change and lifestyle modification information, they had better short-term weight-loss results than their control group counterparts who received only emails for health support rather than having access to the online support system.[81]

---

80 Leahey, Tricia M., and Rena R. Wing. "A Randomized Controlled Pilot Study Testing Three Types of Health Coaches for Obesity Treatment: Professional, Peer, and Mentor." Obesity21, no. 5 (2013): 928-34. doi:10.1002/oby.20271.

81 Imanaka, Mie, Masahiko Ando, Tetsuhisa Kitamura, and Takashi Kawamura. "Effectiveness of Web-Based Self-Disclosure Peer-to-Peer Support for Weight Loss: Randomized Controlled Trial." Journal of Medical Internet Research15, no. 7 (2013). doi:10.2196/jmir.2405.

By having access to the lifestyle changes and behavior progress of their peers, the participants were more successful in losing weight, which speaks to two critical factors when looking at the concept of peer support. It either served as a competitive motivator to other participants when they could see how other people were progressing or sparked inspiration, helping the participants find creative ways to make changes in their own life. Both can be incredibly effective tools that target our innate human behavior of competition and social support.

These studies demonstrate the reason Dr. Eshelman's support group was so successful in lifestyle changes. Facilitating peer interactions constructs a space for people with shared goals to build trust and find support from one another. This support is felt through giving advice, sharing problem-solving strategies, role modeling, and providing emotional support for behavioral change.[82]

At no fault of the busy physician or the overwhelmed patient, there are currently missed opportunities to engage those who are wanting (and needing) to make these diet and physical activity changes. Though all these patients had to complete these lifestyle modifications to be cleared for

82 Gray, Cindy M., Kate Hunt, Nanette Mutrie, Annie S. Anderson, Jim Leishman, Lindsay Dalgarno, and Sally Wyke. "Football Fans in Training: The Development and Optimization of an Intervention Delivered through Professional Sports Clubs to Help Men Lose Weight, Become More Active and Adopt Healthier Eating Habits." BMC Public Health13, no. 1 (2013). doi:10.1186/1471-2458-13-232.

bariatric surgery, the mere fact that they not only continued with Dr. Eshelman's groups after finishing surgery but even went above and beyond the initial expectation demonstrates the power and success of support groups.

Rewarding motivated people with further opportunities to complement their changes can only be a positive way to spur further action. More support groups should be created at local primary care physician offices across the country to support patients asked to make behavioral modifications.

Takeaways

Dr. Eshelman's work demonstrates that the presence of others is incredibly powerful when following bariatric surgery. Community is what enabled her patients to ensure the necessary lifestyle changes they made remained their new norm. Finding commonalities in their goals allowed the results of each patient's bariatric surgery to remain successful. Ultimately, it gifted them an incredible new life, full of support and saturated with healthy habits.

Some key pieces to consider when using a peer support model are as follows:

- Establish health care professional's goals aligned with patients'.
- Use health coach.
- Build trust through transparency.
- Create a safe space to share strategies, advice, and emotional support

- Have facilitator of group to track attendance.
- Peer groups are cost-effective and scalable options.

Another key concept Dr. Eshelman shared with me was mindfulness, both as an approach to eating and an important life skill. Similar to what Sophie Egan wrote about in her book *Devoured*, Dr. Eshelman touched on the power of mindful eating. More on this will be covered in the concluding section of this book.

CHAPTER 10

YOU ARE WHERE YOU LIVE

———

"It's always easier if you're doing something hard if you have other people to do it with," Mick Cornett, the thirty-fifth mayor of Oklahoma City, commented in an interview with *NBC News*.[83]

He was referencing a call to action he made in his eleventh State of the City address in January 2007. After personally struggling with his own weight and the striking, pivotal moment when he learned that Oklahoma City was on the

———

83 "Oklahoma City Mayor Puts City on a Diet." NBCNews. com. January 04, 2008. Accessed June 15, 2019. http://www. nbcnews.com/id/22503467/ns/health-diet_and_nutrition/t/ oklahoma-city-mayor-puts-city-diet/.

list of the most obese cities in the country, he decided he needed to take action.

Symbolically choosing to stand in front of the elephant exhibit at the zoo, Cornett turned to his people on New Year's Eve and said, "This city is going on a diet, and we're going to lose a million pounds."[84]

This chapter will explore how a fourteen-year mayor spearheaded a successful urban planning initiative in Oklahoma City and watched his town lose over a million pounds.

Understanding Community Differences

Before we dive in to the story of Oklahoma City's citywide diet, let us first look at why consideration of a target population's community makeup is essential for providing proper support in addressing lifestyle behaviors.

Both a behavior-change specialist and public health nutritionist, Melissa Antal from Part 2 has worked domestically and internationally to improve maternal and child nutrition for over ten years. Specifically, she has spent much of her time working with the Manoff Group, a business that develops international programs aiming to bring about social and behavioral change for healthy lifestyle promotion.

One of the Manoff Group's main theories is that information is just the beginning. It contends that simply handing

---

84 Cornett, Mick. TED. Accessed June 14, 2019. https://www.ted.com/talks/mick_cornett_how_an_obese_town_lost_a_million_pounds/transcript?language=en.

someone a sheet of facts or providing them resources is not enough to get people to change their behavior. Rather, real change calls for an understanding of the societal norms, culture, and physicality of the surrounding regions.

In one particular instance, the Manoff community health care workers spent many hours taking home visits with counseling cards to follow up after African community members received health information to explore what was feasible. From this research, they determined that instead of just providing new information on maternal health care, the community members needed support that translated into their everyday lives. This required assessment of personal lives, individual resources, motivations, and barriers, as well as anything that may be preventing practice of this behavior.

"We tried our best to design the program in a way that takes feedback from the community about what they want, what they don't want, what they can do," Melissa told me. "You have to look into people's lives, see who people respect, where people spend their time, and who they spend it with in order to reach them."

Sadly, deep consideration for each community's unique needs is missing in current health behavior interventions. Today, doctor's behavioral recommendations are incredibly generic and nonspecific, often making it difficult for patients to adjust the modifications to fit their own lives.

Melissa's job was to design programs and create tools to overcome this barrier of perceived physician ignorance. Her primary goal was to facilitate conversations to learn more about her target population before telling them to change their lifestyle.

Rather than focusing on the individual, Melissa's job required her to approach public health concerns at the community level. Melissa and the Manoff Group alike faced extreme difficulties abroad with receptivity—not unlike patients here in the United States. It was very common for these communities to be close-minded and uninterested in the U.S. government's presentation of health and nutrition education programs.

One way to work around this resistance, Melissa taught me, is a process called formative research. This is an immersive approach to understand the inner workings of a chosen community. While it is time consuming, a lot of anecdotal evidence has shown that this type of investment is indeed worth it to reach community members on a more personalized note.

Defined by the CDC as "the process by which researchers or public health practitioners define a community of interest, determine how to access that community, and describe the attributes of the community that are relevant to a specific public health issue,"[85] the sole purpose of formative research is to tailor operations to local settings in order to identify and

---

85 Center for Disease Control and Prevention. National HIV Behavioral Surveillance System in Men Who Have Sex with Men– Round 4: Formative Research Manual. December 20, 2013

address any barriers of a specific community. This process helps interventionists form an understanding of the behaviors, attitudes, and practices of their target group to explore behavioral determinants. Consideration of these personal, cognitive, economic, and social factors and processes ensures health promotion efforts are both culturally and geographically appropriate.

The key to successful conduction of formative research is 1) establishing and maintaining strong relationships with both the local community members and the providers, and 2) focusing on community outreach.[86] This can be done through qualitative measures such as interviews, focus group discussions, observations, and using a rating/ranking exercise and quantitative measures like surveys. Additionally, project sites can garner community support through meetings with stakeholders and the broader community, utilizing marketing materials, conducting meetings with community advisory boards, and forming collaborations.[87]

Formative research must be conducted before, during, and after implementation of an intervention. Assessment before allows for the program to be planned and designed in a socially sound way, whereas consistent monitoring and evaluation of the framework during the intervention ensures quality delivery throughout. Looking at results upon

---

86 Ibid.
87 Ibid.

completing a formative research intervention permits community members to respond to concerns and offer feedback on the method.

Another positive aspect of formative research is its applicability. Multiple research studies have demonstrated the process is effective at all levels of behavioral interventions, whether they be clinic-based (one-on-one or group), school-based, community-based, or at the population level.[88]

Melissa gave the example of her time working with women in Africa to improve maternal health. If the goal was to change a woman's behavior and her family or the male figure head didn't understand why, it's not only ineffective but also potentially dangerous, as it could lead to domestic violence. While an extreme example, this sheds light on the importance of including surrounding others in behavior modification.

This is representative of a necessary approach when dealing with health at a broad level. In order to get people to listen to health messages, there must exist a mutual respect between the interventionist and the community members at hand. This respect comes from taking the time to understand

---

88 Gittelsohn, Joel, Allan Steckler, Carolyn C. Johnson, Charlotte Pratt, Mira Grieser, Julie Pickrel, Elaine J. Stone, Terry Conway, Derek Coombs, and Lisa K. Staten. "Formative Research in School and Community-based Health Programs and Studies: "state of the Art" and the TAAG Approach." Health Education & Behavior : The Official Publication of the Society for Public Health Education. February 2006. Accessed June 14, 2019. https://www.ncbi.nlm.nih.gov/pmc/articles/PMC2475675/.

each particular community. Different cultural practices—for example, meals and food preparation—need to be considered when presenting information for change.

To me, understanding the context in which a patient lives is one of the most critical pieces of an intervention. Without this consideration, all other efforts might as well be for nothing because of a large disconnect between physician's expectations and the realities of patients' lives.

Another important perspective to consider is the multiple levels of influence in a person's world. The work Melissa did internationally was all based on the social-ecological model of behavior change, which looks at the individual, family, and community level of interactions. This comprehensive approach ensures a more holistic and effective solution is reached by considering many areas that act as influences in someone's life. More on this model will be explored in Chapter 16.

Location, Location, Location

In addition to the cultural makeup, the physical location of a community has the power to affect people's health outcomes. Whether it be positively or negatively, consideration for how an environment shapes an individual's landscape of health decisions is a piece of information critical to creating a wellness intervention.

One negative example is what public health specialists, advocates, and government officials call a "food desert."

A food desert is an area of residency with limited access to fresh, quality, and affordable fruits, vegetables, and other nutritious foods. Typically home to low-income families and individuals, food deserts drastically impact people's dietary decisions, often leading to diets lacking in nutrients.

Rural and minority areas are frequently home to food deserts because they don't have access to large, retail food markets and there is a higher number of fast food and convenience stores where healthy foods are less available.[89]

Let's consider a brief case example. Helen is a sixty-five-year-old woman living in a low-income area in Flint, Michigan. With a decrease in her mobility due to arthritis in her joints from aging, Helen struggles getting around. She also doesn't have a car. Because the closest store to her apartment is the local gas station around the corner, she typically eats a lot of unhealthy and prepackaged foods. Even though she understands the importance of her doctor's recommendation to eat more fruits and vegetables and improve her diet, she struggles to make this a reality and instead continues to shop at the convenience store and not change her purchases—because she simply can't.

Though not all patients find themselves in Helen's shoes, and it depends on the location of the doctor's office, health

---

89 "Access to Healthier Food Retailers - United States, 2011." Centers for Disease Control and Prevention. November 22, 2013. Accessed June 14, 2019. https://www.cdc.gov/mmwr/preview/mmwrhtml/su6203a4.htm?s_cid=su6203a4_x.

care providers should be more in tune with their patient demographics when making recommendations.

In terms of the food desert crisis, the CDC outlined a few ways to navigate improvement of these deserts to in turn create an "oasis." Establishing a community garden and organizing local farmers markets are two options Detroit communities have engaged in. Local governments can improve local transportation for easier access and also change zoning codes or offer other tax and economic incentives to attract retailers with healthier offerings to the area.[90]

A positive example of how a community can impact an individual's health decisions is through an environment conducive to physical activity. Things like neighborhood safety, access to sidewalks, or presence of parks are all factors that support people who want to engage in exercise.

A global study that looked at fourteen cities across the world determined that residential density, public transport, and the number of parks in a city all significantly affect the amount of physical activity a population gets every day. The participants who lived in the least activity-friendly neighborhoods approximately partook in sixty-eight minutes per week of physical activity when compared to eighty-nine a week in those who lived in the most activity-friendly neighborhoods.[91] The activity-friendly label was assessed based on

---

90 Ibid.
91 Sallis, James F., Ester Cerin, Terry L. Conway, Marc A. Adams, Lawrence D. Frank, Michael Pratt, Deborah Salvo, Jasper Schipperijn,

indicators of walkability, public transport access, and park access near the participant's geographic location.

In conclusion, the researchers stated, "Design of urban environments has the potential to contribute substantially to physical activity."[92] This study, like many others, points to the unique role a physical environment can play in reducing the health burden of the physical inactivity pandemic.

One interesting application of this finding is urban planning. Recent research has shown that city planners are increasingly recognizing the influence urban design can have on community health. Urban development teams are pairing up with public health officials to design healthier communities in hopes of fighting the rising prevalence of chronic diseases and physical inactivity.

Melissa readily agreed, saying to me, "This [urban planning for behavior change] is a good example of how you can hit people across their entire world view—from the time they wake up to when they get home from work, there's all these little opportunities to change behavior throughout the day."

As reported in *U.S. News and World Report*, studies show that with decreased car traffic and more opportunities for physical activity, communities experience lower

Graham Smith, Kelli L. Cain, Rachel Davey, Jacqueline Kerr, Poh-Chin Lai, Josef Mitáš, Rodrigo Reis, Olga L. Sarmiento, Grant Schofield, Jens Troelsen, Delfien Van Dyck, Ilse De Bourdeaudhuij, and Neville Owen. "Physical Activity in Relation to Urban Environments in 14 Cities Worldwide: A Cross-sectional Study." The Lancet 387, no. 10034 (2016): 2207-217. doi:10.1016/s0140-6736(15)01284-2.

92 Ibid.

rates of asthma, obesity, diabetes, and other chronic diseases. American Public Health Association Executive Director Georges Benjamin commented to the reporter at *U.S. News,* "City planners should start by thinking about how you can build in a more holistic manner that is more healthy when planning new projects and repairing existing infrastructure."[93]

The American Planning Association mentions different types of "smart growth" in its Planning and Community Health Center. Its list includes building more compact, walkable communities; allowing more mixing of land uses; providing transportation options other than automobiles, including public transit, bicycle, and pedestrian facilities; and balancing jobs and housing to reduce commute times, improve air quality, and reduce reliance on cars.

A final study published in the *Journal of Urban Health* determined from findings that in order to deliver on these examples of urban opportunities for growth, municipalities dedicated to promoting health and activity levels need a new perspective. It suggested the current disconnect between traffic departments, sports offices, and public health sector responsibilities be mended to increase collaboration for

---

93 Galvin, Gaby. "Designing Health Communities Requires Collaboration." U.S. News & World Report. November 1, 2017. Accessed June 14, 2019. https://www.usnews.com/news/healthiest-communities/articles/2017-11-01/how-urban-design-affects-community-health.

effective communication to create common policies that improve the health of its citizens.[94]

This City Is Going on a Diet

A great example of a successful start in urban planning comes from the town of Oklahoma City, Oklahoma, and was spearheaded by fourteen-year mayor Mick Cornett. In his TEDMED talk in Washington, D.C.[95], Cornett told the inspiring story of how together he and his town lost a million pounds. The first necessary step to this movement was his speech at the city zoo in January 2007.

The initial idea to improve the health of the residents of Oklahoma City came from the publication of an infamous "list": the most obese cities in the United States. Coupled with his own weight struggle, the list led Mayor Cornett to examine his city's infrastructure and culture.

"And as I tried to examine how we might deal with obesity, and was taking all of these elements into my mind, I decided that the first thing we needed to do was have a conversation," he recalled in his TED Talk.[96]

---

94 Daumann, Frank, Robin Heinze, Benedikt Römmelt, and Anne Wunderlich. "An Active City Approach for Urban Development." Journal of Urban Health : Bulletin of the New York Academy of Medicine. April 2015. Accessed June 14, 2019. https://www.ncbi.nlm.nih.gov/pmc/articles/PMC4411321/.

95 Cornett, Mick. TED. Accessed June 14, 2019. https://www.ted.com/talks/mick_cornett_how_an_obese_town_lost_a_million_pounds/transcript?language=en.

96 Ibid.

Mick believed the most effective way to initiate his goal of having healthier citizens was to first acknowledge the problem and then engage the public in his famous city-wide diet.

Rather than portraying his proposal in a negative light, the national media helped a great deal with gaining momentum and engaging citizens in the diet. Framing this effort in a positive and encouraging light played a huge role in finding and encouraging the large number of participants who wanted to do something—the website, thiscityisgoingonadiet.com, had over 150,000 after Cornett's appearance on the *Ellen DeGeneres Show*!

Thiscityisgoingonadiet.com featured a number of different resources for citizens who chose to sign up and become a member of the movement. It served as a platform for members to share stories and tips about techniques that worked, offered a place to log and track progress, and also sported many literature resources to read more about obesity, nutrition practices, recipes, and physical activity ideas; it even featured a health journal.

My two favorite options were both representative of utilizing the presence of others. One offered the opportunity to join your own neighborhood group to find people in your area to interact with and to see others' stats to use as motivation. Dubbed "The Power of Two," another feature was pairing with an Accountability Partner. Whoever chose to be paired with a partner met often to work together and encourage each other on their health goals. This helped people find more enthusiasm and energy to achieve more.

The listed benefits on the website are as follows:

- You have a cheerleader and a coach to help you when you feel like giving up.
- Being an accountability partner teaches you about loyalty, friendship, and trustworthiness.
- Knowing someone is counting on you keeps you motivated.
- You can celebrate and work hard with someone who can really understand you.
- Reaching goals is sweeter when it's done together!

What a smart idea!

The initial response was much larger than they had hoped for, which further powered their excitement for future efforts. When people around you are excited about something—when your neighbors, your coworkers, your local waitresses are involved in something—it creates a palpable hype, a contagious excitement about joining something bigger than yourself. This movement not only speaks to the inherent power that exists in numbers, but it also points to the hidden need of a town that was only shared when someone brought attention to it.

After this, conversations began popping up everywhere. In homes between mothers and their children, at school among teachers, at workplaces, churches, you name it. Local running groups started to form. Diners began offering healthy specials dubbed the "mayor's special." New plans for healthier school lunches were developed and workplaces adopted wellness initiatives. People came together across all aspects of the community to take on the challenge of becoming a healthier city.

Mayor Cornett felt the campaign did an incredible job of making obesity a topic of conversation around his town.

"I can tell you that that message about nutrition and health has penetrated in Oklahoma City," he said in an interview with *The Star*. "We're no longer in denial. People still come up to me, if not daily then several times a week, to tell me stories: how much weight they lost, how much weight their spouse lost. That doesn't happen with any other topic."[97]

In my eyes, Oklahoma City's diet demonstrates the unique strength that exists when people are united by a group effort. People throughout all parts of the city were working to reach their goal of losing weight and create a healthier community. And they were doing it together.

Following the awareness campaign, the greatest effort from the city officials came with the passing of the town's third MAPS initiative. While the previous two MAPS initiatives were focused on creating new sports arenas and

---

97 Yang, Jennifer. "Oklahoma Mayor Put His City on a Million-pound Diet. Did It Work?" Thestar.com. November 16, 2015. Accessed June 15, 2019. https://www.thestar.com/news/insight/2015/11/16/oklahoma-mayor-put-his-city-on-a-million-pound-diet-did-it-work.html.

improving the school district to increase the number of residents and businesses, MAPS 3's primary focus was creating a health-focused infrastructure.

"I started examining my city—its culture, its infrastructure—trying to figure out why our specific city seemed to have a problem with obesity," Cornett said in his TED Talk. "I came to the conclusion that we had built an incredible quality of life—if you happened to be a car."

The biggest problem city officials noticed was that Oklahoma City was built around the automobiles. The streets were very wide and had an enormous number of highways, both leading to little walkability. As Mayor Cornett put it, his goal thus became "redesigning their city around people, not cars."[98]

These efforts spread across all aspects of the city, from creating a new central park downtown to building a network of sidewalks all across the city with the goal of connecting neighborhoods to libraries and schools. A significant amount of time and money was put into the revitalization of the urban environment in Oklahoma City.

There was the creation of health and wellness programs for both the inner-city inhabitants and senior citizens, ensuring all residents were accounted for. The streets downtown were made narrower to allow for a bicycle lane,

98 Cornett, Mick. TED. Accessed June 14, 2019. https://www.ted.com/talks/mick_cornett_how_an_obese_town_lost_a_million_pounds/transcript?language=en.

and a huge amount of money went into building a canoe, kayak, and rowing venue that eventually became home to the 2016 U.S. Olympic Trials for canoeing and kayaking. Hundreds of miles of biking, jogging, and walking trails were also built.

In January 2012, only five years after setting the initial goal, Oklahoma City collectively lost a million pounds. The website also kept track of other measures and reported 2,460 inches lost, 4,509 pounds of body fat lost, 3,008,248 miles logged, 8,655,021 minutes of physical activity tracked, and 15,568,165 calories burned. Even more motivating, Oklahoma's capital was nowhere to be found on 2012's updated list of "America's fattest cities."

This leap would not have been possible without Mick Cornett's acknowledgment of his town's obesity epidemic. Without that first conversation sparking efforts citywide, Oklahoma City would not have begun its shift to rewrite its unhealthy ways.

Thomas Glass, a professor of epidemiology with the Global Obesity Prevention Center at Johns Hopkins University, made a thoughtful comparison between obesity efforts and the United States' long battle against tobacco and cigarette use in his interview with *The Star*. The public health movement took many different approaches to stop smoking over the years; he noted, however, that the biggest results showed only once there was a cultural shift among the American public. That is exactly what Mayor Cornett did with his pendulum of a city address in 2007: he halted the momentum of obesity and swung it toward a lifestyle of good health choices.[99]

Cornett humbly concluded his talk by saying, "We have a long way to go. Health is still not something to be proud of in Oklahoma City, but we seemed to have turned a cultural shift in making health a greater priority."

And here he reminds us of a key lesson for long-term health changes—it simply starts with a shift in focus and priority, taking things one at a time to build a future lifetime of wellness.

So how exactly did these efforts pay off?

In a 2017 article published by *U.S. News & World Report* in the "Healthiest Communities" section, Gaby Galvin dubbed it "Oklahoma City's Renaissance." Outlining the inspirational story of how this city lost one million pounds, she explained that the efforts for continued transformation were still going strong.

According to the CDC, obesity rates from 2012 to 2015 in the state of Oklahoma have increased from 32.2 to 33.9 percent, yet in Oklahoma City they have dropped from 31.8 to 29.5 percent. Similarly, the health department's Wellness Score reports show that from 2014 to 2017, Oklahoma City's

---

99 Yang, Jennifer. "Oklahoma Mayor Put His City on a Million-pound Diet. Did It Work?" Thestar.com. November 16, 2015. Accessed June 15, 2019. https://www.thestar.com/news/insight/2015/11/16/oklahoma-mayor-put-his-city-on-a-million-pound-diet-did-it-work.html.

death from stroke dropped 14 percent and death from cardiovascular disease, 5.1 percent. Death from diabetes complications, however, did not significantly change.

Aside from the medical and urban planning revitalization, the local public health department has made proper nutrition habits an expected priority, especially in areas where residents face greater health barriers. For example, one specific plan was creating a two-acre community garden in an area that lacked access to fresh fruits and vegetables.

Although there can be controversy over whether increased awareness is enough to produce significant results, Oklahoma City has demonstrated the power of changing a city's culture and the impact it can have on individual and community health outcomes.

Cornett concluded in his TED Talk, "It may be a twenty-year process to completely turn the ship in the middle of the sea. That started about ten years ago, and you can definitely tell we're headed in the right direction now. Our numbers still aren't great, but they're much better than they used to be."[100]

And that is a goal we can all get behind—turning in the right direction and relying on community support as momentum to carry you forward.

---

100 Ibid.

Takeaways

As much as reflection is helpful for identification of personal contributors to health, understanding how someone's residency affects health choices is an incredibly important aspect of care that providers often don't have the time to consider or talk through with patients when making behavioral recommendations.

Wellness initiatives should strive to consider how the physicality of a surrounding community impacts an individual's ability to make changes in their daily routine. Below are characteristics to consider when creating health promotion plans to ensure longevity:

- Conduct mini formative research of patient population through surveys, focus groups, and interviews to understand target population.
- Locate resources and create list of grocery stores, food banks, and nonprofits that offer fresh fruits and vegetables to give to patients.
- Organize community garden or farmers market efforts.
- Provide patients with a map of local parks, trails, gyms, etc. for places to engage in physical activity.
- Mimic Oklahoma City's communitywide diet and create a challenge for the entire practice with a collective goal.
- Use an online platform where people can track progress and share tips, experiences, and stories.
- Create an "Accountability Partner" program.

CHAPTER 11

POWERED BY
CONNECTION

———

Connecting

Let's consider two scenarios.

Both involve a young, white man, twenty-eight years old and from San Francisco, as well as a sixty-five-year-old black woman from East Oakland.

Jeff, a young professional, has just been diagnosed with clinical depression. In addition to his anxiety medications, he now must take antidepressants and reduce his stress levels. Though surrounded by many people constantly, he continues to feel alone and doesn't quite feel comfortable sharing with his colleagues and friends his diagnosis. His new meds have made him feel foggy and he has a hard time adjusting to life post-diagnosis.

Across the bay, Ruth, a retired school teacher from the notorious East Oakland, struggles from chronic pain. She also has type 2 diabetes and lives alone. On top of her prescribed insulin and NSAIDs, her doctor has recommended she broaden her social network and improve her diet when she can. Both recommendations she understands the importance of but struggles to accomplish.

As time goes on, Jeff grows more distant from his friends and stress from work builds.

Ruth attempts to cook healthier food but doesn't truly know what to make and has problems making it to the grocery store.

Eventually, both well-intentioned patients slide off from managing their conditions aside from taking the prescribed pills and their conditions remain stagnant.

The second case involves Jeff's and Ruth's doctors offering a slightly different recommendation. In addition to telling them they needed to reduce stress, broaden social networks, and change their diet, their physicians informed them of a new program to use as a resource to help them accomplish these things.

Jeff and Ruth both decided it was worth a shot and showed up to the first meeting.

Fast-forward six months. Jeff and Ruth are now close friends. Ruth has learned how to cook healthy, affordable meals to help manage her diabetes. Jeff has a confidant to talk things through with on a bad day. Ruth even drives Jeff to a dentist appointment across town when he has no one else to support him.

In an article from *SFGATE*, an online news site for the Bay Area, "The move from SF to Oakland: What's it really like across the bay?" the author wrote, "A short BART ride separates San Francisco from Oakland, but for many on both sides of the bay, the quick trip feels like a voyage into a different universe."[101]

How is it that two people worlds apart in every aspect of their lives came to be so close? What enabled them both to overcome challenging health obstacles?

While Jeff and Ruth are fictional, the first scenario is a reality many people across the United States face. The second part, about the development of a new program, is most definitely (and happily) true. In this chapter, I will tell you how this unlikely partnership developed. And more importantly, how others can share similar futures.

Prescriptions to Nowhere

Dr. Elizabeth Markle, Ph.D., a licensed psychologist, researcher, and assistant professor of community mental

101 Michelle Robertson, "The Move from SF to Oakland: What's It Really like across the Bay?" SFGate, July 24, 2018, , accessed June 14, 2019, https://www.sfgate.com/expensive-san-francisco/article/moving-from-sf-to-oakland-what-its-like-gig-13089623.php.

health at the California Institute of Integral Studies, has similar beliefs as me. In partnership with Dr. Ben Emmert-Aronson, Ph.D., she co-founded Open Source Wellness, a Community and "Behavioral Pharmacy" in San Francisco dedicated to well-being.

Just as I witnessed in my summer internship at the cardiologist's office, as a primary care behavioral health psychologist, Dr. Markle often saw patients who were given behavioral prescriptions, yet most received no formal instructions or follow-up on where or how to do it.

"It's like handing a patient with diabetes a prescription for insulin and saying, 'Good luck finding that! See you in six months!'" she explained to me in frustration.

Markle's and Emmert-Aronson's extensive background in the healthcare field inspired them to open an easily accessible place that addressed the four main instructions physicians typically recommended to patients: increase physical activity, improve diet, reduce stress, and find social support. Thus, Open Source Wellness was created. Participants join a three-month cohort, meeting weekly to practice these behaviors together in a community. Each week consists of movement, mindfulness, an interactive health lesson, and a meal eaten together in small groups. Each group has a health coach who works with them to meet the goals that matter most to them.

This addresses OSW's universal prescription: Move, Nourish, Connect, Be. This model is accessible, affordable, and flexible, allowing for cultural and contextual adaptation.

There are four different modes of delivery for Open Source Wellness' fulfillment of health behavioral prescriptions. The first model is clinically integrated, embedded within a primary care clinic or hospital. The second model is community-based, with which health care providers refer patients from many different clinics to one community site. The third is the low-income housing model, where this behavioral pharmacy is located within low-income housing. The fourth model

provides corporate wellness within the workplace. All enhance points of contact with struggling patients, which makes Open Source Wellness available to a wide range of people.

OSW's target patient population is low-income patients with diabetes, depression, chronic pain, cardiac disease, or any combination of these chronic diseases. In fact, OSW focuses transdiagnostically because comorbidity of these diseases is the rule rather than the exception.

The CDC has stated that one in four Americans has multiple chronic conditions, all of which last a year or longer, require ongoing medical attention, and limit activities of daily living. In addition, one of the most common underlying causes is the high prevalence of risk factors such as tobacco use and physical inactivity.[102]

---

102 "National Center for Chronic Disease Prevention and Health Promotion | CDC," Centers for Disease Control and Prevention, , accessed June 14, 2019, https://www.cdc.gov/chronicdisease/index.htm.

Drs. Markle and Emmert-Aronson believe that health behavior change initiatives can only be effective when they address the underlying emotional pain often driving maladaptive behaviors. This emotional and social acknowledgment is integral to health care and must not be left to the wayside.

OSW's remedy for poor health outcomes is health and well-being delivery through a small support group setting. This intimate place of community support is paired with assignment to a personal health coach, both of which provide empowering communication throughout the week. The intervention consists of a three-month immersive program of weekly meetings with activities designed to be not only informative but fun, where everyone does the work together.

Upon creating an organization that directly addresses health behavior interventions, both believed in the practicality of this group setting. It is more financially feasible and can reach a wider audience, while also offering a chance for better change through a wide support network.

"Our coaches and small group are so vital," Dr. Emmert-Aronson explained to me. "They are great interpersonally and identify what matters to participants, and helping them access their own internal motivation."

Driven by their mission of "Community IS Medicine," all of OSW's work is dedicated to promoting that sense of social support. Their focus is experiential learning—it's not just talking about health behaviors but actually doing them in and with their surrounding community. They pride themselves on having a joyful and social approach, so patients can feel rewarded in the work they do, therefore making their efforts sustainable.

Take, for example, another success story the pair shared with me. Bertha (name changed) had been chronically depressed for over two decades. Despondent and, for lack of a better word, numb, she had been on a variety of antidepressant and anti-anxiety medications for that same amount of time. In her own words, she said, "I have not stopped crying for twenty years."

In conventional terms, however, she was medically stable. As she was on medications and taking them regularly, the only additional advice she was given was to find social support and reduce her stress.

Given the lack of a democratized delivery system for this advice, Dr. Markle called this a "prescription to nowhere." And it's not just Bertha who ends up suffering. Providers, communities, systems, and patients all feel its effects.

Luckily, Bertha got referred to a new organization called Open Source Wellness. She was told it was a new delivery system for all the behavioral recommendations she had been receiving.

After being assigned to a small group and health coach, she began regularly attending the sessions. She slowly made connections with other people in her surrounding communities, learned the art of meditation, and even started cooking for herself.

Upon completing the program, Bertha applied to be a peer leader with OSW. She began helping to create the program for other participants, taking on leadership in a way she had been unable to for years. In addition to discontinuing her medications, she now regularly brags, "I'm not crying! For the first time in twenty years, I'm not crying."

"She really reengaged with life in a phenomenal way," Dr. Emmert-Aronson shared.

And that is how true social support can and should work.

Connectedness through OSW is what enabled Jeff and Ruth in the beginning of this chapter to uncover their unlikely partnership they could lean on in times of need to find success. Peer engagement is also what guided Bertha out of depression, spurred seventy-year-old Charley to quit smoking, and showed Sarah with chronic knee pain the beauty of movement. *Names have been changed but conditions and outcomes are real.**

Clinical Application

Open Source Wellness has helped not only patients but also health care providers.

To enhance understanding and increase communication between providers and Open Source Wellness, OSW offer a workshop where health care professionals could participate in an event with current participants to fully understand the care their patients would receive.

Coined "Providers' Night," doctors, chiropractors, therapists, and other health care providers from the Bay Area gathered together for an immersive night at Open Source Wellness to learn how they are fighting chronic diseases.

These health care providers enjoyed a night full of healthful activities, sometimes alongside their patients. The sessions include a dance movement class, a meditation gathering, and a plant-based community dinner. "It can be incredibly powerful for providers and their patients to connect outside of the clinic setting, and for patients to show their providers the changes they've made. I think for many providers it reminds them why they went into medicine in the first place," Dr. Emmert-Aronson said.

Drs. Markle and Emmert-Aronson have found these nights foundational for providers to fully understand the model, and often lead to them championing Open Source Wellness, and lifestyle medicine more broadly, within their respective clinics.

Emmert-Aronsonspoke to me about the strong clinical need for physician and patient support in the health promotion world.

"Many physicians recognize the importance of behavioral modifications, and give what we think of as behavioral prescriptions: eat better, exercise more, reduce your stress. However," he continued, "without an accessible, affordable delivery system, these are prescriptions to nowhere. We have found that providers are grateful to finally have a resource to share with their patients, a behavioral pharmacy for their prescriptions."

Markle and Emmert-Aronson have created exactly that—a place where referred patients can receive the support they need when doctors tell them to change their diet or physical activity. Patients at OSW are referred by a variety of health care professionals, including primary care doctors, psychologists, social workers, endocrinologists, cardiologists, and community college counselors.

Results

There is much to be learned from Markle and Emmert-Aronson's creation of a behavioral pharmacy. Having both practiced in the medical system, they know and understand the ins and outs of working in such a (broken) system. They too were frustrated yet came up with a solution that is excitedly working!

Driven by data and gold standard measures for tracking, Open Source Wellness is committed to giving care that has been proven to work. OSW's results show there is a qualitative increase in their patient's sense of connectedness, vitality, and activation.

The findings have also demonstrated improved behavioral and mental health measures. OSW's client population showed drops of 47 percent in depression scores (PHQ-9, 14.5

to 7.7), increases in weekly exercise from eighty-two to 123 minutes, and an increased fruit and vegetable consumption from five to six servings daily.

Of great clinical significance is the biomarker improvement seen in the hypertensive subset population. There was an average drop in blood pressure of almost twenty points from 146/77 to 130/77.

Perhaps the most striking outcome was the change in acute care utilization. OSW examined emergency department visits and unplanned hospitalizations for the six months preceding group participation and the six months following group completion. They found a 77 percent decrease in acute care utilization, from a total of twenty-two visits to only five.

Even though they've found great success in the beginning years of their practice, Markle and Emmert-Aronson shared with me that the challenge with this type of work is always matter of funding. Specifically, the difficulty lies in not getting reimbursement for their services from insurers.

Despite this very real, very tough challenge, when asked if they believed a systemwide shift could be done, in tandem they replied, "Absolutely." I could practically hear their smiling, determined souls through the phone, further fueling my passion for this field.

Emmert-Aronson continued, "Just like there are currently systematic pressures *against* health, with challenges due to social determinants of health and financial incentives for intensive treatment rather than preventative care, we can create systematic pressure *for* health."

The key for that pressure? Perhaps not surprisingly, it's ... the presence of others.

"In addition to policy changes, this is where community is really important," he finished. "Through group support we can actually make the healthy decision the easy and fun decision. **That** will ultimately reverse our health crisis."

Emmert-Aronson and Markle tackled the issue of insurance reimbursement using community. Through the clinical model, the OSW program is scheduled, charted, and billed as a Group Medical Visit (GMV). This allows for a single provider to bill for fifteen to twenty patients instead of the eight to ten a provider would typically see individually. Ultimately, this group work allows the program to dramatically amplify its reach and effectiveness for both patients and providers.

It also lends nicely to gaining momentum. There's power in numbers. Through increasing the number of people OSW can help, a wider pool of data can be collected. More comprehensive data thus increases the likelihood of continual success and builds a good case for outside support.

A few months after my interview with OSW, I saw wonderful news that solidified my belief that Markle and Emmert-Aronson were huge players in this national call for revamped solutions in the health behavior world.

Excitedly, Open Source Wellness found a sounding board to get recognition for the important work it is doing.

Winner of the Scattergood Innovation Award for Behavioral Health in March 2019, Open Source Wellness received $25,000 to help spread its work into the national conversation about transforming health.

Even being named a finalist helped raise awareness of this increasingly prevalent public health concern—it encouraged a dialogue among behavioral health innovators and gave OSW the space to present at the National Council for Behavioral Health conference of 2019 in Nashville, Tennessee.

It is people like Markle and Emmert-Aronson, as well as projects like OSW and the other nineteen NatCon finalists, that are necessary for starting the conversation and ensuring efforts are made on a wider scale.

Next Steps

So, what exactly can be done?

Organizations like OSW should be used as primary models for a clear direction forward. Utilizing their framework and further supporting their movement efforts are definitive next steps.

As Emmert-Aronson and Markle have demonstrated, community can be used to help individuals make necessary lifestyle changes. But they have also shown us it is what *can* and *will* get efforts like these noticed.

There's a notion that more bodies, more results, more passion will drive this solution onward to help countless others than the people of Oakland, California. It will take, however, the ever-important community to help get them there.

A few ways to carry it forward would be: finding sources of funding through grant proposals, identifying investors, or pairing up with similar projects and organizations for joint support. OSW is currently entertaining partnerships with an emergency department, a Veteran's Association Medical Center, and a rural health clinic.

Another, simpler avenue on the individual level would be volunteering, raising awareness specifically through social media outlets, and establishing partnerships with local high schools and colleges.

In its application for the Scattergood Innovation Award, OSW described its goal: "Ultimately, we aspire to show results at organizational and national levels over the course of our growth, and are working with providers, insurers, and integrated delivery systems to build the clinical and financial case for its widespread adoption."

So, while OSW makes efforts to broaden its outreach, it will also continue to focus on the home front, guiding its patients in making lifestyle changes that will save their lives.

"It's really the small victories day in and day out that keep it alive for us," Markle humbly shared with me.

Taking things one at a time, after all, enhances sustainability of actions and drives results.

Takeaways

- Use OSW as model for behavioral health efforts across the country.
- Create mini behavioral pharmacy at local physician's office through hiring of behavioral pharmacist.
- Work in groups and bill as GMV.
- Find ways to directly support OSW and help it gain national attention for potential country- and systemwide adoption.

CHAPTER 12

CREATING
A COMMUNITY

———

Let's revisit Brian from Advantage Strength.

Right on the front wall of Advantage's gym in bold red paint lies the important Advantage mantra: "Modest improvement, consistently done."

Brian understands, however, that modesty is hard to sell—which is where the presence of others comes in.

Aside from determining a more meaningful reason, or the right *why*, of making a health change, the other key part of Brian's client success is his targeted establishment of a community.

The Hidden Cost of Loneliness

According to a study conducted by AARP, the nation's largest nonprofit organization for empowering adult Americans, over 33 percent of adult Americans are chronically lonely[103]; another study from the University of California–San Francisco found that 43 percent of adults suffer from chronic loneliness[104].

John Cacioppo, director of the University of Chicago's Center for Cognitive and Social Neuroscience, has been studying loneliness for over twenty years. In an interview with *Fortune* in 2016, he stated that chronic loneliness levels are indeed on the rise[105].

There have also been numerous mentions of a "loneliness epidemic" sweeping the nation from a variety of news sources, such as the *Huffington Post*, the *New Yorker*, *Forbes*, *Time*, the *Boston Globe*, the *New York Times*, and the *Washington Post* as well as seen in movements like the Cost of Loneliness Project.

103 G. Oscar Anderson, "Loneliness Among Older Adults: A National Survey of Adults 45," AARP, September 01, 2010, , accessed June 14, 2019, https://www.aarp.org/research/topics/life/info-2014/loneliness_2010.html.

104 Leland Kim, "Loneliness Linked to Serious Health Problems and Death Among Elderly," Loneliness Linked to Serious Health Problems and Death Among Elderly | UC San Francisco, June 18, 2012, , accessed June 14, 2019, https://www.ucsf.edu/news/2012/06/98644/loneliness-linked-serious-health-problems-and-death-among-elderly.

105 "Chronic Loneliness Is a Modern-Day Epidemic," Fortune, , accessed June 14, 2019, http://fortune.com/2016/06/22/loneliness-is-a-modern-day-epidemic/.

This issue directly impacts health for a host of reasons. Loneliness induces the release of our stress hormone cortisol. Enhanced and excess levels of cortisol can lead to a variety of symptoms, all of which negatively affect your health. A few symptoms include high blood pressure, osteoporosis, and weight gain in both the abdomen and face[106]. Too much cortisol can even increase carbohydrate cravings[107].

Additionally, loneliness not only leads to depression and anxiety but can also increase the odds of premature death by 26 percent.[108]

So how can a health promotion program mitigate this?

By creating a space to feel peer support.

When describing the community at Advantage, one filled with board game nights, spike-ball tournaments, and handwritten postcards, Brian absolutely lit up. Laughing, he described to me an action figure ad a member had created featuring each of the three staff. It proudly hangs on the wall near the entrance.

106 "Cortisol," You and Your Hormones, , accessed June 14, 2019, http://www.yourhormones.info/hormones/cortisol/.

107 Ariana M. Chao et al., "Stress, Cortisol, and Other Appetite-related Hormones: Prospective Prediction of 6-month Changes in Food Cravings and Weight," Obesity 25, no. 4 (2017): , doi:10.1002/oby.21790.

108 "Chronic Loneliness Is a Modern-Day Epidemic." Fortune. Accessed June 14, 2019. http://fortune.com/2016/06/22/loneliness-is-a-modern-day-epidemic/.

"Knowing they are at home thinking about the gym when they aren't here at the gym is a really cool thing to see," he told me.

So, why exactly did Brian begin to foster this sort of genuine human community within his goal of physical health?

Chronic loneliness is typically defined as the negative feeling of isolation due to lack of meaningful, intimate, and reciprocal interactions. An important distinction is between the subjective feeling of loneliness and the tangible reality of social isolation—both of which have been shown to affect well-being.

Loneliness doesn't just affect people mentally and emotionally; it also takes a drastic toll on your physical health.

A wide array of academic research suggests loneliness can play a role in the development of many chronic diseases such as obesity, gastrointestinal disease, metabolic syndrome, type II diabetes, and cardiovascular disease.[109]

I am by no means stating that just because someone is lonely they will get type II diabetes or have a heart attack. Just as with any chronic disease, there are far too many factors to isolate and name a singular cause.

It is, however, a noteworthy risk factor for many adverse health conditions, specifically those tied to lifestyle.

Cacioppo also made an important distinction in his interview with *Fortune*: "People aren't dying of loneliness. But

---

109 "The Cost of Loneliness Project," The Cost of Loneliness Project, , accessed June 14, 2019, https://www.thecostofloneliness.org/.

they are dying of cardiovascular diseases, cancer, accidents, suicide and diabetes," he clarified. "Based on your genetics and your environmental history, loneliness can make these conditions strike earlier than they otherwise would have."

At Advantage, mitigating this risk starts with the first conversation. Before anyone joins, they are offered a free three-week trial. The trial begins with an individual consultation where Brian seeks to get to know the person and talks about what exactly they are looking to get out of the experience. The emphasis rests on supporting the needs of each individual, as everyone responds to coaching styles differently. This very first encounter enables a personal connection to be made.

Advantage is unique in the sense that each workout is individualized to a specific person, yet it is run as a group-style class. Before the lifting session begins, there is a group stretch, dynamic warm-up, and then a power warm-up. Only after the members have completed these together do they move on to their own personalized weight-training plan.

At the end of the trial, instead of trying to sell a membership, Brian engages in an honest conversation to determine if it was a right fit for that person. It is this dedication to personal connection that often leads to not only the joining of the Advantage family but also a membership for the long term.

Recently, movements to counteract loneliness have been gaining momentum. The Cost of Loneliness Project is a group seeking national acknowledgment of loneliness as an urgent social and public health crisis. It calls for recognition to combat this imperative health care issue as it has devastating consequences across many domains.

Eradicating loneliness in a person attempting a health behavior change can often be simple, inexpensive, and quick. For example, remembering key details can go a long way. Asking questions about how their presentation at work went or checking in about their son's football game is an easy yet often overlooked touch.

"When someone feels valued, it makes them want to put in more work for you and themselves," Brian stated.

Every day at Advantage a new "Would You Rather" question or a riddle is handwritten on the chalkboard hanging in front of the warm up area. While members stretch and roll-out before their workout, the conversation always works its way around to the question of the day. Home to many good-natured debates, the turfed space allows individuals to voice opinions and be heard. Often, it brings out personal experiences, whether light-hearted or serious, that people are happy to both share and listen to.

Most people don't go to the gym because they love to work out. It's often seen as an obligation, a required thing on their to-do list. This is why Brian strives to make his members feel valued and supported in a group setting, as well as personally.

Brian sending out personalized video message in emails, creating community events, and showing gratitude to the people at Advantage makes them feel special and included. The more someone feels they belong to something, the more motivated they are to stick with the workouts and want to give back.

One member at Advantage, a doctor of physical rehabilitation medicine at the University of Michigan, shared with me, "I need that accountability. It's just so much easier to bail on a workout when you don't have people wondering where you are."

I personally got the chance to work as an intern with Brian at Advantage. During my year working with Brian and all his clients, I so clearly saw how deeply the culture of community was embedded into Advantage's structure. Brian's goal was to create not just a community, but a full-on lifestyle.

Every event, every little touch Brian adds, despite the apparent simplicity and modesty, is purposeful. And it all circles back to community.

A critical doctrine at Advantage is to keep people engaged in working out and coming back. When the people surrounding you every morning at your 6 a.m. workout class become your friends, it is much easier to roll out of bed in the morning.

Lifestyle Medicine

Community, the presence of others, social support, peer interaction—whatever name is used, at its core, this concept greatly lessens the consequential repercussions of loneliness and in turn creates an opportunity for additional well-being.

Adequate exercise and proper nutrition are known to enhance both physical and mental health. Both have been acknowledged as forms of medicine through different movements. "Exercise Is Medicine," an initiative launched by the American College of Sports Medicine and the American Medical Association, with support from the surgeon general, encourages physicians and health care providers to include physical activity in their treatment plans. The Food as Medicine movement, dubbed a "brewing revolution" by a *National Public Radio* article, is also suggestive of this momentum. Physicians and medical institutions around the country are making food a formal part of treatment plans to prevent and manage diseases through diet.

An additional movement should be formed to combat loneliness and enhance people's feeling of well-being and opportunity for health—one of peer support. If an intervention program ties in the community aspect, you have a three-in-one medication allowing the treatment of multiple health issues in one.

Though not all people consider themselves extroverts, there exists the inherent evolutionary aspect of community and its importance to our survival as a species. Leaning into that notion for health programs is a critical piece that offers sustained efforts.

Further, similar to Young's Stepladders concept, there is a neurological component to how Brian is successful with his clients.

A model he picked up from his personal research, as Brian commits to always providing quality, evidence-based work, is implementing D.O.S.E.

This acronym stands for Dopamine, Oxytocin, Serotonin, and Endorphins, all important neurotransmitters that encourage repeated action.

For surges of dopamine, Advantage incorporates goals for its clients to reach. Every time a member completes a four-week program, they get a gold sticker on their workout folder. Seemingly juvenile, the gold stars in reality have been a huge hit. Members are constantly wanting to finish to get another star, whether to compete with their peers or to make their folders seem "fuller." It also allows them to channel that inner child hidden among the throes of adulthood.

Oxytocin comes in when the trainers make physical contact with their members for a job well done, such as a high-five for completing a difficult exercise.

Serotonin (as well as dopamine) can play a role when members check off the exercises on their sheet like a to-do list.

Endorphins are what follow the exercise itself and produce a feel-good feeling. Linking a positive experience to exercise, and Advantage in particular, keeps members returning day in and day out.

In this chapter we have uncovered the powerful impact incorporating the presence of others into a health program can have. Be it to serve as competition, support, or to further fight other potential chronic diseases, social interaction is a critical piece to any habit promotion effort.

Takeaways

Programs should seek to build a community within a wellness intervention to increase adherence. Below are some ways to do that within a wellness program:

- Create support groups within the wellness program.
- Pair up individuals.
- Offer personal touches wherever possible through team-building activities, engaging questions, etc.
- Listen to clients.
- Check in and reach out to people who miss a session.
- Don't be afraid to make it fun!

CHAPTER 13

IT TAKES A VILLAGE

"We are hard-wired for community. Doing things in isolation isn't sustainable," Kerry Minshew MA/LPC/NCC, a behavioral specialist at St. Joseph Mercy Health System, shared with me.

Kerry was one of the three medical professionals I had the honor of working alongside during my time at St. Joseph Mercy's ShapeDown Weight Management Program. I have mentioned my time working at ShapeDown throughout this book and will continue to sprinkle examples throughout, because it is tangible, firsthand experience that taught me a lot of what I know.

Combining Sean Young's research on community and my experience as the exercise specialist at ShapeDown, this chapter explores why the presence of others can be pivotal in keeping people engaged in healthy behaviors years down the line.

Passion

My time with the ShapeDown program at Saint Joseph Mercy Health System was hands down one of the best experiences I have ever had. Through the families' openness with their everyday struggles, I was able to find ways to offer support. ShapeDown demonstrated to me the power of community.

To me, community was getting invited to a young girl's quinceañera after working with her on accomplishing her personal goals of exercising four days a week and cutting out soda from her diet during an eight-week class. Community was when a stubborn teenager who initially didn't want to take the class came back after successfully completing the program to be a mentor for the new kids. It's families who come to the program for a third time because it became so interwoven into their story, a life-saving necessity. I saw community when one parent shared a struggle from their childhood and was comforted by another and offered sound advice left and right by those surrounding him.

Not only did ShapeDown allow me to pursue my passion of helping people live healthy lives, it also taught me an incredible amount about myself, as did the people around me—my mentors and the participating families included.

Adam, my boss at Premier Cardiovascular Specialists the summer I worked as an exercise physiologist intern, introduced me to the ShapeDown program. It was one of the many summer days that four out of our eight scheduled stress-test patients were no-shows; on those days, we had extra time to sit next to the treadmill and talk. On this particular day, he was telling me about the internship he had with Michigan Heart, the cardiovascular care center at St. Joseph Mercy hospital. He proceeded to tell me about a program that gave him the chance to help overweight and obese kids and their families learn healthy behaviors. Intrigued, I asked him countless questions, begging him to tell me more. After my questions got old, he gave me the contact information of the program coordinator, and the rest of the day I envisioned myself getting involved.

This happened right around the time I officially informed my coach of my decision to medically retire from the team. Despite being heartbroken, I told myself I needed to make the most of my year off the team and actually do something useful with my time, otherwise I'd be wasting an opportunity. I didn't want to further perpetuate the sadness and negativity surrounding no longer being able to compete for fear of becoming trapped, so outward I looked.

After emailing the program coordinator, Beth, I set up a time to shadow a class at the end of the summer to get a feel for the program. At the end of my shadowing experience, I fell in love and officially became a volunteer. For the next nine months I would spend every Monday night from 5 to 9 p.m. working with the ShapeDown community, eventually getting the opportunity to become the head exercise specialist. From it, I learned a great deal about the barriers people face, but more importantly, I learned how to help guide people toward well-being.

ShapeDown

Beth Darnell BSW, the ShapeDown program coordinator, has worked with the class for more than twenty-three years and has enriched thousands of families' lives. Initially a medical social worker, Beth found herself constantly overwhelmed from the stress of work, which left her little energy to take care of her own health needs. At her husband's suggestion, she began engaging in daily physical activity and eating healthier meals to better manage the stress of her job and realized she felt a load of difference. "As my daily exercise and fun physical activities increased and my meals became healthier, my weight automatically normalized. I left the 'dieting' mentality behind and was in the best physical and emotional state I had ever been in since before college," she passionately recalled.

Upon returning to work after the birth of her son, Beth learned there was an opportunity to teach the counseling portion at and coordinate the ShapeDown Weight Management Program for children, teens, and parents. Incredibly excited she had the chance to teach others about the success she had with transforming her lifestyle, she jumped at the opportunity and changed her career focus from assisting families during traumatic life events to helping them manage weight and health behaviors.

Beth eventually recruited Jennie Hanh, RD, CDE, a clinical nutritionist at the Center for Diabetes and Nutrition Education at St. Joseph, and Kerry Minshew, a fellow nutrition educator she knew from the Physical Education and Nutrition Working Together (PE-Nut) program to be the nutritionist and behavioral counselor, respectively, for the ShapeDown program. It is through this program they all grew together as advocacies for health and wellness.

When I first met the three of them, I began as a volunteer. Beth, Jennie, and Kerry are three incredibly selfless and hard-working health care professionals who devoted all their time and effort to making the ShapeDown program a quality and meaningful experience. Similar to Beth's circumstance, an opening for the exercise specialist position became available and I excitedly got offered the opportunity and took it. Switching to a primary role rather than an accessory volunteer allowed me to collaborate with Jennie, Beth, Kerry, and the parents and kids to work together as a team to create effective lessons on how healthy eating, an active lifestyle, and effective communication promote weight loss and family unity.

What ensued was months of rewarding work, lessons learned, and countless connections. Despite being incredibly difficult watching people struggle with the reality of their lives, I loved trying to find ways to support each individual family and each member. For example, I once naively suggested to a mom and her daughter that they go on a bike ride after work to enjoy movement. Hearing her blunt reply of "I can't fit on a bike" was both embarrassing for me and informative. If it weren't for her honesty and vulnerability in making that statement, I would not have learned that everyone's starting place is different, and that what works for one person might not be the solution for another.

Driven to guide that particular family to a workable solution rather than becoming just another well-intentioned bystander who didn't grasp their reality, I spent over an hour attempting to perfect a customized at-home circuit full of their favorite exercises. Regardless of whether this mom and daughter duo ended up using the circuit sheet I created, their smiles when I handed it over the next week spoke volumes of their appreciation for being seen.

So what exactly is ShapeDown? ShapeDown, Healthy Families, Healthy Kids is a family program offered at the St. Joseph Mercy Health System that teaches families how to engage in a healthy lifestyle so they may thrive in other aspects of their lives. Holistically focused, ShapeDown believes in the power of movement and preparing healthy foods for enjoyment rather than intense workouts and dieting. The class is an eight-week program with meetings once a week currently offered at three different locations within the St. Joseph Mercy Health System.

Families are typically referred by their pediatric physicians. Once the families agree to sign up, the child and their guardian must meet with the staff for an initial appointment. This helps both parties to get to know one another, as the staff shares more about the program and answers any questions. Together, clients and staffers determine an individualized plan of action for the upcoming weeks. Following this, the caregiver and child attend the weekly sessions with other families to actively engage as a unit in critical tools to facilitate long-term change, such as effective role-modeling to improve self-esteem, or teaching practices to bolster the awareness of detrimental health behavior patterns.

A typical schedule of the class involves a thirty-minute group meeting with all family members and staff to reflect on the previous week and set goals for the upcoming one. Next, the children, teens, and parents were separated into three groups that rotated between the health professionals for thirty-minute intervals. The three classes consisted of a nutrition demonstration with Jennie Hahn, the registered dietitian; a behavior discussion with Kerry Minshew, the licensed counselor and behavioral specialist; and a physical activity or game with me or the exercise specialist on staff.

In the kitchen, the kids and teens had the chance to cook a new meal or snack for their parents and try the foods they prepare. They also had a mini nutrition lesson on eating habits and the nutrient contents of common snacks and meals. Meals ranged from homemade Greek yogurt parfaits with granola, nuts, and fresh fruit, to kale chips and sauteed vegetables, to bean dip wraps with a taco salad. I found the most beneficial and awe-striking demonstration to families was always when we showed them a soda bottle filled with the exact amount of sugar that was in each drink. They were consistently in disbelief!

The behavior meetings were informal discussions on topics such as goal-setting and stress outlets for the kids and adolescents, and role modeling and parenting styles for the adults. Kerry does a wonderful job guiding the conversation yet still letting dialogue flow naturally as she addresses common concerns and allows suggestions from other members. Often, people just need a safe space to share and learn from one another to take next steps.

I thoroughly enjoyed the physical activity sessions. While it was challenging at first to find exercises that fit all levels of ability, the process was ultimately rewarding when I was able to find a balance for each group. For the duration they were with me I would teach them simple ways to move at home, how to use certain exercise equipment such as weights and resistance bands, and most importantly that physical activity can seamlessly be added throughout the day if you are creative; there need not be hourlong cardio sessions, especially at the beginning of the process. Emphasizing that "exercise" can be easy and fun was always my primary goal of each session.

Following the eight class sessions, there is a follow-up to discuss progress and make goals for how the family will continue to put the tools they learn into practice going forward. There is a final follow-up after three months to check in and promote accountability with maintaining their goals. It was not uncommon to see the same families retake the program for further emphasis of the lessons they learned.

ShapeDown leaves the time and space for families to have both individual consultations with each specialist, in addition to providing a group dynamic. Kerry, Jennie, and I all had the chance to meet with each family and child before and after the class to personalize the approach and address health issues specific to each family.

"Group classes are the key to our success. Our community forms a strong bond, coming together to learn, exchange ideas, and support one another," Beth told me. "It is very difficult to change eating, movement, and behavior habits. It does 'take a village' to make major lifestyle change happen."

Group classes can be extremely powerful for helping people achieve goals that take a long time. Often, I found myself longing to provide clients with ongoing support that would last beyond the duration of the class. Jennie shared this sentiment. When asked what she would change about the program if she could, she answered, "It takes a long time to establish habits and the program is only ten weeks long. I would love to offer an advanced ShapeDown class for the graduates," she explains. "Those old habits tend to sneak back quickly."

Community can mitigate the bridge of needing constant reassurance or a scheduled program to maintain the needs. The community could effectively function as "the class" once the class has ended and all the information has been dispersed.

Upon asking Kerry if she believes people can change if they aren't internally motivated, she shared with me that ultimately they can't. "We can use logic and big-picture thinking to get people on board for a short while. That's why diets work in the short term (*I'm going to lose weight, lower my blood pressure, have more energy*). However, when life happens, those things fly out the window." Sharing the viewpoint of what we uncovered earlier in this book, she stated, "You need to find meaning to what you're doing that goes beyond what you hear in the doctor's office. You need to find your *why*. Once you do, the *how* works itself out."

Beth further agreed that a conversation about why change is important to long-term health from a doctor requires more depth if there is hope for long-term change. "Ultimately, the parent does have to be motivated on some level to make change happen," she said. "The doctor referral may be the starting point. If this brings them to the class, it is our job to engage and educate and take every opportunity to move the needle just a bit towards health in this family's life."

Both believe that community is the biggest way to move patients in a positive direction. The structure of a ten-week class is great for helping families set weekly goals together and for holding each other accountable. A built community can act as a buffer to the all-too-common slide in internal motivation when "life" gets in the way.

Force 2: Community

"A community will only lead to lasting change if its members are engaged," Sean Young wrote in *Stick With It* on his second force, community[110].

Young determined a method that kept 94 percent of his research participants engaged in a target health behavior after twelve weeks of making the change—and a whopping 84 percent a year and a half after the study ended. He credits this to creating an *it* factor that ensured participants kept up the changes. Communal interventions must be *engaging* to be fully effective in assisting members sustain changes.

To create this engagement, Young stated that each community, aside from simply existing as a group with shared characteristics, must have what he calls a social magnet. Defined as "a magnetic force that keeps people participating," a social magnet is a necessary piece of any health behavior intervention, for it has embedded within it social accountability and enjoyment.

---

110 Sean Young, Stick with It: A Scientifically Proven Process for Changing Your Life -- for Good (New York: Harper, 2018).

To demonstrate, he used the example of gym buddies. Young claimed that having a partner simply accompanying one to the gym is not sufficient for long-term engagement for its surface-level approach. Over time, the mere presence of someone else will be less and less effective in motivating someone to engage in physical activity (typically) unless there are additional factors. Conversely, a gym buddy that has "social magnetic" qualities will create a drive to continually make those changes. For example, the partner may send you articles on a new circuit to try, text you when you can't make it, or tag you in a motivational video on Facebook. This added layer of involvement further enhances engagement and keeps people participating.

Young also found peer mentors to be effective as partners during behavior change attempts, With proper training, people who have already been successful in making a target change themselves can be additional factor contributing to a social magnetic pull as they have firsthand experience. In addition to a partner's presence alongside a patient at the gym, added forms of accountability create a deeper sense of community that call for continual engagement.

Young's research and description perfectly mirrors Brian Sipotz's community at Advantage Strength and Conditioning explored in Chapter 3. Advantage contains many "social magnets" such as having a group of committed individuals who share similar values, game nights, and team 5ks that serve to connect, and members who hold each other accountable.

Similarly, ShapeDown's biggest asset to engagement, in the program and beyond, stems from the support network created by the families.

"Parents and guardians from all walks of life come together looking for answers to the same question: how do we help our child become as healthy as possible?" Beth emphasized.

To Beth, the common thread of wanting the best for their children ties the families together and keeps them engaged in the group classes. Regardless of race, class, or family history, all ShapeDown families are united by the struggle of having children who are classified as clinically overweight or obese and long for a different life.

Throughout his research, Young and his colleagues struggled with certain labels or groupings being stigmatizing, which prevented his initial subjects from participating.

Conversely, Beth has found that the stigma typically associated with being labeled overweight or obese is actually a driving force in creating the community at ShapeDown. This commonality creates a compassionate and understanding space that minimizes the judgment and in turn fosters growth. This reiterates the importance of not only having a community, but having one that is nonjudgmental and willing to be honest with themselves and their peers. Getting to interact on such a personal level with people who share similar struggles develops a robust support system. The parents, adolescents, and children all take turns serving as a role model for their classmates. This connection fosters a positive and encouraging environment, helping families feel comfortable making changes.

Beth finds it particularly interesting (and beneficial!) that the diagnosis has different root causes yet manifests in the same way. Whether the unhealthy behaviors are the result of negative habits learned in a parent's childhood, overindulgent meals on vacations, or food insecurity, every member of the ShapeDown program is ultimately there to learn ways to be proactive with their physical, nutritional, and emotional health.

Kerry works intimately with each group, getting the chance to explore all the differing dynamics up close. Purposefully held in a circle facing each other, Kerry facilitates group discussions around eight common themes to help build up wellness habits. Topics such as parenting styles, stress-eating, mental health, personal barriers/strengths, and role-modeling are all covered within these discussions.

The group setting allows parents to explore their own story and learn from others all while receiving supplemental support from the health professional. Kerry commented on the power of this group dynamic: "What I like to tell my groups is that everybody's voice is important. We all have some wisdom to share with the group: a failure, a success, advice given to us by others. What makes the group dynamic work is that we all learn from each other."

Jennie also believes the parents greatly benefit from hearing others' stories. "Parents often state they feel very supported. Especially when they share their great ideas with others. They don't feel so alone," she concluded.

The Hows

Of course, simply knowing you need a community isn't enough. Forming a new, beneficial community can present challenges. Through their research, Young and his colleagues pursued the goal of overcoming the barriers facing group formations. From their many years of investigation, Young and his team found six necessary components for the creation of a successful community.

They are as follows: the need to trust, the need to fit in, the need for self-worth, the need for a social magnet, the need to be rewarded, and the need to feel empowered[111]. All these needs were met in Young's specific undertaking, creating an HIV online community for at-risk males. He accomplished a successful group through the presence of a peer mentor or role model. This is what kept his participants engaged, even up to a year and a half after the study ended.

Trust is a critical component of any relationship. From trust comes honesty, and honesty is necessary for guiding people to making successful changes. Specifically in a group setting, if individuals don't feel comfortable sharing, there will be limited information for a health professional to provide personalized and meaningful solutions to accomplishing

---

111 Ibid.

health goals. Kerry shared with me ShapeDown's key to creating trust. "We focus on the two commonalities we share: (1) we're all trying to live healthier lives, and (2) it's hard. No matter what our background is, these changes are difficult." Teaching the values as something every human being can learn, rather than singling out an individual, unites both the members and providers alike, creating a safe space where people feel comfortable sharing.

When people feel empowered, they believe in their own ability to make changes. Lisa Quast, a contributor at *Forbes*, explored six ways to empower others to succeed. Her ideas consist of sharing information, creating clear goals, teaching people it is okay to make mistakes, celebrating failures as well as successes, supporting a learning environment through discussions of potential situations, and slowly transferring responsibility to the patients[112]. Kerry concurred, sharing with me "When there are others around us who are working on the same goals, consistency is easier. Community is what inspires us to do better."

Some other simple ways to increase confidence within a group setting that I have learned are noticing and acknowledging people's abilities and strengths, giving sincere compliments, listening intently to encourage continual sharing,

112 Lisa Quast, "6 Ways To Empower Others To Succeed," Forbes, August 21, 2012, , accessed June 15, 2019, https://www.forbes.com/sites/lisaquast/2011/02/28/6-ways-to-empower-others-to-succeed/#487498275c62.

and honoring autonomy by allowing patients to come up with their own answers and ideas.

This may translate by having mini "warm-up" activities before the start of each group meeting, such as complimenting your neighbor on something they did well or providing members with a scenario and asking how they might go about tackling the situation. ShapeDown employs this strategy by having five common goals for the program: five or more fruit and vegetable servings a day, four hours of family or social time, three servings of dairy, two hours or less of screen time per day, and one hour of physical activity per day. At the start of each meeting, each parent and child have to share one of those target health behaviors they did well in the previous week and one that was difficult. Sharing goals as well as individual progress of those goals highlights a sense of community and empowerment.

These are just brief ways to incorporate Young's findings. Other health professionals or wellness providers may have other views on ways to increase their patients' sense of trust, fitting in, self-worth, empowerment, being rewarded, or incorporating a social magnet.

On the fiscal and clinical side of *how*, Beth pointed out that to be affordable for their qualifying families, they have to be creative. "It is a bit complicated," she admitted. Despite being complicated, their commitment has helped all qualifying families engage in the program. They are able to bill for the medical nutrition therapy portion of the program.

The additional exercise and counseling services are covered by the amount St. Joseph Mercy's health care system gives back to the community under funds reserved for "community benefit" and delivered through a scholarship program. ShapeDown demonstrates one way health behavior interventions in a group setting can be covered.

As stated, creating a community is one of the most essential pieces to ensuring long-term engagement in an activity; it becomes imperative when the target behavior is difficult, as it often feels when it comes to remedying long-standing health habits. The presence of a tight-knit group of people increases the scale of any program, deepens engagement, and facilitates human connection.

Takeaways

At the end of the day, communities must be adaptable. Providers may seek comfort knowing there is not one correct way to function within a group of people, as each is unique in its own way. In order to capitalize on the powerful presence of others, health professionals must turn to their members to understand their uniqueness and deliver a program fitting for that particular group. There are governing principles, however, that we have uncovered in this chapter that must exist at each group's core in order to deliver on the long-term effectiveness. Once these foundational principles are met, communities can take on a life of their own and thrive.

- A program must contain these components to capitalize on implementing an intervention in the group setting:
- Members and health professionals must be open, honest, and supportive.
- Communities or partners must have a "social magnet" tying members in.
- The group must meet more than once a week and longer than eight weeks to solidify habits.
- The community as a whole should aim to meet Young's six needs (trust, acceptance, self-worth, social magnet, reward, empowerment).
- Providers may make a list of the many supportive communities that already exist in their area.
- Health professionals could work with local health care systems to inquire about community funds.

PART 4

R

O

O

Tailor to the individual

You have what you need, and together we will find it.

—THE SPIRIT OF MI

Part 4 examines why consideration for individual characteristics, whether physical, emotional, or cultural, is of the utmost importance when creating a sustainable health improvement plan.

Today in the current medical paradigm, there exists missed opportunities for tailoring behavioral recommendations and treatment plans to individual patients. In my experience working at a cardiologist's office, it was as generic as checking a box on the stress report form of "Improve diet" and "Increase Physical Activity"—regardless of the patient's age, gender, residency, or even preexisting medical conditions! Every person received the same three or four lined treatment recommendations and was asked to come in for a follow-up in a few months.

Though it is understandable (but *not* acceptable) how the system has gotten to this point, all in the name of efficiency, I believe nonspecific recommendations are further perpetuating the issue of patients not adhering to their behavioral prescriptions. And, quite honestly, why should we expect them to? If patients receive standardized care, a broad, blanketed approach that is given to every other person, there are few reasons tying them to making the prescribed changes. Rather, it becomes just another *should* on their to-do list that is most often forgotten immediately upon leaving the physician's office.

Patients going to see doctors have an inherent expectation that the doctor will examine a particular condition and treat it as specifically as possible in order for you to heal as quickly as possible. I don't believe making behavioral recommendations should be any different. Now, I want to make it very clear that I have the utmost respect for every doctor and physician in this country. I don't believe they are failing patients by making brief behavioral suggestions; rather, I feel it is the system at large failing both health care professionals by preventing them from doing their job and patients from taking charge of their own health and subsequently their lives.

Two parts of the modern day Hippocratic Oath are as follows: "I will remember that there is art to medicine as well as science, and that warmth, sympathy, and understanding may outweigh the surgeon's knife or the chemist's drug. ... I will prevent disease whenever I can, for prevention is preferable to cure." [113] It is time for the medical system to allow room for physicians to fulfill an oath they took upon graduation from medical school. I hope the future holds a place where a health care professional or trained wellness coach can take the time to get to know their patients to leave them with a plan that guides them to a lifetime of wellness free from chronic diseases.

One of the more obvious elements that helped me remain active upon quitting the team was not limiting myself to just running. I began to try other forms of activity—whether it was a yoga class, biking, going on the elliptical, or taking a kickboxing class, I was always searching for new ways to incorporate movement into my life. Opting to walk or bike to class instead of taking the bus was another option I liked (except when it was snowing or negative 40 degrees during the "Polar Vortex"- then I most definitely rode the bus). Finding something I enjoyed that kept me interested was a huge part of ensuring I still worked out.

---

113   "Evolution of Medical Ethics." The Hippocratic Oath. Accessed June 15, 2019. https://owlspace-ccm.rice.edu/access/content/user/ecy1/ Nazi Human Experimentation/Pages/Hippocratic Oath-modern. html.

I also had a difficult time adjusting to having to cook meals on my own after finishing my time on the team. Being in season year round with cross-country, indoor, and outdoor track, I had the privilege of having free breakfast every morning in a "Grab 'n' Go" style with options of bagels, yogurt, fresh fruit, egg sandwiches, cereal, oatmeal, and granola bars, as well as having a full course, buffet-style dinner offered four nights of the week, all provided by the athletic department. Without these convenient and healthy meals at my fingertips, I had to identify what worked for me personally to ensure I ate properly and did not succumb to the temptation of eating cheap junk food or eating out for meals.

Aside from making it a rule to grocery shop every Sunday, one technique I found that worked best for me was taking turns with my roommate cooking each other dinner. Knowing that I had to provide a meal for my friend motivated me to cook something she was proud of. An additional bonus was that half of the week I did not need to cook anything because she was cooking for me.

Another activity that helped was sending a picture of my lunch to my team's nutritionist every Tuesday and Thursday. Finding ways to hold me accountable helped me stick to my goals of eating a sound diet. It was my fear of letting people down and longing to please others that made these particulars approaches helpful in keeping up my healthy eating.

Identifying personal preferences is one of the easiest ways a medical professional or wellness program can personalize a health behavior plan for individuals. The more someone enjoys what they are doing, the more likely they will be to continue engagement in that activity. Similarly, if there is someone who can guide a patient in finding creative ways to make an action that feels like a chore more appealing, it may significantly increase their odds of continuing with the behavior.

Just as helpful can be finding out what serves as people's motivators or inspirations. Working with a patient who is willing to talk things through can lead to identification of techniques that work for each individual. It was only after a conversation with my dietitian that together we came up with the idea of sending a picture as proof I had packed a nutritious lunch. I can vividly recall nights in my kitchen adding bags of carrots, peppers, and cucumbers or including dairy products like yogurt for calcium when making my lunch because I didn't want to "fail" in my text at lunch the next day.

It is important to acknowledge that there is not one proper form of exercise or one correct way to include physical activity in your life. Just as there is no perfect diet or meal or grocery list, there are countless ways of living a healthy lifestyle for the countless, unique individuals in this country. This notion must be emphasized and reiterated to patients, particularly because of a common misconception that efforts don't count unless exercise lasts longer than an hour or you burn X amount of calories or your diet is vegetarian, vegan, or gluten-, sugar-, or fat-free. While these methods may work for some, they won't work for a large majority of Americans. Honoring your own personal preferences and seeking out ways you find enjoyable and fun is necessary if your goal is for the long haul.

Another way to consider the individual when treating behaviors is getting a firmer understanding of the inner workings of each patient and their life. Whether it be learning where they live, who their family members are, or what cultural norms or patterns they may have learned growing up, looking at the factors that consistently make up and influence someone's behaviors is essential if the goal is to change those behaviors.

Physicians are incredibly busy and constantly swamped with many responsibilities. Part 4 explores different ways within the medical system that health care professionals can seek to know individual patients on a deeper level to make more personalized treatment plans. It also uncovers *why* personalization is so important when it comes to long-term adherence. The feasibility of having a trained wellness coach or program built within a primary care physicians office will also be explored.

Here's to honoring the individual, for the power to change exists within all of us. Sometimes all it takes is guidance in finding it.

CHAPTER 14

MEET WHERE THEY'RE AT

———

Say you came home one night to find you had been robbed. Your new flat screen TV missing, your wife's jewelry gone—your house in its entirety eerily misplaced.

Upon the police arresting a suspect and ensuring his culpability, would you feel inclined to follow up with the young prisoner and write him a letter? Do you imagine yourself believing in the raw power of human connection enough to continue years of correspondence with him in hopes of supporting him to change?

Dr. John Piette, Ph.D., did just that, fully embodying the spirit he has taught and researched for decades.

This chapter explores how despite stacked odds, environmental influences, and learned behaviors, there exists a way to shift the trajectory of someone's life.

It all lies in the art of honoring the individual, while silently guiding them forward to change.

Brief Interventions

"You know, this is really real. This is where people are at and things don't always work," Dr. Piette, a health behavior/health education professor at the University of Michigan's School of Public Health, explained to me.

Also co-director of the university's Center for Managing Chronic Disease, Dr. Piette is a global leader in the field of improving access to self-management support for chronic diseases such as diabetes, cardiovascular disease, and chronic pain. His primary focus is developing mobile health interventions for socioeconomically vulnerable people in both the United States and Latin America to assist patients in health monitoring and behavior changes.

Dr. Piette was first inspired in the sustainability of health behaviors during his research with Intimate Partner Violence (IVP). After providing victims of sexual violence and assault with preventative screening measures, tools to change, and resources for help, a large majority of the women continued to stay in an abusive relationship.

This perplexed him to no end. After education and directed resources, there still existed rutted behaviors.

While he acknowledged the complexities of such a situation, Dr. Piette became fascinated with what worked in getting people to change their patterns. He sought to uncover the answer of what motivates people to make a drastic, life-altering shift.

What came next was an extensive dive into interventional research across a wide spectrum of patient populations. A resounding answer lay in the realm of brief interventions and the multiple modes through which they can be delivered.

The driving belief behind the field of brief interventions (BI) is that behaviors are the main causes of chronic diseases. Therefore, it is not heart disease, cancer, or diabetes that causes death, but rather tobacco, alcohol consumption, physical inactivity, and a poor diet.

Typically, a BI is a time-efficient, evidence-based intervention that aims to be the first step of supporting a patient in changing a problematic health behavior. It is in essence a simple and quick method delivered at teachable moments.

While it's difficult to address stable behaviors, most BIs seek to target people in the moderate risk group of whatever risky behavior they are engaging in. For example, if a woman went in to her annual check-up at her primary care doctor's office and mentioned on the screening survey that she was a light smoker (typically smoking between one to ten cigarettes a day), the doctor might follow up with the remaining appointment time to assess which stage of change this patient was at within the Transtheoretical Model/Stages of Change

Model and begin to use "change talk" to transition the patient to a path of treatment.

Dr. Piette greatly believes in the power of these interventions—so much so that he takes time from teaching at the graduate level once a semester to give undergraduate students the skills needed to participate in behavioral services within community-based organizations. The class focuses on successful strategies for promoting behavior change using brief interventions.

As a public health minor, I had the chance to take his course, "Changing Health Behaviors: What Works." Looking back, this class single-handedly sparked my desire to use the field of brief interventions for weight and diet conversations. It was only when I worked the next summer at the cardiologist's office that I saw the great need for this service and the tangible setting in which such an intervention could be implemented.

In the beginning, the primary focus was to understand the process of SBIRT as a whole, and then move on to the more nuanced applications.

Brief Interventions are a critical piece of the SBIRT model (Screening, Brief Intervention, and Referral to Treatment), which is an evidence-based practice used to assess, reduce, and prevent problematic health behaviors. It is most commonly used with alcohol or tobacco dependence, as those are the areas with the most extensive research; however, the BI section of the model is currently being applied to domestic violence cases, chronic pain, and physical inactivity.

The SBIRT model first gained momentum after the publishing of a report in 1990 by the Institute of Medicine titled *Broadening the Base of Treatment for Alcohol Problems.* After the initial publication, decades of research ensued worldwide to determine effectiveness of treatment, both with the screening tools and the intervention.

The largest contribution was made when the World Health Organization took interest. The WHO recognized the importance of SBIRT and began focusing resources on research to develop screening tests, implement the interventions, and broadly determine how to integrate it into the health care systems of countries around the world.[114]

Today, the SBIRT model is most commonly used in emergency departments. As of 2006, the Committee on Trauma of the American College of Surgeons has recommended that all Level I and II trauma centers be equipped to use SBIRT screening tools and further that Level I centers offer a brief intervention when necessary.[115]

---

114 Agerwala, Suneel M., and Elinore F. Mccance-Katz. "Integrating Screening, Brief Intervention, and Referral to Treatment (SBIRT) into Clinical Practice Settings: A Brief Review." Journal of Psychoactive Drugs 44, no. 4 (2012): 307-17. doi:10.1080/02791072.2012.7201 69.

115 Soderstrom, Carl A., Carlo C. Diclemente, Patricia C. Dischinger, J. Richard Hebel, David R. Mcduff, Kimberly Mitchell Auman, and Joseph A. Kufera. "A Controlled Trial of Brief Intervention Versus Brief Advice for At-Risk Drinking Trauma Center Patients." The

Additionally, there is very strong evidence supporting the use of SBIRT in the primary care setting.[116] Though not a required course in medical schools, SAMHSA (Substance Abuse and Mental Health Services Administration) has developed and funded the creation of SBIRT Medical Residency Programs that focus on teaching medical residents the skills of SBIRT and how to implement it into their practice.[117] The American Medical Association has also approved several billing codes that allow for reimbursement for providing these services.

The Art of Motivational Interviewing

Dr. Piette's class primarily focused on two types of BIs: motivational interviewing (MI) and cognitive behavioral therapy (CBT).

Though cognitive behavioral therapy can be incredibly powerful, a majority of our class focused on determining evidence-based practices and motivational interviewing for its ease of incorporation into the health care setting. CBT should only be implemented by trained mental health counselors.

Journal of Trauma: Injury, Infection, and Critical Care 62, no. 5 (2007): 1102-112. doi:10.1097/ta.0b013e31804bdb26.

116 Ibid.

117 Agerwala, Suneel M., and Elinore F. Mccance-Katz. "Integrating Screening, Brief Intervention, and Referral to Treatment (SBIRT) into Clinical Practice Settings: A Brief Review." Journal of Psychoactive Drugs 44, no. 4 (2012): 307-17. doi:10.1080/02791072.2012.7201 69.

One of Dr. Piette's favorite class activities was watching numerous clips of motivational interviewing examples.

After watching countless mock interviews using the MI technique, I became incredibly curious and passionate about the field. It was such a smooth and seamless way to help people! I particularly loved the empathetic and patient-forward nature of the approach. To me, it was absolutely brilliant.

That is why when I saw a posting for a motivational interviewing workshop at the University of Michigan Hospital, I jumped at the chance to attend. The two-night conference was an exceptional program that furthered my knowledge in this field and allowed me to work with other health care professionals on eliciting change.

At its core, the technique of motivational interviewing involves a direct, patient-centered conversation used to address ambivalence and enhance a person's motivation in regard to changing a targeted health behavior. A dance of sorts, MI requires a strong balance of both upholding the "spirit of MI," which honors the individual through collaboration, compassion, evocation, and acceptance, while also nudging them in direction of committing to action for change.

Collaboration emphasizes the importance of working *with* patients and honoring the fact that they know themselves best. Compassion follows the notion of giving priority to patients' needs and assuming they are doing the best they can in any given situation. Evocation is a strength-focused premise that seeks to remind physicians to draw existing motivation out from within the patient instead of seeking to implant it themselves. The final core pillar of the "MI spirit" is that of acceptance, which is made up of the four key components of absolute worth, affirmation, accurate empathy, and autonomy.

Absolute worth is the reminder that each human being has innate worth. The second value of affirmation draws and points out individual strengths to help enhance perceived capability. Accurate empathy is the responsive, active listening of the patient, which is followed up by the value of autonomy, ultimately respecting the patient's say in their own life. Using these values allows for meeting the patient where they are at. Care and consideration for the patient's current state is an invaluable tool for guiding them to a change.

In the textbook *Motivational Interviewing: Helping People Change* (3rd edition), the authors wrote, "When done well, MI involves listening more than telling. It does not operate from a deficiency model that seeks to instill knowledge, insight, skills, correct thinking, or even motivation. Rather, the counselor seeks to evoke the client's own motivation, with confidence in the human desire and capacity to grow in positive directions." [118]

Limiting the typical patient-doctor hierarchical dynamic permits the individual's pace and perspective to be heard. As

118 Miller, William Richard., and Stephen Rollnick. Motivational Interviewing: Helping People Change. New York: Guilford Press, 2013.

a result, this often leads to an enhanced sense of autonomy and confidence in the patient—setting them up nicely to be successful.

More emphasis should be placed on this field in the current system. Finding quick ways to honor the individual while providing guidance is a necessary direction more fields should implement.

Heck, in class I often daydreamed about there being a specific position at a doctor's office just for brief interventionists working with patients on lifestyle habits: a position that blended the skills of a nutritionist, a medical social worker, and a public health/health promotion specialist trained in using and embodying the spirit of MI.

MI Tools and Example Script

Within MI there are a variety of tools a professional may use to help meet the patient at whatever stage they may be at and then gently guide them toward thinking of change.

Some common tools to evoke or respond to change talk:

- **The confidence ruler**: "On a scale of 1 to 10, with 10 being very confident, how confident are you that you could stop drinking soda today?" Then follow up with restatement and question, "What made you say 6 as opposed to a 3?"

- **The importance ruler**: "On a scale of 1 to 10, with 10 being incredibly important, how important is increasing your physical activity to you? ... Why an 8 and not a 5?"

- **OARS**:
  - Open-ended questions for more detail
  - Affirming the patient's beliefs for understanding or finding strengths for confidence
  - Reflecting what the patient has said
  - Summarizing the narrative you as a provider are hearing
- **Looking Back and Looking Forward:** Attempt to uncover hidden strengths and accomplishments from past and look forward to establish future goals and values.
- **Elicit-Provide-Elicit:** (Asking permission, listening, informing)
  - **E:** "Are you okay if I share with you some information about gaining weight?" or "What do you already know about how gaining weight has affected the goals you spoke with me about?"
  - **P:** Reflect what they say back, emphasize autonomy, or share information
  - **E:** Restate reaction, address potential next steps

Next, I will provide some example questions and statements a provider might use within a Motivational Interviewing session to help move along the conversation. All statements and questions below are taken from a handout titled "Improving Provider-Patient Care in Preventing Weight Bias" from The Rudd Center for Food Policy and Obesity at Yale University.

Validation: "I can understand why you feel that way"

Acknowledgement of autonomy: "It's up to you to decide if and when you are ready to make lifestyle changes."

Reiteration: "I hear you saying that you are not ready to lose weight right now."

Taking Small Steps: "After talking about this, and doing the exercise, if you feel you would like to make some changes, the next step won't be jumping into action – we can begin with some preparation work."

Reinforcement: "It's great that you feel good about your decision to make some lifestyle changes; you are taking important steps to improve your health."

Pros and Cons: "Using this worksheet, what is one benefit of losing weight? What is one drawback of losing weight?"

Targeting opportunities for change: "Looking at your eating habits, I think the biggest benefits would come from switching from whole milk dairy products to fat-free dairy products. What do you think?"

Identifying Obstacles: "Have you ever attempted weight loss before? What was helpful? What kinds of problems would you expect in making those changes now? How do you think you could deal with them?"

Providing Support: "Which family members or friends could support you as you make this change? How could they support you? Is there anything else I can do to help?"[119]

---

119 "The Rudd Center for Food Policy and Obesity Www ..." Accessed June 14, 2019. http://www.uconnruddcenter.org/files/Pdfs/MI Example scripts.pdf.

These are just a few examples of things a provider may say with their patient during a motivational interview session. All of the above phrases demonstrate the "spirit" of MI in that the provider serves as a sounding board to meet the patient where they are currently at. Rather than talking down to the patient and lecturing about how to be healthier, MI allows the provider to tactically guide a patient to uncover personalized solutions that are suited for sustainment.

One study that looked at the use of MI and Physical Activity Prescriptions (PAP) as a treatment plan found that the use of MI significantly increased leisure exercise time and improved health-related variables in hypertensive patients.[120] It is important to note, however, that only professionals specifically trained in Motivational Interviewing should be having these conversations with patients as there is an art to ensuring it simultaneously flows and also yields results. Incorporating MI into health behavior interventions should be a goal of many healthcare providers for its efficiency and effectiveness. Consideration for implementation is highly recommended moving forward for health and wellness professionals. If done correctly, MI can help many people change habits that are critical for overall health outcomes.

---

120 Sjöling, Mats, Kristina Lundberg, Erling Englund, Anton Westman, and Miek C. Jong. "Effectiveness of Motivational Interviewing and Physical Activity on Prescription on Leisure Exercise Time in Subjects Suffering from Mild to Moderate Hypertension." BMC Research Notes 4, no. 1 (2011). doi:10.1186/1756-0500-4-352.

Anything Counts

Dr. Piette himself has also struggled to remain physically active. Previously considered a recreational runner, he developed bursitis of the greater trochanter and had to stop.

"It really turned me off to exercising for a decade or so," he chuckled.

This phenomenon is incredibly common. Dr. Michelle Segar spent years exploring how your attitude toward exercise greatly affects the probability of consistent engagement. Though he knew it was important to remain active, Dr. Piette consistently found problems with the many modes of physical activity available to him. Particularly, when it came to swimming, he couldn't stand the thought of the commute to the pool, getting in cold water, the act of swimming itself, and then leaving all cold and wet to drive back home. A negative experience in something he liked prevented him from seeking out new ways to move.

One of the reasons he was always searching for an excuse to not partake in exercise was simply because he didn't like any of them! No longer able to throw on a pair of shoes and jump out the door to run, Dr. Piette struggled to find not only the joy but also convenience in other exercises.

What ensued was the search for the right exercise. Eventually, he stumbled across something that worked for him: he discovered his love for and the simplicity of weightlifting. He now works on his strength and lifts weights three to four times a week. The best part? He has a weight set at home in his basement, allowing for ease of access.

Dr. Piette was successful in increasing his own physical activity level after a bad experience by finding a way to reengage in an exercise that was easy and enjoyable for him. Yet if people don't have the education, credentials, or support to point this out to them, it typically gets left untouched.

If more opportunities for this creative dialogue existed within the current system, there would be an increased rate of adherence for the behavioral prescriptions that are often made. Meeting the patient where they are at while gently guiding them to realizations can offer the space for changes to grow.

The field of brief interventions has shown us that time doesn't have to be a limiting factor in encouraging people to make a change. Using a technique like motivational interviewing can uncover a lot of what is already within the patient to allow for a personalized, unique plan of action.

When it comes down to it, our society is often quick to tell us the "right" way to do something. Whether it is a certain body type, how to dress, what to eat, or ways to exercise, if you don't adhere to the societal expectations of a certain activity, you often experience a feeling of failure. Simply put, having an expert to help someone find a physical activity or approach to food that works for them, or even give them the permission to try something new, is an incredible power that yields results.

As Dr. Piette told me, "More emphasis needs to be placed on just movement and motion as opposed to 'working out.'"

I will tell a brief story as an example.

One night at ShapeDown, I was leading the teen group in their exercises for the night. During our stretches, we were talking about how their exercise plans had been going for that week. One girl shared with me that she didn't make it to the gym at all. Since she felt no activities were as good as going to the gym, she simply did nothing.

Though that line of thinking doesn't logically make sense in terms of physical activity, our country currently operates under the understanding that if you don't go to the gym or lift weights or spin for an hour, the exercise doesn't count.

Luckily, because of my education and training, I had the chance to intervene and talk with her about the importance of being physically active even if it isn't for the hour she would have had at the gym. I got to work with her individually to come up with a plan for how she could add in movement at her house when she can't make it to the gym.

The next week, much to my delight, she returned saying she accomplished the goal we had set for the week. All it took was a quick conversation to uncover her personal preferences and help her find ways she believed she could move more at home.

The Power of Acknowledgment

Let's revisit the scenario from the start of this chapter.

Though a misguided teenager and someone struggling to get the recommended amount of exercise are in vastly different situations, there's a critical similarity that Dr. Piette brought to light.

At their core lies potential—someone longing for change who doesn't quite know the next step. Dr. Piette exemplified the power that nonjudgmental acknowledgement can hold for a person in this position.

Over the course of years and many letters, Dr. Piette and the prisoner had developed a relationship of sorts. Less of a friendship and more so a simple human connection, Dr. Piette merely took the time to acknowledge the presence of another human being. And through it, he found the voice of a young man wanting to be heard.

As Dr. Piette found himself taking on the role of a mentor to this young man, it brought to light the enormous role your environment and upbringing can play in the direction of your life. When a human being is not given the opportunity or resources to thrive, it is incredibly challenging to shift their trajectory. Having the time and resources to assist made helping the young man easy for Dr. Piette. A lot can be done when you have the proper tools to support someone.

Dr. Piette likes to think he made a difference in the young man's life. Full of hope, the prisoner has written to Dr. Piette about his plans for the future, some of which consist of finding a job and "doing good things with his life."

After decades of work in health education, Dr. Piette fully acknowledges both the transient nature of such situations as well as the unpredictability of an individual's capability for success.

A sage in the field, Dr. Piette reminded me, "It's not helpful to have a fatalistic attitude in this field, but it is important to be realistic."

With a 60 percent chance of resentencing against the young man, Piette admits no one really knows what will happen when he gets out. Similar to implementing brief interventions in a clinical setting or teaching big ideas to students, you won't always know the effect it can have on the direction of people's lives. And at the end of the day, providers need to accept the reality that they may not be able to help every single individual they interact with.

Yet, despite this humanistic flaw, this "handicap" that is limited knowledge of the future, Dr. Piette has continued to teach, to research, and to write to the young man all these years. Just as health professionals should continue to support the countless patients needing to change lifestyle

It seems that despite his occasional disheartened skepticism, Dr. Piette does, in fact, believe in the ability and power of the human spirit to change for the better. All it takes is a little bit of kindness and guidance to help change the trajectory of someone's life.

Takeaways

Dr. Piette and his class completely changed the course of my professional life. His teachings opened my eyes to a realm of healthcare that I didn't know existed and now firmly believe should be practiced in all health promotion and education settings. Below are ways to implement brief interventions in a health behavior program, both tangibly and in spirit.

- Consider MI training for healthcare professionals working with patients on lifestyle changes.
- Explore other BIs such as cognitive behavioral therapy or time-limited family/group therapy.
- Honor the individual.
- Always treat patients with respect, practice empathy, and serve as a pillar of support.
- Remind yourself, your nurses, doctors, and practice of your mission often and continue to believe in your work.

CHAPTER 15

EMPATHY REVEALED

———

"People really need an emotional connection to make a lifestyle change," Jaclyn* (*name changed*) NP established.

Jaclyn is a family nurse practitioner who works at a weight loss clinic in Chicago. Along with a physician, she is the lead medical provider overseeing the practice's whole team of medical professionals ranging from physician assistants and nurses to other nurse practitioners.

Whether the goal is to lose ten pounds for a class reunion or losing enough weight to avoid a major operation like bariatric surgery, the sole goal of her clinic is to help patients lose weight.

Aside from the typical treatment plans of prescribing appetite suppressants and educating on portion sizes, Jaclyn believes long-term success can be found by creating an established, warm environment between clinician and patient.

This chapter will explore the key components for initiating the development of this type of relationship, all of which stem from treating the whole person and honoring the individual.

Time

First and foremost, providers need time. Both in the duration of appointments and frequency, having enough time is critical in establishing the type of relationship that sets someone up for success. Because the sole purpose of the clinic is to provide weight-loss assistance, Jaclyn is not limited to a regimented two-minute conversation about weight at a fifteen-minute yearly check-up appointment like countless other providers across the United States. Instead, she has the ability to adjust the time of the appointment based on an individual's need.

This opportunity to delve in, she believes, is one of the biggest assets of a clinic like hers as opposed to primary care or cardiologist offices. Additionally, Jaclyn gets to see her patients on either a weekly or monthly basis. This further offers the weight-loss providers time to build a relationship with their patients, as opposed to primary care physicians and other health care professionals who only get to spend a few minutes, if any, on lifestyle habits.

Finally, treatment duration at her clinic has no limit. At their practice, the average treatment visits typically last anywhere from a few months to a few years. The medical professionals have the chance to work with their patients as long as it continues to work for them.

Personal Connection

The next step is establishing a personal connection. Jaclyn described how important it is for people to feel comfortable when they begin to tackle the challenge of losing weight. Providing patients with an environment they trust is safe is necessary if you want them to open up about the hard stuff.

For example, if people don't feel they can come in and share when they have a hard day because their dog died or are stressed because they are in the middle of transitioning jobs, they are less likely to then share about the deeper issues at hand, such as their problematic eating behaviors. Creating a space where the patient feels okay opening up is a large part of helping someone change their lifestyle, specifically in losing weight. Three ways for a provider to foster the development of this specific space are demonstrating relatability, acknowledging the difficult nature of losing weight, and fostering a partnership with the client.

Jaclyn herself struggles with maintaining weight. She believes her ability to relate to patients in this way adds a layer of support and understanding to her meetings. While not every provider needs to understand this process firsthand, demonstrating the understanding that weight loss is a difficult and long process is useful for establishing rapport. It also helps someone to adjust their expectations by preparing for the upcoming challenges.

It is my experience with the healthcare field that more often than not, it is difficult for physicians to comprehend why people simply can't eat better and exercise more. Even more frustrating, the doctors sometimes allow this belief to show in their interactions with the individual. While I do believe physicians care deeply about their patients' well-being, it is difficult for them to hide their own personal beliefs and attitudes when addressing something as personal as changing lifestyle. In their eyes, losing weight has a simple fix.

For example, I have mentioned my volunteer position with the ShapeDown program. At a prospective patient outreach event where we traveled to a local primary care physician's office to explain the program, we had the chance to talk with a doctor about one of the patients he identified as a qualifier for the program. After explaining the multiple approaches he has taken with this specific family, he made a comment in passing that didn't sit well with me.

"Despite what the mom says, clearly, her son is not eating nothing." Chuckling, yet shaking his head, he concluded, "You don't get that heavy by eating nothing."

Clearly frustrated, he continued to explain how he doesn't understand why the mom couldn't just feed him less. I tell this story not to bash a hard-working physician, but because it exemplifies the many existing barriers faced when working in this field. Here we have a doctor, who, from the sounds of it, has met with this family many times to talk over the effects of childhood obesity and guide them in seeking help, yet has seen no results. Having done everything he is supposed to do, he can't grasp why the young boy still hasn't lost weight.

His belief that simply having the five-year-old boy eat less will yield weight loss stands as a roadblock to accomplishing that exact goal. While I believe there are many ways to turn this situation around, one way would be acknowledgment from the physician that reversing overweight/obesity is incredibly challenging. Demonstrating to the families or the individual required to lose weight that the physician understands how it is both emotionally and physically overwhelming is important.

"It's a huge emotional undertaking to even call and make an appointment for most people, let alone walking through the door, sitting in the waiting room, and then talking to someone at length about what you're struggling with," Jaclyn passionately described. "That is an emotional journey in and of itself, let alone uncovering how you got to be 125 pounds overweight in the first place."

Recognition of difficulty by the physician will lead to a smoother process on both ends of the equation. Doctors will have realistic expectations and the patient will feel understood, both of which can lead to long-term success. A program for sustainable behavior change would require the health promoter to be patient and understanding, or at the very least employ techniques that display these important characteristics.

Similar to acknowledging the difficulty of losing weight, pointing out the universality of this dilemma is critical. Emphasizing that many people across the country also deal with this can be incredibly beneficial to the patient's mental attitude and can make them feel they are not alone. Even setting aside the concept of weight, sharing with the overweight or obese patient that every single person, regardless of age, sex, or size, should seek to incorporate more physical activity and a healthier diet into their lives destigmatizes the whole interaction.

Most physicians struggle to steer clear of imposing hierarchical roles. Though doctors have lots of clinical knowledge and skills, a program or intervention must set that role aside and in turn replace it with understanding and patience. This is a constant battle many Americans face when meeting with their physicians. Doctors talking down to patients can belittle their confidence, which is a crucial piece of attaining their goals. With an asymmetrical relationship, there exists the need to leave room for empowerment and growth, which can be stifled by the inherent power dynamic of the patient-physician interaction.

One systematic review published in 2015 looked at fifty-seven articles to explore the patient experience in communicating with a primary care physician. The authors sought to explore the communication difficulties that persisted between patients and physicians to better understand the patient perspective in order to improve care. With a subtitle of "Intercultural Encounters and a Balance Between Vulnerability and Integrity," the researchers hoped to uncover ways to find that balance.

Ninety-three percent of the studies reviewed reported negative patient experiences occurring as a result of the patient feeling vulnerable.[121] They found this feeling of vulnerability was resultant of three experiences: being treated with disrespect, experiencing pressure due to time constraints, and feeling helpless due to dominance of biomedical culture in the encounter. In other words, a conversation saturated in medical jargon placed a larger emphasis on the biological aspects of the patient's symptoms with little to no regard for the psychosocial implications of their condition—for example, the emotional impact of the illness on their life.

The review reported that most patients did not feel comfortable raising the psychosocial impact of their illness and instead waited for the physician to bring it up—which the physician didn't. Some patients even described the negative experience as feeling like a child due to the paternalistic manner in which the physician decided the treatment plan,

---

121 Rocque, Rhea, and Yvan Leanza. "A Systematic Review of Patients' Experiences in Communicating with Primary Care Physicians: Intercultural Encounters and a Balance between Vulnerability and Integrity." Plos One 10, no. 10 (2015). doi:10.1371/journal.pone.0139577.

resorted to complicated jargon, and neglected the patient's own expertise of the illness.[122]

To counterbalance these negative experiences, the authors determined there must be superior relational skills and a tailored approach to care. By treating patients with dignity and respect, doctors can help patients retain a sense of integrity. Ultimately, the findings underlined the necessity for physicians to remain aware of and sensitive to the cultural and microcultural factors at play during communication in order to develop a tailored intervention to patient preferences for satisfactory experiences.[123]

Another article published by *Science Daily* found that 65 percent of patient satisfaction was attributed to physician empathy.[124] To enhance the patient experience and improve adherence outcomes, a provider—and subsequently a wellness program—should include expressions of empathy.

A blog post on eVisit, a telemedicine provider, shared six ways to improve physician empathy. They are as follows: remember personal details, spend an extra minute on each visit, make eye contact, show support, put yourself in

---

122 Ibid.

123 Ibid.

124 American Academy of Orthopaedic Surgeons. "Physician empathy a key driver of patient satisfaction: New study supports enhanced physician-patient communication training." ScienceDaily. www.sciencedaily.com/releases/2016/03/160301114118.htm (accessed June 12, 2019).

the patient's shoes, and get feedback from your patients.[125] Another blog post by Ameritech outlined three additional ways: practice active listening, challenge your own stereotypes and prejudices, and try to pay attention to the nonverbal cues.[126] These lists demonstrate small ways to practice kindness and understanding within the four walls of the exam room.

The third criterion that assists in building a strong connection between the interventionist and the patient is to establish a partnership between the two. Laying out initially that both the provider and the person have unique roles to play builds the necessary foundation for maximization of the intervention.

The physician must hold up their end by providing education, resources, and support, but the individual also needs to follow through on the work at home. Relaying this expectation early on sets the tone for the remainder of the session that the results are not dependent on one person. Finding ways to foster this team mentality is critical in longevity of the intervention.

---

125 Iafolla, Teresa. "Improve Physician Empathy in 7 Simple Steps." Improve Physician Empathy in 7 Simple Steps. Accessed June 15, 2019. https://blog.evisit.com/improve-physician-empathy-in-7-simple-steps.
126 "Tips for Showing Empathy When Providing Healthcare." Ameritech College of Healthcare. April 12, 2018. Accessed June 15, 2019. https://www.ameritech.edu/blog/empathy-when-providing-care/.

Consideration of Culture

Another overarching theme in delivering a successful intervention for weight loss is understanding the personal and cultural background of the individual. There are always varying aspects of someone's situation that either support or hinder their relationship with wellness, specifically when it comes to diet. Tailoring the treatment to the individual at hand must not be overlooked.

First, a familiarity with the influence culture has on food is necessary to provide patients with personalized support. Jaclyn's clinic is situated in a really diverse area of Chicago, opening her up to a broad spectrum of patients and cultures. Of Polish descent, Jaclyn experienced a big learning curve when she first started working with Latinx and black patients. Seeking to understand where these patients were coming from diet-wise, she made it a point to learn about the typical diet of different cultures and the patients' knowledge base so as to better understand what their struggles might be.

To demonstrate, she explained to me that many of the Latinx patients she sees have type 2 diabetes. It is not uncommon for a Latinx diet to contain a high percentage of rice and beans. What she has found is that these patients were never taught that white rice is a high glycemic index food high, rich in carbohydrates that our body converts to sugar. For a diabetes patient told to avoid sugar, this becomes a huge problem.

Understanding a family dynamic is also important when considering an individual. "You can really learn a lot about someone by what their family brings to a party," Jaclyn emphasized. Are there salads and vegetables or pizzas and chips? "Something like this can represent their everyday struggles, the patterns that are genetically woven since childhood."

A great example is with a teenager I worked with in the ShapeDown program. After a night in the kitchen making fruit salads and homemade veggie dip from nonfat plain Greek yogurt, our dietician inquired if she would consider bringing this to her next family party.

She laughed and said, "Heck, no. No one would touch it."

She went on to explain, rather excitedly, that at her family get-togethers there was only ever fried chicken, mac and cheese, and other comfort foods. This is entirely representative of one of the struggles she faces. As a fifteen-year-old, she is most likely not going to seek out her own healthy alternative in lieu of foods that have become her favorite from years of familial influence—thus making the difficult undertaking of losing weight an even more challenging task.

This is why the people Jaclyn treats who have family support are typically the ones who have more success. Trying to overwrite a lifetime of learned behaviors is incredibly tough. It can be done, however, and the first step lies in both the practitioner's and the patient's understanding of these food habits.

Acknowledging the Individual

Another consideration when developing a personalized support program, Jaclyn explained, is digging at the deeper root of an individual's food decisions as well as assessing their motivation levels.

"Changing health behaviors, and specifically diet, is a multifaceted thing. You need to understand where their motivation is and where their starting place is in this lifestyle change shift and then go from there," she highlighted.

As an example, she mentioned one of her clients who ate McDonald's every morning for breakfast. Instead of simply explaining to the patient that he needs to stop eating McDonald's because it is incredibly high in unhealthy fats, sugar, carbs, and sodium and severely impacting his health, Jaclyn sought to understand why he was choosing to eat the fast food in the first place.

Do you eat McDonald's because it's cheap? Is it because the drive-thru is fast and you have limited time in the morning? Did you simply like the taste?

Jaclyn believes these are the questions that a lot of the times go unasked. It is about getting to the root of their food behaviors and really asking the right questions that allow for a firmer grasp on where the client is coming from. It is also helpful to find solutions!

She continued, "Being able to sit down with the people and see where their struggles are and then problem solving together is critical. There's not really a broad spectrum of 'these are the five tips for weight loss' like you see on Facebook or online—it is so much more complex. Everyone is very different."

It is through acknowledgment of these individual differences that true strides can be made. There is no cookie-cutter approach to tackle losing weight. Low-carb diets, becoming vegetarian or vegan, keto diets, gluten-free—just like we explored in Part 1, none of these methods work for everyone. Therefore, it is important to treat these health behavior interventions as a trial-and-error process until the correct fit can be made.

Lack of Motivation

All of this is well and good if the patient is, in fact, motivated. But what can be done when someone doesn't really want the help?

Because Jaclyn's clinic does not accept insurance or have recommendations, all the patients who receive care are paying out of pocket and at some level want to be there. She does, however, work with the occasional patient who struggles with wanting to participate. Typically, it goes along the lines of *My aunt recommended I come here; she found success with your clinic, but I don't think I need help. I feel like I'm doing fine, not quite sure why I'm here,* etc. Using the transtheoretical model of behavior change, someone like this would fall in either the contemplation (getting ready) or preparation (ready) stages.

Jaclyn stated, "As a provider you put out what you put out and if they want to pick it up, great, but the thing about behavioral change and lifestyle modification is that a huge part of it is a patient's readiness to change and where they are on the transtheoretical model. Things like how open they are to it, what kind of problems they have, what barriers they face personally, are they ready for the education or just ready for you to invite them to be there—all are important considerations."

It is not uncommon, however, for certain people to shut down her efforts completely.

In a situation like that, Jaclyn's approach is to just sit back and jump in wherever she can. Even if it is just talking about one manageable thing—such as limiting their consumption of sugary sodas and replacing it with flavored, carbonated water—can be big. Even one little change has the potential to go a long way. Regardless of where a patient is at, Jaclyn advised whenever you can to really understand where the patient is and just try to fit something in in hopes of making one small change for someone. Little things can still make a big difference.

Successful Trends

Jaclyn has seen everything from excitement over losing just six pounds to huge transformations—big enough that you wouldn't recognize the person if they walked through the door. In her view, the biggest success and inspiration comes when people who were crying at their initial appointment leave on their last day smiling, in new clothes, and no longer needing to take their diabetes medications because they've lost weight and are able to control it.

When talking about the success of her patients, Jaclyn believes the trend differentiating between someone who is successful and those who are not involves two things. The first is sugar.

A common problem in our society, especially the United States as a whole, is sugar. People tend to think of sugar as only being in ice cream and candy bars, but there seems to be a large disconnect that exists today. From sports drinks and juices to bread and ketchup, sugar is in almost every processed food, constituting a majority of our grocery stores.

"It's a matter of making sure that people are aware of what, when, and how much they are putting into their bodies, and for so many people in the U.S. it is sugar. When we can help find ways to reduce their sugar intake we see huge results," Jaclyn shared.

There are many ways Jaclyn suggested to limit sugar intake—replacing sugary drinks with flavored water, limiting the amount of fast food eaten in a week, understanding the role sugar is filling for you. Do you eat when you're lonely, when you're stressed, when you're happy? These answers can help shed light on a deeper reliance on sugar that offers a clearer perspective on ways to change.

Once the weight is lost, the best predictor of weight-loss maintenance in Jaclyn's patients is their engagement in physical activity. Sadly, it is not uncommon for someone to lose 75+ pounds while a patient at the clinic, and then return a year or two later having gained fifty pounds of it back. The people who remain at a stable weight are those who exercise regularly.

"It is important for the provider to point out the habit changes that someone has made and then continue to encourage it and help find ways to make it stick," Jaclyn suggested.

In summary, all of Jaclyn's techniques point to the same thing: acknowledging the totality of an individual. In order to be effective with an intervention, the patient must be considered from all angles of their life. Whether it is family background, cultural influences, or personal beliefs, creating an environment where a person in their entirety is recognized leads to successful results in the patient's life.

Takeaways

Jaclyn's clinic offers services that should be more widely accessible to all patients who need to shift their lifestyle. Our future medical system should find the space to have wellness consultations on lifestyle changes embedded within the mainstream avenues of health care such as primary care physicians and cardiologists offices. At the very least, I wish these services were covered by insurance so more people have access to them. Until then, we can just learn from them what works.

Health Promotion programs should include:

- Time/flexibility with scheduling.
- Establishment of a personal connection between provider and patient.
- Enhanced rapport between patient-provider through practicing empathy, minimizing vulnerability, and tailoring approach.
- Acknowledgement of difficulty and psychosocial impacts of making huge lifestyle changes.
- Meeting the patient where they are at and give what you can.
- Focus on minimizing sugar intake and maintaining physical activity to keep weight down.

CHAPTER 16

THE LONE STARFISH

———

"Our lives begin to end the day we become silent about the things that matter."

With an email signature featuring this quote from Martin Luther King Jr., Dr. White-Perkins M.D., Ph.D., has dedicated her life to serving urban, underserved communities in improving their health and well-being.

This chapter explores her unique approach to targeting health care disparities and how it translates to getting people to change their behaviors.

Finding a Natural Leader

A senior staff physician of family medicine at the Henry Ford Medical Center, Dr. White-Perkins also spends her time working as a clinical associate professor of behavioral health at Wayne State's Medical School in Detroit and serves as the director of the Institute on Multicultural Health. Her primary focus as a clinician, professor, and researcher is providing primary care services and developing community-based health promotion programs specifically for racial and ethnic minorities who experience health care disparities.

Dr. White-Perkins has worked on several research projects and health care service initiatives in Detroit seeking to screen individuals and find the best ways to promote health in those who have limited access to care. One such project involved partnering with the Blue Cross Blue Shield insurance company (BCBS) of Michigan, where they trained a male community health worker to go to local barber shops and enroll customers in hypertension screening and then provide education.

While funding was an issue and they had to stop halfway through, the tested model was deemed feasible as they had high participation from many barbershops the whole duration of the study. Through this, Dr. White-Perkins found that having screenings at a spot in a local area where many men frequented was a great way to engage people from the community. It offered a seamless way to incorporate health care into people's lives by meeting them in their daily life.

Additionally, having consent of a respected community member, such as the barber, shows others it is okay and leads to increased engagement. The nature of the intervention, however, made it difficult for follow-ups to see if the hypertensive people actually connected with a further resource, which spurred Dr. White-Perkins' next round of research.

After having done a lot of screening work within the community, Dr. White-Perkins and her team were able to shift their focus from identification of at-risk patients to outreach services that provided them with access to community health care workers. The community health care workers acted as a resource that would connect people with a trained professional in the area to receive the proper care.

For one of her next projects, she paired up with fifty congregations to implement a safe community, nursing, and health ministry program. They took natural leaders from the churches across the Detroit metro area and partnered with the Henry Ford Health System. The idea was to give already existing community leaders resources and training to improve the health of their community members as they already had a space to offer a meaningful impact.

"These community leaders offer more trust and breadth when it comes to sustainable health behavior changes," she explained to me.

The community leaders Dr. White-Perkins refers to are typically called opinion leaders, but can also have the title of champions, lay health advisers, or health advocates. Defined as people who influence the opinions, attitudes, beliefs, motivations, and behaviors of others[127], opinion leaders are used

127 Valente, Thomas W., and Patchareeya Pumpuang. "Identifying Opinion Leaders to Promote Behavior Change." Health Education

in public health to gain support for and implement community health programs.

Business Dictionary highlights another important aspect of peer leaders, stating they are influential members of a community, group, or society to whom others turn for advice, opinions, and views. Most likely because of this personalized advising and firsthand knowledge of people's real lives, programs using opinion leaders are generally considered more effective than programs that don't incorporate them.[128] Opinion leaders can also ensure the effectiveness of health programs by removing barriers to change and increasing the rate of the diffusion of new innovations within the community.[129]

One systematic review examined close to 200 studies on the use of opinion leaders in promoting behavior change. This specific article identified ten techniques used to effectively identify and recruit these opinion leaders within a community. They are as follows: celebrities, self-selection, self-identification, staff selection, positional approach, judges' ratings and technique, expert identification, and the remaining three fall under the larger category of peer nominations.[130]

& Behavior 34, no. 6 (2006): 881-96. doi:10.1177/1090198106297855.

128 Ibid.

129 Valente, T. W., and R. L. Davis. "Accelerating the Diffusion of Innovations Using Opinion Leaders." The ANNALS of the American Academy of Political and Social Science 566, no. 1 (1999): 55-67. doi: 10.1177/000271629956600105.

130 Valente, Thomas W., and Patchareeya Pumpuang. "Identifying Opinion Leaders to Promote Behavior Change." Health Education

The authors suggested using a tailored combination of the above methods to select more effective leaders to improve program effectiveness. For example, they stated a person identified through expert identification and peer nominations is most likely a highly regarded and well-suited opinion leader, whereas using the combined methods of self-identification and peer nominations might get you a leader to whom others look to for advice and require less training because they are motivated. Regardless of the chosen identification methods, research affirmed that using multiple methods in tandem will offer an opportunity to compare different types of leaders and facilitate the identification of those who are important for motivating and sustaining behavior change.

Despite well-meaning efforts of public health officials, someone is most likely to listen to and respect the things someone says if they already put their faith in them for other things. Having an established mentor deliver teachings about private things such as chronic illnesses offers a more personal touch to topics that are often very difficult to talk about. Further, it gives their efforts a chance to have a longer effect, for their lives are already intertwined. Researchers Valente and Pumpuang backed this notion by stating opinion leader development and training is often the one tangible benefit left behind by community-based programs and offers the

& Behavior 34, no. 6 (2006): 881-96. doi:10.1177/1090198106297855.

chance to continually influence community members long after the program is dismantled.

The idea of community participation and ownership is an integral part of generating support and engagement in prevention activities at the community level. It is through this community-based health promotion model that those factors deemed essential for proper implementation can be reached.

The community-based model is reflected in numerous prevention programs funded by both federal health agencies and private foundations that have targeted entire communities for intervention.[131] The Task Force on Community Preventive Services established by the CDC and the Institute of Medicine's Committee on Capitalizing on Social Science and Behavioral Research to Improve the Public's Health are two such examples that have endorsed this social environment perspective for health promotion.[132]

This community- and population-based focus is representative of the current shift in health promotion efforts directly from the individual to further encompassing an individual's outside influences for a broader perspective of care.

131 Kreuter, Marshall W., Nicole A. Lezin, and Laura A. Young. "Evaluating Community-Based Collaborative Mechanisms: Implications for Practitioners." Health Promotion Practice 1, no. 1 (2000): 49-63. doi:10.1177/152483990000100109.
132 Emmons, Karen M., Elizabeth M. Barbeau, Caitlin Gutheil, Jo Ellen Stryker, and Anne M. Stoddard. "Social Influences, Social Context, and Health Behaviors Among Working-Class, Multi-Ethnic Adults." Health Education & Behavior 34, no. 2 (2006): 315-34. doi:10.1177/1090198106288011.

Dr. White-Perkins finished by saying, "Empowering the natural helpers already in the community allows for a more lasting impact."

Community outreach is just one piece of integrating health promotion efforts across the totality of an individual's world. Other environmental influences that affect health behaviors must also be considered to fully tailor a wellness program to an individual.

A Multifactorial Approach

If our goal as a nation is to address the widespread effects of obesity, we must also act against the systemic roots of inequality that have permeated our culture. It is a difficult task for many reasons, with the primary issue being these effects can be felt at every level of a person's world.

Race, religious beliefs, socioeconomic status, poverty, gender identities, systemic inequalities—all concepts that people struggle to address—are exactly the ones that are deeply tied to so many negative health outcomes.

"The work around health disparities really requires you to address and really talk about the very topics that we are socialized not to bring up," Dr. White-Perkins told me.

It is incredibly difficult to address a nationwide issue and not mention the very factors contributing to the problem. So many of these topics are taught in medical school as simply risk factors of health, yet not broadly explored with the humanitarian consideration they deserve.

Daniel Stokols, Ph.D., a former professor and dean of the School of Social Ecology at the University of California–Irvine; Judd Allen, Ph.D., president of Human Resources Inc.; and Richard Bellingham, Ed.D., president of New Possibilities, agreed in a research paper they wrote on the social ecology of health promotion. "Lifestyle-change programs that proceed in a 'linear' fashion to modify specific health behaviors often neglect the contextual circumstances that lead to high relapse and attrition rates once the interventions have ended," they wrote. "And certain health risks-such as exposure to community violence, obesity, teen pregnancy, substance abuse, financial barriers to medical and preventive services, and lack of adequate health insurance-remain segmented, particularly among low-income and minority groups in the population."[133]

This paper was published in 1996—before I was even born. Sadly, as a nation, we still face the same problems today that we did twenty-two years ago. There is still a need to consider and describe the interactive characteristics of influence that underlie an individual's health outcomes when creating a health promotion program.

Dr. White-Perkins looks to avoid having this narrow perspective when working with her patients and families. To

---

133 Stokols, Daniel, Judd Allen, and Richard L. Bellingham. "The Social Ecology of Health Promotion: Implications for Research and Practice." American Journal of Health Promotion 10, no. 4 (1996): 247-51. doi:10.4278/0890-1171-10.4.247.

ensure this, she takes a more psychosocial approach, where she looks at the context in which individual patients live. She particularly loves working with patients when she gets to peel back the layers for a firmer grasp on where they work, play, worship, reside—all allowing her to better understand the individual and determine ways to empower them in making healthier behavior choices.

"If we are really going to have an impact on health outcomes for those who are the most vulnerable, the most marginalized, health systems need to be prepared to work at all levels," she passionately stated.

The levels to which she is referring are personal, interpersonal, familial, communal, and societal; they all stem from the social-ecological model. This theory-based framework, often used in the realm of public health for preventative care, explores the dynamic relationship between an individual and their surrounding environment. Specifically, it looks at how these different influences impact health behaviors.

The social-ecological model offers a physician, an interventionist, or any medical professional a way to attack the problem behavior from a variety of lenses. It allows room for consideration of macro-level influences that may not otherwise be addressed except at the policy level.

One example is assessing the patient's support system—family or otherwise. After reviewing numerous randomized controlled trials on the role family involvement plays in weight control, weight maintenance, and weight-loss interventions, McLean et al. concluded in their systematic review that spouse involvement increased effectiveness of the interventions.[134] Further, in the reviewed studies that included children, beneficial effects were seen when greater numbers of behavior change techniques were taught to both the parents and children. The paper ended by stating that the development of future interventions can be improved by paying careful attention to which family members are targeted in the intervention. Specifically, it is necessary to note how each member is involved in the goal setting-process, how they provide support, and finally if they receive any sort of training in behavior change techniques. This study highlights the importance of considering the social support system of every individual when creating an intervention plan.

In order for interventions to change beliefs and behavioral skills, there must exist support across all levels of influence, not just at the familial level. The programs are likely to work better when policies and environments complement the more personal levels when supporting the targeted behavior changes. Similarly, environmental changes like Oklahoma City's urban planning shift is not sufficient by itself to alter lifestyle habits. Rather, a partnership among all constituents is called for.

134 Mclean, N., S. Griffin, K. Toney, and W. Hardeman. "Family Involvement in Weight Control, Weight Maintenance and Weight-loss Interventions: A Systematic Review of Randomised Trials." International Journal of Obesity 27, no. 9 (2003): 987-1005. doi:10.1038/sj.ijo.0802383.

Let's consider the simple example of opening a gym in a small town. Access to an indoor workout facility may have little impact on increasing physical activity levels unless coupled with a marketing and education campaign, affordable prices, and individuals receive support from their family members in making it a priority. There must be a partnership between levels of influence if an intervention hopes to take root. Another option would be creating an intervention that targets all levels of a person's world, which would happen only by means of a conversation with the individual to consider the unique influences of that particular life.

In another review paper titled "Social Ecological Approaches to Individuals and Their Contexts: Twenty Years of *Health Education & Behavior* Health Promotion Interventions," the researchers concluded that though social ecological models have long been recommended to guide public health practice, the extent to which they are actually applied in health promotion interventions is unclear.[135] Upon conducting a review of over 150 articles from the past twenty years, they found that more articles described interventions that focused on individual and interpersonal characteristics as opposed to community, institutional, or policy factors.[136]

---

135 Golden, Shelley D., and Jo Anne L. Earp. "Social Ecological Approaches to Individuals and Their Contexts." Health Education & Behavior 39, no. 3 (2012): 364-72. doi:10.1177/1090198111418634.
136 Ibid.

Additionally, they determined that when an intervention narrowed in on the topics of nutrition and physical activity, the social ecological model was more successfully adopted, suggesting this framework can work well with efforts for improving diet and increasing physical activity. In conclusion, the authors called for an enhancement in training, research, and health education theory to better foster successful efforts in modifying social and political environments for health improvement. [137]

Dr. White-Perkins also believes that taking a personal level approach can be finite. Limiting the impact to within the four walls of the clinic sheds light on other problem areas needing attention that are contributing to the problem.

"When you look at that community and population level, you start to realize there must also be some upstream factors that are contributing to certain patterns of disease and illness," Dr. White-Perkins explained.

As an example, the rampant rise of financial inequality has been shown to increase toxic stress levels within the family setting. Research has shown these increased levels of toxic stress from situations such as extreme poverty or food scarcity can create behavioral problems such as ADD or ADHD and negative coping habits in children and adolescents. These negative effects can in turn impact their long-term health with the presence of diseases like obesity, heart

---

137 Ibid.

disease, or drug abuse.[138] To combat disparities, interventions must work at the individual level, the interpersonal level, and the broader structural levels within and outside the health system.

Macro and political effects have the power to impact the social and economic standing of a population. These broad level influences have ground effects that are then translated at the household level. Take, for example, poverty. One such example is the Affordable Care Act, which resulted in access to health care insurance for millions of Americans lacking it. Regardless of political stance, this is just one demonstration of the effects policy can have on people's health, good or bad.

A literature review sought to examine the dietary behaviors of Americans least likely to meet the USDA guidelines for the recommended daily servings of fruits and vegetables (non-Hispanic black people and those with lower incomes), to explore the integration of socio-ecological concepts into health promotion programs.

Robinson discovered that dietary behaviors and fruit and vegetable intake among African Americans are the result of a complex interplay of personal, cultural, and environmental factors that are perfectly described by the socio-ecological model. Her results are displayed below:

---

138 "The Effects of Toxic Stress on Children | Henry Ford." LiveWell. February 21, 2019. Accessed June 15, 2019. https://henryfordlivewell.com/child-experiencing-toxic-stress/.

Intrapersonal level: Taste preferences, habits, nutritional knowledge, cooking skills.

Interpersonal level/social environment: Cultural traditions, social traditions, role expectations that impact eating practices, patterns within peer groups, friends, and family.

Organizational/Community/Public Policy: Environmental factors that affect food access and availability.[139]

Robinson's findings demonstrate how incredibly useful it is to have an understanding of the personal, social, and environmental influences of an individual when providing someone with a wellness plan. To ensure problematic behaviors will be changed and the change will be maintained after treatment, an intervention must be fitting to all parts of an individual's world. Understanding these factors and barriers allows for a more culturally sound and sensitive strategy for implementation.

In Chapter 3 of the 2015–20 Dietary Guidelines from Health.gov, the social-ecological model was also explored. Titled, "Everyone Has a Role in Supporting Healthy Eating Patterns," this document examined how the Social-Ecological model can help health professionals understand the layers of influence that shape a person's food and physical activity choices.

---

139 Robinson, Tanya. "Applying the Socio-ecological Model to Improving Fruit and Vegetable Intake Among Low-Income African Americans." Journal of Community Health 33, no. 6 (2008): 395-406. doi:10.1007/s10900-008-9109-5.

It stated, "Consistent evidence shows that implementing multiple changes at various levels of the Social-Ecological Model is effective in improving eating and physical activity behaviors."[140]

For example, findings demonstrate that school policy changes in food availability during lunch alters children's buying behavior. Individual factors such as age, sex, SES, or community settings like schools, worksites, food service, and retail establishments, all influence beverage and food consumption and physical activity levels in individuals. Even factors at the sector level like health care, government, and education policies all largely impact health.

Whether by examining a family dynamic or exploring resources in a community, the social-ecological model allows room for understanding the multiple roles of relationships and social dynamics at play in someone's life. Acknowledging these different factors assists in the development of specific strategies to promote well-being in each individual. It allows the practitioner to identify any potential barriers or facilitators that may exist in a patient's life to help them hurdle the health problem at hand. At all levels there exists the opportunity to play unique and equally important roles in making sustainable changes for the long term.

---

140 "Chapter 3 Everyone Has a Role in Supporting Healthy Eating Patterns." Chapter 3 Introduction - 2015-2020 Dietary Guidelines. Accessed June 15, 2019. https://health.gov/dietaryguidelines/2015/guidelines/chapter-3/.

Honoring the Individual

Different from most physicians, Dr. White-Perkins actively seeks to avoid working under the assumption of common implicit biases. Her approach is one free of blame and judgment, both of which are critical pieces when working with patients who need to change a lifestyle. A doctor will not be successful when they imply to a patient who needs to lose weight that it's all their fault because of the food they are eating—even if it is unintentional. Often, this is the reason social workers are brought in as interface between the patient and doctor for these critical yet sensitive conversations. It is their approach that typically yields smoother results when working against these issues as opposed to doctors.

My professor, Dr. Hawkins, Ph.D., shared this all-too-common sentiment one day during my social work class. During her time working as a medical social worker in the labor and delivery unit, she shared with us that it was common for doctors and nurses alike to consistently refer her to patients when a difficult conversation about lifestyle needed to be had. She stated that sadly there was lots of tiptoeing and judgment around these patients before she was allowed the space to intervene and get to the root issue.

Dr. Hawkins was also taught to work under a strengths-based perspective, commonly used in social work practice. Similar to motivational interviewing, which we will explore in the next chapter, this approach operates under the assumption that everyone possesses strengths and that focusing on them diminishes temptation to further engage in their negative behaviors. Instead of focusing on the client's problems and deficits, this approach highlights their abilities, talents, and resources to assist them with their problems and goals.

Fostering a cooperative and mutually respectful relationship promotes identification of the problem behavior and allows for establishment of rapport. It is this connection that will ensure a smooth delivery of the intervention and progress that yields results.

Ideally, as a health system and society, we will find solutions that reach the broader aspects of our lives. We must administer interventions that address all levels of societal influences so we can find these lasting solutions, as grand of a task it may seem.

I often get frustrated thinking about the vast numbers of patients who need support in making behavior changes and don't have access to quality care. In our conversation, however, Dr. White-Perkins gently reminded me to not get overwhelmed with the idea of how many people there are in this country to help.

As both a family medicine physician and a systemic health disparities researcher, she has learned to keep a balanced perspective of how and who she can help.

She likened it to a story I often heard and loved as a child growing up. It went a little something like this:

One day a man was walking along the beach when he noticed a boy picking something up and gently throwing it into the ocean. Approaching the boy, he asked, "What are you doing?" The youth replied, "Throwing starfish back into the ocean. The surf is up and the tide is going out. If I don't throw them back, they'll die." "Son," the man said, "don't you realize there are miles and miles of beach and hundreds and hundreds of starfish? You can't make a difference!" After listening politely, the boy bent down, picked up another starfish and threw it back into the surf. Then, smiling at the man, he said, "I made a difference for that one."

—LOREN EISLEY

It is here we can fully appreciate the importance of focusing on each individual in their entirety. Honing in on the personal characteristics of each client leaves room for more effective solutions to be created—what works for one person may not work for another.

And at the end of the day, any health care provider treating the patient in front of them to the best of their ability is something we should all stand behind. I just believe we can and should take that next leap to providing more space for tailoring face-time to the patient at hand.

Dr. Perkins firmly believes consideration for your environmental influences must be taken into account when seeking to address a health behavior problem. And in light of the pervasive, systemic issues that exist in our country, if you're in the direct line of assistance, you must focus on helping one person at a time with care for these different levels.

As the Rural Health Information Hub, an organization supported by the Health Resources and Services Administration (HRSA) of the U.S. Department of Health and Human Services, stated in its *Healthy People 2020* movement, "Because significant and dynamic inter-relationships exist among these different levels of health determinants, interventions are most likely to be effective when they address determinants at all levels."[141]

To summarize, tailoring to the individual and understanding where patients are at in their life allows for personalized treatment that is more successful than generic behavioral prescriptions, especially in the long run.

Takeaways

Though she stressed the importance of working within a community to gain the support of their surrounding peers, Dr. White-Perkins largely believes consideration of the individual and their circumstances is critical for caring for a patient. Below are some ways to incorporate this

141 "Rural Health Information Hub." Social Determinants of Health for Rural People Introduction. Accessed June 15, 2019. https://www.ruralhealthinfo.org/topics/social-determinants-of-health.

consideration into a wellness program or lifestyle intervention to help patients achieve behavioral changes for the long term:

- Identify opinion leader from patient population base to serve as liaison between providers and serve as influencer of target behaviors.
- Wellness programs *must* consider the whole person and look at the broader levels of influences in patients' lives.
- Ask patients (or have them complete worksheet) to identify the perceived strengths and barriers they face at each level of influence in their life.
- Have brainstorming session with patient on how to best tailor the program to highlight strengths in their life.
- Help find solutions to overcome mentioned barriers.
- Do your best to help every individual.

CHAPTER 17

TOOLS FOR TARGETING
THE INDIVIDUAL

———

Aside from Stepladders and Community, Sean Young uncovered five more essential forces required for behavior change that are scientifically proven in his book *Stick with It: A Scientifically Proven Process for Changing Your Life for Good*. I believe the remaining five forces of his SCIENCE acronym can fall under one general concept—honoring the individual.

In a podcast interview on the Jordan Harbinger show, Young explained a critical piece that must be understood and clearly depicted at all levels when working with a patient in the realm of behavior change:

"Don't change the person; change the process."[142]

Programs to support individuals must not be about changing the person, but rather adjusting the process to meet each person where they are at. In other words, it is *tailoring* wellness programs to the individual that will lead to long-term success.

"We must make small tweaks to the way we do things, target the small processes within the context of our lives," he stated.[143]

Successful health behavior efforts do come down to the power of the individual, but not in the way people commonly think. This chapter explores what changes to the process must be made to ensure longevity of such efforts.

Important

If education alone and spending more money is not the answer to spur long-term engagement in individuals, what truly drives engagement? How can we possibly get people to do things not dependent on internal motivation or grit?

Young's third force is "Important." Ensuring that the behavior at hand is actually important to the person making the change is an obvious yet commonly overlooked aspect in the medical world. When giving a patient a behavioral

142 "Sean Young | Changing Your Life for Good with SCIENCE." Interview. Www.jordanharbinger.com (audio blog). Accessed June 12, 2019.

143 Ibid.

recommendation, medical professionals believe the mere facts or future consequences of the disease will be enough to spark inspiration for change. Yet research shows this is often not enough to make a difference for everyone. In fact, our mind is great at taking care of our current selves but actually perceives our future selves as strangers.

Jason Mitchell, a researcher at Harvard, in partnership with C. Neil Macrae from the University of Aberdeen in Scotland and colleagues, has conducted many studies exploring the role temporal distance plays in imagining different perceptions of self.

In one study, researchers asked people how much they, or a stranger, would enjoy engaging in some activity both the next day and in a year from now. The fMRI reports of the ventromedial prefrontal cortex, a region associated with perceptions of pleasure, decision-making, and the conceptions of self, found that for some people, thinking about an activity in the future led to brain activity similar to when thinking about another person.[144] In other cases, the neural activation patterns associated with thinking about the far-future scenario were similar to those of thinking about the current self.

---

144 Mitchell, Jason P., Jessica Schirmer, Daniel L. Ames, and Daniel T. Gilbert. "Medial Prefrontal Cortex Predicts Intertemporal Choice." Journal of Cognitive Neuroscience 23, no. 4 (2011): 857-66. doi:10.1162/jocn.2010.21479.

To solidify their findings, another study was published later, which found that while simulations of an event in the near future were dominated by a first-person representation of the self, the perspective switched to a third-person depiction when the event was located in the distant future.[145]

"This failure to identify with your future-self lines up with the tendencies towards short-term now-ness, as opposed to long-term planning," Cass Sunstein wrote in an opinion blog for *Bloomberg*.[146]

This helps explain why people are prone to things like procrastination, failure to save money, and engagement in unhealthy behaviors. Despite knowing the harmful long-term effects, some people can't perceive that the negative consequences of their actions will impact themselves; rather, their brain processes it as happening to someone else.

Another study conducted by Mitchell and colleagues sought to remedy this failing and found that rates of saving money increased when connections between your current and future selves were strengthened. This can be done by using a mental imagery strategy called spatial visual

---

145 Macrae, C. Neil, Jason P. Mitchell, Kirsten A. Tait, Diana L. Mcnamara, Marius Golubickis, Pavlos P. Topalidis, and Brittany M. Christian. "Turning I into Me: Imagining Your Future Self." Consciousness and Cognition 37 (2015): 207-13. doi:10.1016/j.concog.2015.09.009.

146 Schultz, Colin. "Some People See Their Future-Selves as Strangers." Smithsonian.com. October 29, 2012. Accessed June 15, 2019. https://www.smithsonianmag.com/smart-news/some-people-see-their-future-selves-as-strangers-98378412/.

perspective that ties visual bodily awareness to the mental imagery task of imagining your future self.[147]

Further, in a study that looked at how people can increase their monetary saving behavior, it has been stated that when the future self shares similarities with the present self, when it is viewed in vivid and realistic terms, and when it is seen in a positive light, people are more willing to make choices today that may benefit them at some point in the years to come.[148] This can be done by showing participants a digital representation of their future selves, by instructing subjects to take on the perspective of an elderly individual in a certain scenario, or by having participants implicitly associate two concepts together in a positive light.[149]

To translate this to the realm of health behaviors, one study found in comparison to a control group, when participants were shown a virtual version of themselves gaining weight, they were more likely to go to the gym[150]. Though

---

147 Macrae, C. Neil, Jason P. Mitchell, Marius Golubickis, Nerissa S. P. Ho, Rain Sherlock, Raffaella Parlongo, Olivia C. M. Simpson, and Brittany M. Christian. "Saving for Your Future Self: The Role of Imaginary Experiences." Self and Identity 16, no. 4 (2016): 384-98. doi:10.1080/15298868.2016.1264465.

148 Hershfield, Hal E., Daniel G. Goldstein, William F. Sharpe, Jesse Fox, Leo Yeykelis, Laura L. Carstensen, and Jeremy N. Bailenson. "Increasing Saving Behavior Through Age-Progressed Renderings of the Future Self." Journal of Marketing Research 48, no. SPL (2011). doi:10.1509/jmkr.48.spl.s23.

149 Ibid.

150 Fox, Jesse, and Jeremy N. Bailenson. "Virtual Self-Modeling: The Effects of Vicarious Reinforcement and Identification on Exercise Behaviors." Media Psychology 12, no. 1 (2009): 1-25. doi:10.1080/15213260802669474.

not always fiscally feasible or time-efficient for medical practitioners to implement the use of virtual reality into their practices, finding a personalized way to tie current decisions to future consequences is important.

A more accessible format to address the cause-and-effect nature of future decision-making is through a thought exercise. This potential solution based on Hershfield's findings has to do with making the emotional consequences of current decisions clear. Besides a visual demonstration, another option would be having participants answer questions in a "day-in-the-life" format from the perspective of an older individual with a certain health condition.

For example, an exercise might be as follows: *Imagine you are a sixty-five-year-old woman who is morbidly obese, suffers from type II diabetes and hypertension, and has trouble walking around. Your daughter just had her first child, making you a grandma. How do you think your daily routine might be impacted by your health conditions? Would it affect your ability to help your daughter transition into motherhood? How do you imagine it might limit your interactions with your new granddaughter?*

By having someone taking the perspective of an elderly individual, there is the potential for choosing significantly more later rewards and a boost of engagement in positive behaviors.[151] You can further increase the effectiveness of

---

151 Hershfield, Hal E., Daniel G. Goldstein, William F. Sharpe, Jesse Fox, Leo Yeykelis, Laura L. Carstensen, and Jeremy N. Bailenson.

this intervention by tailoring it to the individual and seeking to understand their future wishes and goals.

I unknowingly used this method when deciding to leave the team. With repeated urgings from my dad and other family members, I was constantly asked to think about the future consequences of breaking multiple bones at such a young age. They encouraged me to think about the life I wanted to live going forward and to assess if my actions now would prevent that from happening.

My dad is ultimately the one who got this to click for me. Knowing my longing to be a mom one day, as well as my passion for movement all too well, he asked me how I'd feel if I couldn't play outside and run around with my kids because I broke my feet too many times when I was younger. Sitting there, imagining a future reality where I *couldn't* play sports with my kids or go on a run by myself when things got too overwhelming quite honestly (excuse my language) scared the shit out of me. It was ultimately the visualization of such a life rather than my aunts' and uncles' verbal warnings that showed me the risk I was taking should I choose to gamble my bone health a fifth time by competing my senior year.

Even more critical, as Young mentioned in his interview, is taking care to not further demotivate a patient by making

"Increasing Saving Behavior Through Age-Progressed Renderings of the Future Self." Journal of Marketing Research 48, no. SPL (2011). doi:10.1509/jmkr.48.spl.s23.

them feel inadequate. My dad didn't make me feel lesser for choosing to leave the team; he supported my decision and pointed out how it aligned with my future goals. Further, his tactic more deeply resonated with me than the repeated negative advice I constantly received from others telling me I was clearly harming my body and making the wrong decision by continuing to compete.

Simply informing someone that something is wrong, unhealthy, or dangerous and making them feel bad about their decisions are not tools of inspiration that will lead to change. In fact, most commonly, such an approach will do the opposite of what we want, further stagnating someone's progress. I know every time someone told me I should stop running competitively, my immediate was response was to run more. Similarly, when people who know their diet isn't the greatest are constantly told to change it, this non-supportive approach prevents them from change.

A more successful approach would be connecting with the patient to find a way to make the necessary changes more relevant to their lives, just like my dad did. As Young showed, people will keep doing things they find important. At the end of the day, tasks won't get done when they are not in some way meaningful to the individual at hand.

Another important (no pun intended) distinction Young wanted to make was that there's no one personality best suited for long-term changes. "The good news is," he wrote, "people don't have to be born motivated to follow through with new things."[152]

In fact, most psychologist researchers don't believe there is such a thing as a motivated personality. Instead, the large determining factors of people's actions result from the context they find themselves in when making the decision. The people who surround you, the environment in which you live, and your understanding of the benefits of doing said action all greatly influence your participation.

So even at the surface level if someone doesn't feel that eating more vegetables is important to them, Young's research showed there are ways to get people to do something regardless of their interest level or motivation. While many chronic disease patients sadly face many barriers, having a professional help them find ways to work around the challenges to seek out a positive environment would allow opportunities for more success.

Young outlined a few ways to make a goal behavior important to someone through narrowing down importance to three large incentives: money, social connections, and health. While he acknowledged that everyone is different and that not everyone will be entirely motivated by these three things, he provides much research to depict that underlying most human decisions in this day and age are capital gains, social benefits, or improved health. Understanding

---

152 Young, Sean. Stick with It: A Scientifically Proven Process for Changing Your Life -- for Good. New York: Harper, 2018.

the patient enough to find what is meaningful to them is a necessary part of the equation. And despite motivation not always being present, there are always ways to enhance it to use in tandem with the other seven forces.

Easy

Similar to the Stepladder and Important forces, the "Easy" force is one that most people think they understand, yet Young redefined it in a way to ensure lasting behavior changes. Simply put, things that are easy for us to do, we will continue to do.

One night at ShapeDown in the teen exercise group, our topic was stress reduction. The goal of this particular session was to introduce how stretching, yoga, and other forms of physical activity can serve as a means of reducing stress and anxiety. I shared with them how personally, running had always been a way for me to step outside the stressors of my everyday life. I explained how it served as a safe haven of sorts and grounded me in a way nothing else ever had. I encouraged them to find their own personal outlet to help them more smoothly incorporate movement into their lives so they too could feel the benefits. As we moved on to the next activity, one girl quietly commented, "That only works because running is easy for you." Due to limited time and being in a group setting, I left her with the quick reply that different things work for different people. I just happened to like running, whereas I knew she preferred playing softball.

And this is true. Every person has particular interests, passions, and abilities that all affect engagement. Yet her statement illuminates a very common misconception often hiding behind inaction—this idea that someone like her could never be a runner because she wasn't built like one, it's too hard for her, or she's never done it before, etc. prevents someone from even trying. This overwriting of ability by stating she isn't motivated or disciplined enough are common societal and personal driving beliefs preventing countless Americans from engaging in physical activity every day.

The young girl in my class was more than right—running is, in fact, easy for me. And I could sit here and expound the cries of society by saying that it is simply because I am a hard worker and she is not, that I spent hours, days, weeks, years devoting myself to the sport to get better where she hasn't—but that wouldn't paint the whole picture. While those things are true and I did indeed spend more than half my life dedicated to running year-round for improvement, there are also the facts of my upbringing. Because I was born into a family that had a certain set of genes, a safe community where I could run the streets alone at age ten, and access to a top-ranked middle and high school track team, I had the opportunities to be successful at running that my young friend did not. Knowing this, I believe it is our duty to help others find ways to more easily incorporate movement and eating well into their busy, unique lives.

After class, I met with the young girl to further talk with her and her family to create a plan to help them increase their exercise. They shared with me that they had started going to the community gym but were lost about what to do. An easy solution—I created a guided workout plan with pictures for them based on their preferences to start using at the gym. It was a success as they continued going to the gym, but became a problem when "life" began catching up with them and they stopped going as frequently. Typically, they would go to the gym late at night, which led to later dinners, later bedtimes, and less time for homework. All it took to help get them back on track was a simple conversation with them to help figure out logistics on how they could go earlier in the day right after school. Sometimes the most simple solutions can be overlooked or unsuccessful because there is no collaboration.

Young took this simple idea and backed it with years of research. One way to enhance feelings of ease, he found, is by limiting choices. In interviews, he uses the personal example of purposeful parking at work. As a professor on UCLA's campus, Young strategically parks his car past the campus gym. He also makes it a point to pack a gym bag and carry it with him to work. By the time the end of the work day rolls around, he needs to walk past the gym, with a gym bag, to get in his car and go home. At that point, he stated, it is actually more inconvenient for him to *not* stop and work out. Seeking out the path of least resistance is what drives his engagement.

Barry Schwartz, a psychologist, professor, and frequent *New York Times* editorial contributor, also explored the idea of limiting choice in his "Paradox of Choice" TEDGlobal talk in 2005.

"With so many options to choose from, people find it very difficult to choose at all," he explained. "It's so damn hard to decide, that you'll just put it off till tomorrow, and then tomorrow and then tomorrow and tomorrow, and, of course, tomorrow never comes."[153] This is apparent in the messages our society sends about physical activity and dieting. There are way too many paths to take that claim they will show people results, so ultimately the task is put off and their health efforts never take off.

Schwartz also discussed the intersection of excess choices and expectations, a concept I believe is further contributing to lack of engagement in physical activity and poor diets across the United States. "Adding options to people's lives can't help but increase the expectations people have about how good those options will be. And what that's going to produce is less satisfaction with results, even when they're good results," he stated.[154]

This inherent expectation of perfection that comes from a society drowning in fitness and nutrition options causes individuals to stop trying. If they can't find the perfect

153 Schwartz, Barry. TED. Accessed June 15, 2019. https://www.ted.com/talks/barry_schwartz_on_the_paradox_of_choice?language=en.
154 Ibid.

solution or master a certain approach to dieting or exercise that worked for someone else, they feel defeated. This defeat and unsatisfactory completion lends to inaction and stopped efforts for betterment.

"What I'm telling you is that these expensive, complicated choices—it's not simply that they don't help. They actually hurt. They actually make us worse off," Schwartz emphasized.[155] Though talking about the effects of material affluence on industrial societies at large, this sentiment can most definitely be applied directly to the diet and fitness industry. There's a belief that the most expensive diet plan, need-to-have FitBit, or exclusive gym membership will be *the* answer to our failed attempts at self-improvement. Yet, ironically, it is what's preventing us from achieving our wellness goals.

This calls for a back-to-the basics plan both for food and exercise. Despite slowly seeing this return to whole-health diets and more functional movement in recent years, I still feel a cultural shift and acceptance of this simplicity is called for. Highlighting this idea within the health care system could speed up this shift to a more holistic approach.

To make it easier on people looking to make health changes, our solutions must be simple and easy. There must be limited options offered based on personal preferences to reduce paralysis, defeat, and inaction and in turn increase engagement.

---

155 Ibid.

Grocery stores like Trader Joe's and Costco Wholesale, whether knowingly or not, also make use of having limited options and their success shows in consumer data reports. Data science professionals have ranked Trader Joe's number one in customer preference two years in a row because of this. Jack Houston interviewed Barry Schwartz in a *Business Insider* article to uncover why Trader Joe's choice limitation is so successful.

To demonstrate, Houston counted the number of pasta sauces, olive oils, and cereals at his local market. They had 144 pasta sauces, 44 olive oils, and 172 cereals. Trader Joe's, on the other hand, had only 14 pasta sauces, 14 olive oils, and 39 cereals to choose from. Though Schwartz suggested Trader Joe's did this inadvertently and rather used it to control costs, he does believe it plays a role in simplifying the shopping experience and limiting consumer stress.[156]

"When you give people too many options, they get paralyzed instead of liberated," Schwartz explained, echoing the main thesis of his book *The Paradox of Choice: Why More Is Less.*[157] Trader Joe's enhanced consumers' experience by limiting stress and offering them ease of choice.

A program targeting health behaviors should seek to work with an individual to find the easiest way for them to engage

156 Houston, Jack. "A Psychologist Explains How Trader Joe's Gets You to Spend More Money." Business Insider. February 19, 2019. Accessed June 15, 2019. https://www.businessinsider.com/trader-joes-how-gets-you-spend-money-psychologist-2019-1.

157 Ibid.

in a health change. After all, people are often their own greatest experts. With guidance, they would be able to create
a plan that works smoothly based on their life circumstances.

Neurohacks

Another way to override bad habits and problematic
behaviors, Young shared, is to trick your brain! Coined
Neurohacks, Young's fifth force demonstrates how the brain
wants to be efficient. By completing something every day,
regardless of how small, new neural pathways begin to form.

An example Young likes to use is that of a man who had
recently gotten divorced. Not an amicable divorce—this
man and his ex-wife had many problems that created a vast
amount of turmoil and stress. One day, the man got a noti-
fication email that it was time to reset his password. This
was where he had the inspiration to change his password to
4giveher. Logging in multiple times a day was at first a painful
experience. It forced him to relive his new reality: that he was
no longer married and had been hurt by someone he loved.

As time went on, it began to get easier. As I am sure you
might have guessed, this man one day found himself no longer bitter and indeed realized he had forgiven his ex-wife.
Though there are most likely many contributing factors that
shifted his attitude, here the repetition of his password served
as a fundamental key to resetting his brain. This man later
went on to use the same technique to help him quit smoking.
At a five-year follow-up, the man was still tobacco-free—an

incredible feat. This man's success with using a neural hack suggests that quick mental shortcuts might actually change the brain to do things it couldn't do before. The changing of a password, whether it be 4giveher or quitsmokingnow, merely skims the surface of the incredible power our minds hold.

Translating this concept to the health promotion world shifts a current societal understanding upside down. Currently, there exists the notion that all it takes for someone to eat more vegetables or to run a marathon or to be successful—really, at anything at all—is willpower and motivation with sprinkles of visualization.

People are taught it all starts in the brain, but Young and his colleagues have found that the reverse idea is actually true. "I think it's just kind of a downer to us because we think we have to be motivated to do things and when we don't want to do them we get down," he says in the *Art of Manliness* podcast.[158] While visualization exercises and positive thinking are no doubt incredibly powerful and important tools, they are not the sole way to find success. It is tangible, repeated actions that will lead to successful habit formation rather than the commanding attitude of grit. Only after an action becomes saturated in daily routine will that attitude follow. Mind follows body follows mind.

---

158 "Podcast #329: Stick With It — The Science of Behavior Change." Interview. Art of Manliness (audio blog), August 10, 2017. Accessed June 12, 2019.

As Young further explained in the interview, "We first need to teach ourselves we can actually do it. We can't just have our brains telling our bodies to do something; we actually need our body to teach our brain, 'Hey, I already did that. I can totally keep doing this.'"[159]

For example, in my case, I now can wake up early in the morning to run not simply because I am motivated, but because I have done it frequently and often enough that my brain believes I am a runner: *I must be a runner if I run every day. And if I am a runner, I must run.* My brain then perceives running as a necessity of sorts to keep using the most efficient pathways it has worked hard to form.

The best part? It doesn't matter how many times you've failed; brain plasticity allows a fresh start to override any negative behavior with a new and healthier response. Brain plasticity refers to the brain's ability to change and establish new connections throughout life. This is great news for people who think it's too late to change their ways!

Captivating

Young's sixth force is called "Captivating." This simply explores how, in order for someone to keep doing things, they must be rewarded for doing them. Efforts must seek to engage the patient at hand and keep them interested to ensure they remain doing it.

---

159 Ibid.

This is as simple of a concept as making physical activity fun for someone. If people are enjoying themselves, they will forget to be preoccupied with how difficult the task at hand is and seamlessly complete it without realizing.

A captivating activity also lends nicely to repetition. If someone enjoys doing something, they will keep doing it! Repeated action allows behaviors to be solidified. Identifying activities that individuals deem personally enjoyable ensures they will continue to do them, ultimately helping them establish a new routine.

Finding a method that successfully captures someone's attention can only come from conversing with the individual at hand. Every person finds different things engaging, and every life is uniquely complex. It is up to the wellness provider to determine ways to personalize plans, for what works for one may not work for another.

Engrained

Repetition ties in perfectly with Young's seventh force "Engrained." Habits are formed when something is done over and over again, no matter how small the task is. It is through routine actions that pathways are etched into the brain, creating these neuronal connections. Even if it is as quick as doing five pushups every morning immediately upon waking up, eventually it becomes the norm, both consciously and subconsciously.

One mantra I've consistently told my sisters and mom when they were frustrated with themselves in changing a bad habit would be "start with acknowledgment."

I would proceed to tell them, "The fact that you're frustrated shows you've already done half the work—acknowledging when you slip up and need to act differently."

Perhaps subconsciously gleaned from AA support groups, there's this idea that the first step on the road to recovery is recognizing you have a problem; this can be incredibly powerful. Having enough awareness to recognize that your behaviors are detrimental to your well-being is huge! It signals that, on some level, you are frustrated and ready to do something about it.

To demonstrate, take this example with my little sister. When my sister shared with me that she felt down on herself for eating too many bags of Sour Patch Kids or a whole jar of Nutella in just a few days, I encouraged her to simply sit with the fact that she was upset. Rather than telling her to stop eating them immediately, I had her focus and become aware of that voice of frustration every time she ate too many sweets. That's all. Strictly listen to that voice and do nothing further.

Eventually, she began noticing it all the time. "Quite honestly, it just became sort of a nuisance," she told me. "I'd become annoyed with myself for eating too many sweets, would notice the annoyance, and then hear your voice telling me to just sit with it. At a certain point," she continued,

"I just didn't want to deal with it anymore. So I stopped eating them."

Consistent acknowledgment of a problem eventually becomes a driving power that carries people forward toward changing it. In combination with the themes uncovered in ROOTs and Young's forces, acknowledgment works as a catalyst. For only following this foundation of acceptance can work begin to fix it.

Takeaways

This chapter took a look at the remaining parts of Sean Young's SCIENCE framework. His work has shown us that interventions must be important to the individual, engaging, make use of neurohacks, captivating, and become engrained in order to see long-lasting change in your habits. Below are some ideas to implement within a health promotion program based on my and Young's research:

- Seek to understand personally compelling reasons to ensure programs are important and captivating to the individual at hand.
- Tie personally relevant incentives to behavioral tasks based on patient population base.
- Create wellness tasks that are easy to implement for individual in the context of their lives.
- Foster a positive wellness culture by shifting focus from diets and fitness trends to simple diet and movement tasks.

- Incorporate thought experiments to target emotional, realistic, and vivid future-self conceptions to positively influence long-term choices.
- Limit patient's behavioral options when it comes to treatment plans— make it easy for them and minimize choice.
- Tailor approaches to the individual and make it meaningful to each person.
- Consider use of "neurohacks" by offering suggestions of changing passwords or repeatedly and consistently writing down goals.
- Target increased acknowledgement of negative behaviors in patients and encourage sitting with the frustration.
- Ask patient to count how many times a day they experience frustration with their behaviors or engage in wishful thinking that things were different.

CHAPTER 18

THE QUESTION OF INSURANCE

———

Prioritizing Financial Gains

Unfortunately, we can't have a conversation about medicine and health care without also addressing financial restrictions and, more specifically, insurance coverage. Ah, there it is. The elephant in the room, so to speak, surrounding my new health care field-wide proposition. I'll be honest: it is an extremely disruptive and stubborn barrier standing in the way of my idea. Though I don't have the most widespread knowledge, and this chapter will merely skim the surface, I acknowledge it is a very real obstacle that prevents a lot of changes from happening within the medical system.

Numerous studies have shown that our nation's health care is by far the most expensive in the world. The problem? We don't have the health profile to show for it. Not even making the Bloomberg Global Health Index list of the twenty-five healthiest countries, the United States, despite being a developed country, has noteworthy health risks (high blood pressure, tobacco use, obesity), lower life expectancy, and more chronic disease-driven death than many of its counterparts. Even former President Barack Obama spoke to the present economic health care crisis. "The greatest threat to America's fiscal health," he said in a speech at the White House, "is not Social Security. ... By a wide margin, the biggest threat to our nation's balance sheet is the skyrocketing cost of health care."[160]

In an article from the *New Yorker*, Atul Gawande explored "The Cost Conundrum" of U.S. health care. In particular, he looks at McAllen, Texas, the second most expensive health care market in the country, to determine how exactly this crisis came to be and what can potentially be done to combat it.

After controlling for numerous factors, such as diet, health, socioeconomic status, by comparing two similar border towns in size, location, and circumstance (McAllen and El Paso), Gawande discovered the Medicare cost per

---

160 "Remarks by the President on Fiscal Policy." National Archives and Records Administration. Accessed June 15, 2019. https://obamawhitehouse.archives.gov/the-press-office/2011/04/13/remarks-president-fiscal-policy.

enrollee was drastically different ($14,946 vs. $7,504) due to the marked differences in the amount of care ordered for patients. For example, patients in McAllen received more operations, diagnostic tests, hospital admissions, specialist visits, and home nursing care than in El Paso.[161] Another common theme in these "high-cost regions" is significantly less low-cost preventative service and primary care options. In other words, he made (and heavily supported through research) the controversial claim that medical costs are so high because of a system that seeks to run any and all possible tests to maximize financial gains, despite it not always being the best option for the patient.

So what exactly does this all mean in the realm of health behavior change?

My argument is that, sadly, in the current system, medical decisions are increasingly dictated by maximizing financial gain. In order for new ideas and propositions to be accepted into the current system, there must be incentives for both physicians and insurance companies for the implementation of more preventative health programs. Additionally, there would need to be solid evidence and research demonstrating that these new types of programs would be effective for health outcomes.

---

161 Gawande, Atul, and Atul Gawande. "The Cost Conundrum." The New Yorker. June 19, 2017. Accessed June 15, 2019. https://www.newyorker.com/magazine/2009/06/01/the-cost-conundrum.

Offering services not covered by insurance does allow for more flexibility in the way Jaclyn and her weight loss staff from Chapter 15 support patients looking to lose weight. Despite limiting the number of people her clinic is able to help when compared to primary care physicians and cardiologists, Jaclyn's practice isn't confined to the rigid structure that other health care professionals are. They never have to deal with the question of billing for a service or asking if it is medically necessary and justifiable; they aren't confined to a certain amount of time they are able to spend with each patient and can instead go at their own pace. The downfall to services without insurance coverage, however, is limiting the pool of people who can afford their services. And, specifically when it comes to battling overweight and obesity, medical weight-loss clinics that don't accept insurance, especially Medicare or Medicaid, barely skim the surface of people in the United States who need medical help in losing weight.

Current Coverage

Currently, there are a few programs and services covered by insurance that target overweight and obese individuals to help get them the support they need when tackling their physicians commonly prescribed behavioral recommendations.

According to WebMD, under the Affordable Care Act most health insurance plans, including all plans purchased through the marketplace, now include obesity screening and counseling, with no copays or deductibles. "What consumers should count on, expect and demand, is what's called intensive behavioral support for obesity," said Ted Kyle, spokesman for the Obesity Society in an interview with WebMD. "It should be covered by all insurance plans under the Affordable Care Act."[162]

The articles pointed out, however, that there is no exact definition of what obesity counseling must include and that these offerings vary from plan to plan, making it sneakily difficult for patients to receive these services. "Bottom line is health plans are riddled with inconsistencies about covering medically necessary care for this chronic disease and for prevention of its complications," Kyle finished.[163] Though there has been an apparent shift in health consciousness on the part of insurers, they continue to make things murky by leaving plan details unclear, ultimately leaving it up to the patient to challenge their health plans to get the services they are legally entitled to.

In a more positive light, after this ACA expansion of health mandates for obesity, policies from 2015–2016 listed twenty-three states as having a specific health benefit requirement of covering bariatric and gastric bypass surgery and sixteen states include coverage and reimbursement for dietary or nutritional screening, counseling and/or therapy for obesity,

162 "3 Weight Loss Services Your Plan May Cover." WebMD. Accessed June 15, 2019. https://blogs.webmd.com/public-health/20150519/3-weight-loss-services-your-plan-may-cover.

163 Ibid.

sometimes including weight-loss programs. In addition to weight loss surgeries and nutritional counseling, in some cases FDA-approved weight-loss medication for individuals with a BMI of 27 or higher might also be covered.

Generally, the chances of weight-loss support being covered by insurance seem to improve if the person has a weight-related health condition such as heart disease, hypertension, obesity, or diabetes. And most all of the services offered are at the individual level.

If a patient meets all required criteria, Medicare will cover a diabetes prevention program, which neatly falls under the umbrella of a lifestyle change program. Diabetes prevention programs are a proven health behavior change program that helps prevent type II diabetes in at-risk patients. The program has sixteen sessions offered in a group setting over a six-month period. The class covers a multitude of topics, including tips on how to get more exercise and strategies to help control weight, and it provides you with a behavior coach trained to keep people motivated. If the patient completes that core session and meets certain weight-loss and attendance goals, they will receive six more months of follow-up sessions to help maintain the learned healthy habits.

From Drs. Markle and Emmert-Aronson at Open Source Wellness, we learned that behavior change sessions can be billed as Group Medical Visits to insurance companies. We also saw that the ShapeDown program is supported by St.

Joseph Mercy Trinity Health System through offering scholarships to families in need.

Based on Dr. Kate Lorig's research at Stanford University's Patient Education Research Center, the Center for Healthy Aging also laid out ways community organizations can ways to be covered under insurance. Titled "Health and Behavior Assessment and Intervention (HBAI) Services Coverage of Chronic Disease Self-Management Education Medicare and Medicare Advantage," this tip sheet's primary aim is to help community-based organizations in collaboration with a physician and/or non-physician practitioner to provide evidence-based preventative health programs for individuals who have one or more chronic diseases.

They state that in 2002, six CPT codes (a medical code used to report to physicians, health insurance companies, and accreditation organizations) were added to the system to address the behavioral, social, and psychosocial barriers to the self-management of one or more chronic diseases.[164] It further provided the information that all Medicare Advantage plans are mandated to cover HBAI services by particular providers such as physicians, nurse practitioners, licensed clinical psychologists, and licensed clinical social workers.[165]

---

164 "Health and Behavior Assessment and Intervention (HBAI) Services Coverage of Chronic Disease Self-Management Education Medicare and Medicare Advantage." National Council on Aging. Accessed June 12, 2019.

165 Ibid.

Lay leaders or community health workers can also lead the class if under the supervision of the authorized provider.

For billing, the claims must be submitted under the NPI number of the licensed individual. They also provide a list of many codes that the medical providers can file claims under Medicare Part B (Initial Health and Behavior assessment, Individual intervention, Health and Behavior intervention service provided in a group setting), each billed in fifteen-minute increments. For further guidance, the authors provide a sample reimbursement model for organizations to use to create programs.

Future Directions

An article from *Very Well Health* in 2019 shared that insurers are trending toward prevention care on some plans. There has been an increase in wellness options being offered in the last year, including gym memberships, weight-loss clinics, weight-loss surgery, massage therapy, and smoking cessation programs.[166] For example, some United Health Care plans include 10–50 percent discounts on specific health club memberships, which can save people money upon joining.

166 Norris, Louise. "What Do I Need to Know About Health Insurance Changes for 2019?" Verywell Health. December 25, 2018. Accessed June 15, 2019. https://www.verywellhealth.com/health-insurance-changes-facts-before-enrollment-4151694.

Another interesting thing to consider is the future direction of healthcare in general. With the advancement of technology, there has been an increasing shift to at-home care via telehealth. Telehealth is a broad term that encompasses a variety of technologies and methods used to deliver virtual medical, health, and education services to a patient remotely. Today, telehealth is being used for a variety of medical services.

"For most of the past half century, the best place for a physician visit was at their office or clinic, which had replaced the house call," Merrill Goozner, editor of *Modern Health Care*, wrote in an op-ed. "With the advance of new technologies like video conferencing, telehealth and remote monitoring, many patients are realizing the best access point for physician care is once again their home."[167] The Mayo Clinic outlined a variety of ways telehealth is currently being implemented: mobile phone uploads of daily logs, educational videos, apps that track and record important data such as vital signs or personal health information.[168]

Video chat sessions with a dietitian, nurse, psychologist, or health coach are also becoming increasingly popular. One example is FruitStreet, an online platform for lifestyle disease

---

167 Goozner, Merrill. "Editorial: The Paradigm Is Shifting." Modern Healthcare. March 09, 2019. Accessed June 15, 2019. https://www.modernhealthcare.com/opinion-editorial/editorial-paradigm-shifting.

168 "Managing Your Health in the Age of Wi-Fi." Mayo Clinic. August 16, 2017. Accessed June 15, 2019. https://www.mayoclinic.org/healthy-lifestyle/consumer-health/in-depth/telehealth/art-20044878.

management that was created by physicians independently all across the country. It is now the official CDC Diabetes Prevention Program and is covered by insurance. One part of this course is video conferencing with a health coach, as well as access to over twenty-five interactive lessons on topics like healthy eating, cooking, exercise, stress management, and sleep.

Home-based or telehealth interventions can be more cost-effective than traditional visits because they can be delivered by a physician assistant, nurse, or home health aide and also limit time spent and minimize transportation costs.

A ROOT program could have success being implemented as an online program. Trained behavioral health specialists and wellness coaches could offer care and treatment by meeting patients where they are at. Rather than offered at a primary care office, this option lays out an easy way for patients to incorporate a session into their daily lives, without causing a major disruption. This could further increase participation levels, which would positively affect adherence.

Takeaways

From this research, I have concluded that going forward there is hope for more behavioral health services that will be made available to a wide range of patients, specifically ones requiring a change in lifestyle habits such as diet and physical activity.

Potentially feasible ways to make a program with ROOTs billable and covered by insurance to reach as many people as possible are as follows:

- Bill as GMV.
- Hire billable providers at PCP such as a physician, nurse practitioner, LCSW, or a LCP.
- Follow the Center for Healthy Aging's HBAI Tip Sheet.
- Further collect research to demonstrate effectiveness of group setting and lobby insurance agencies.
- Provide list of services patients qualify for and have coverage for.
- Find hospitals that prioritize funds for health behavior management initiatives.

CHAPTER 19

WORKPLACE WELLNESS

———

In April 2019, there were 129.21 million Americans that were employed full time.[169] Additionally, according to the Bureau of Labor Statistics, the average American works 44 hours per week, or 8.8 hours per day.[170] With an average of 6.8 hours of sleep per night,[171] this means that over half of people's waking hours are spent at the workplace.

An estimated 71.6 percent of American adults in the 2015–16 calendar year were found to be either overweight or

---

169 "U.S.: Number of Full-time Workers in April 2019." Statista. Accessed June 15, 2019. https://www.statista.com/statistics/192361/unadjusted-monthly-number-of-full-time-employees-in-the-us/.

170 Forwardist. "A Brief History of the 8-hour Workday, Which Changed How Americans Work." CNBC. May 05, 2017. Accessed June 15, 2019. https://www.cnbc.com/2017/05/03/how-the-8-hour-workday-changed-how-americans-work.html.

171 Gallup, Inc. "In U.S., 40% Get Less Than Recommended Amount of Sleep." Gallup.com. Accessed June 15, 2019. https://news.gallup.com/poll/166553/less-recommended-amount-sleep.aspx.

obese[172]. As a large percentage of these adults are employed, the workplace offers a huge target space for controlled interventions. Not only does it have the time and space, it also creates the opportunity to access a vast amount of funds to provide quality care.

According to the IBISWorld Industry Report on Corporate Wellness Services in the United States, the employee wellness sector is almost an $8 billion industry with the expectation to grow up to 7.8 percent by 2021.[173] Further, the global corporate wellness market size is projected to reach USD 90.7 billion by 2026.[174]

A potential solution to this insurance barrier, a ROOT program would be best suited for implementation in the world of Workplace Wellness.

Let's take a look.

Workplace Wellness

"Workplace wellness seems like a very natural fit—people are safer, more productive, feel better and generally

172 "FastStats - Overweight Prevalence." Centers for Disease Control and Prevention. Accessed June 15, 2019. https://www.cdc.gov/nchs/fastats/obesity-overweight.htm.

173 "Industry Market Research, Reports, and Statistics." IBISWorld. Accessed June 15, 2019. https://www.ibisworld.com/industry-trends/specialized-market-research-reports/life-sciences/wellness-services/corporate-wellness-services.html.

174 "Corporate Wellness Market Worth $90.7 Billion By 2026 | CAGR 6.8%." Market Research Reports & Consulting. Accessed June 15, 2019. https://www.grandviewresearch.com/press-release/global-corporate-wellness-market.

have a better attitude if their health is better because it is not a weight dragging them down," Mary Marzec, Ph.D., thoughtfully shared with me over tea one morning.

I first met Dr. Marzec at the University of Michigan's School of Kinesiology career fair. After chatting with her at her booth about the rise of chronic diseases and how to best target the individuals that suffer from them, my mind began whirring. I was further inspired when I went to a talk she gave later that week on her research findings in the realm of workplace wellness.

With a master's in bio-statistics and Ph.D. in kinesiology, the primary focus of her academic studies work was exploring determinants of workplace absenteeism and helping organizations create cultures that support health. She has been in the area of workplace wellness for 14 years.

All workplace programs have the common denominators of wanting people to be healthy and minimizing illnesses and diseases to enhance employee satisfaction and productivity and limit absenteeism. In essence, there is a blanket approach that most companies follow when implementing a health and wellness program to achieve these goals. For example, they typically offer incentives, insurance drops, gym memberships, health benefits, or even cash to reward employee participation. Despite following the same general principles, there are vast differences across varying companies in the effectiveness of such initiatives, often reflected by low engagement.

Dr. Marzec used her academic background to develop a data program that assessed a company's culture surrounding health. This assessment included surveys with questions like *How supported do you feel in your leadership around health and well-being?* that were solely focused around wellness and health culture at a company. Through data analysis, Dr. Marzec was able to assign each company a "Culture Score" and found there was a significant correlation between overweight and obesity and lower culture scores.

She uncovered that the critical issue separating companies was not, in fact, ineffective wellness programs, but rather the surrounding environment that affected employee behaviors. "One of the differences in whether or not people participate in these programs, or take advantage of them, is the underlying culture," Dr. Marzec told me.

Dr. Marzec is now a senior scientist at Virgin Pulse, the world's largest digital employee well-being and engagement company dedicated to providing personalized wellness solutions to build engagement in wellness programs. There, she counsels companies on how to create a more effective culture and environment to support employees in making health behavior changes or maintaining habits and improve their quality of life.

Incredibly invigorated, I felt her research findings and work on culture greatly aligned with my uncovered ROOT framework. She happily agreed to talk with me further about her involvement in wellness programming. It was there

I learned a great deal and felt I found my answer to tackling the rise of chronic disease rates in the United States and helping people find lasting solutions.

As we will explore in this chapter, Dr. Marzec determined that the problem of wellness program uptake lies in the previously established *culture* of a company. She taught me why this happens by exploring the different barriers that currently exist, as well as by looking at how we can shift those misaligned cultures and the future direction of the corporate wellness sector.

Why the Workplace?

Where the medical field is notorious for slow system changes resulting from reliance on legislative-level changes, corporate America is fast-paced and always looking for ways to improve. Especially with incredible technological advances, there's constant competition among employers to be the best and offer the greatest benefits all in hopes of retaining employees. In a time when pensions are going away, health care benefits are not what they used to be, and people have the ability to apply to jobs all across the country, there is little motivating employees to stay at a company. Dr. Marzec feels the challenges of retention and recruitment are why more and more companies are leaning into wellness.

Though she hated to generalize, Dr. Marzec shared with me her belief that millennials have driven a lot of this positive change in the workplace. "They don't put up with bad experiences at work— they expect a certain level of experience and service as employees. If they have a punitive manager, a manager who doesn't care about them or their health, it simply isn't tolerated and they'll find another job."

In pursuit of personal as well as professional growth, the upcoming generation will go to great lengths to have a positive work experience. People are feeling increasingly more comfortable only staying at a job for two or three years and then moving on to something else if they aren't satisfied. Even older, more experienced workers are questioning why they should stay five, ten more years if the work environment isn't supportive or positive now. "The other thing companies don't realize is that factors like job dissatisfaction are health risks in themselves," Dr. Marzec said. "People are more likely to have higher health care costs in the next three to five years if they are not satisfied with their job."

Companies are increasingly turning to third-party vendors like Virgin Pulse to help them make these changes. Fewer companies are doing them internally because it is time- and labor-intensive and they don't have the staffing. Further, wellness companies are putting in lots of effort to deliver effective, cutting-edge results to meet employers' demands. "Employers are sophisticated in many ways. They want results, and they're holding the third-party vendors accountable to deliver on effective solutions," Dr. Marzec explained.

It is this high speed, evolving workplace landscape that makes employers the perfect target for implementing behavior change programs. Dr. Marzec firmly agreed: "Eight to 12 hours a day, 40+ hours a week at work—that's your biggest opportunity."

Workplace Barriers

Though Virgin Pulse implements the same general program across all its clients, there are vast differences in the effectiveness. Like previously mentioned, Dr. Marzec's research shows this is largely due to how the culture at the office or workplace welcomes these initiatives.

Dr. Marzec has identified three common levels within an organization that typically breed this unsupportive culture. These misalignments can exist at multiple layers of an organization's hierarchy.

"I usually think of it in terms of your leadership support at the top, your policies, your manager support, and then coworkers," Dr. Marzec clarified. "All are different avenues that can breed either toxic or supportive environments."

Policy

People often view health as an external entity, something that exists separate from their everyday lives. This sentiment of health behaviors being done behind closed doors, outside of daily life, is often carried over into the workplace. Even when companies say wellness is a priority they still encourage people to do it outside of work and expect it to be done on their own time. At some companies, there are even rules and policies stating you can't exercise on company time.

She uses the example of some companies requiring employees to sign a waiver that states they will only exercise on break time, because if they get hurt, it turns into a legal safety issue. If someone is injured on the clock, it becomes a recordable incident and then must be processed through OSHA, Occupational Safety and Health Administration and corporate becomes involved. It becomes an extreme hassle and liability to even attempt to get exercise in at work, often preventing the employees who are motivated to do something from doing so.

The other way policy can prevent people from engaging in healthy behaviors at the workplace are ones that affect decisions about food. It is not uncommon for offices to be surrounded by junk food. When people are in that environment for eight or more hours a day and the only options are processed foods that come from a vending machine, they will make negative decisions out of convenience. Sticking to healthy eating plans becomes difficult when options are so limited.

Even with things as seemingly little as company events or business lunches, if the food is catered and full of unhealthy options, the company is displaying one culture and asking employees to live another. It can become confusing when expectations and communicated messages don't match up with the reality. As simple a fix as changing the types of food offered at an event or, if the budget allows, buying healthy vending machines can begin to shift that negative culture at the workplace.

Dr. Marzec got incredibly excited when talking about the newest addition to one of the sites she frequents. "They now have these little machines that have water that is flavored. You can choose your flavor of water, whether or not its sparkling," she happily explained. Following through on wellness from a policy perspective is crucial for shifting the culture at workplaces.

Though seemingly obvious, it is not always this apparent at the ground level. "I talk to leaders and sort of make that connection for them. It isn't that they don't care about employee health and wellness; it's just that they haven't always connected the fact that their ordering pizzas at every event and asking people to lose weight don't align with the wellness program," she shared with me. This change ultimately starts with the leaders of companies because they are the ones enacting the policies that get passed on to the managers to enforce, which the employees are then expected to follow. These levels are much more connected than they appear—cohesion must exist between all parties.

It is not uncommon for well-being programs at the workplace to cause backlash because of these inconsistent ideals. It mostly has to do with the way they are integrated with and tied to benefits and health insurance premiums. The original idea makes sense, if your employees are going to put in the time and work to improve their health, it is nice to give them rewards. In Dr. Marzec's experience, however, the reality is that people often struggle with knowing where to send the forms in, forget to turn them in, didn't understand how it paid off, or experienced a timing issue with the processing. "It becomes almost more like a punishment than a choice," she stated. "It can even come across as punitive, and the implementation is tricky."

Manager

Dr. Marzec passionately described to me how imperative it is to have a manager on board with the company's wellness efforts when looking for long-term engagement in health behaviors.

Judgment on the job is a prime reason there can be a lack of engagement in employee initiatives.Even when there are well-meaning company offerings for wellness, such as yoga classes or a lunch walking groups, if the resounding mentality of the employees is *I don't have enough time and have multiple competing deadlines to meet,* or if an employee leaves at lunch and is on their way to the walking group and the manager comments, *Gee, I wish I had time to walk,* an offhand comment, particularly from a supervisor, can really discourage that employee and others from walking on their lunch break. there is no way the employee will attempt to go on a walk on their lunch break ever again. Fear of work ethic critique can be a powerful motivator, overwriting any prior established wellness behaviors at the office.

Similarly, as another example, Dr. Marzec told me about one project that she worked on with the California Department of Health. Funded by the CDC, on the day of the ribbon cutting for new walking routes that were made available. If people didn't see their manager there, they completely turned around and went straight back to their desk because they didn't know if it was okay or not. This signifies the importance of having managerial support in wellness initiatives.

To demonstrate how simple a shift in managerial support can be, Dr. Marzec asked me to imagine a call center. I envisioned countless desks of workers with headsets, sitting in their chairs at desks for hours on end, day in and day out. She shared with me that the shift in this scenario can be as simple as the manager walking around saying, "Time to get up and stretch!"

"Not that everybody will do it, but even the manager just saying it's important for you to take care of yourself during the day makes a big difference on the job," she highlighted. "The mentality shifts to *My manager actually just cares about me.*"

This transition leaves workers both with a sense of duty and pride. Out of respect to their leader and fellow coworkers, people begin to get up and partake in the daily stretch, adding movement into their life. It begins to act as a sort of positive peer pressure force.

In a *Harvard Business Review* article from 2011, Peter Fuda and Richard Badham explored how leaders spark and sustain change. Similar to what Dr. Marzec described to me within the huddles, Fuda and Badham discussed something they call "the snowball." Using Clynton Bartholomeusz, the CEO of a large German beauty company, as an example, Fuda and Badham explained that by standing up in front of his top sixty managers to admit his failings, acknowledge his need to change problematic behaviors, and outline future goals, he was able to set a model and plan for others to follow.[175] In the authors' words, Clynton set a snowball loose at the top of a mountain engaging and inspiring his employees to follow suit.

"The snowball represents a cycle of mutual accountability that creates momentum for change. It starts rolling when a leader opens himself up," they wrote. "This act of humility is seen as courageous and inspires others to follow suit. As more members of the team join the process (and those causing drag are removed), the snowball becomes more tightly compacted and almost impossible to stop."[176]

When a leader is willing to be open and acknowledge their own shortcomings, it shows employees that it's okay to struggle, that openness is acceptable and that they too

---

175 Badham, Peter FudaRichard. "Fire, Snowball, Mask, Movie: How Leaders Spark and Sustain Change." Harvard Business Review. August 01, 2014. Accessed June 15, 2019. https://hbr.org/2011/11/fire-snowball-mask-movie-how-leaders-spark-and-sustain-change.

176 Ibid.

should follow suit and begin to work toward changing their behavior. To make the manager that Dr. Marzec mentioned even more successful, upon introducing the topic of stretching, they may begin with a story about how they too struggle to practice wellness and movement during the day and that there is the shared goal of supporting everybody to work on it together.

People in positions of power have a responsibility, not only to their company and daily work, but also to the employees below them who are, whether consciously or not, turn in to them for cues on how to act.

Creating the space for engagement in wellness activities throughout the workday, personally engaging in health initiatives, and supporting subordinates in taking care of themselves are just a few ways Dr. Marzec shared with me on how managers have the power to shift the culture at worksites to encourage healthier behaviors in employees.

Coworkers

Coworkers also have the ability to influence, whether negatively or positively, the direction wellness initiatives can take.

While it might not be apparent that individuals at this level can impact the way health promotion programs are taken up, Dr. Marzec describes numerous ways in which they can serve both themselves and their peers from the bottom up.

A typical way companies try to engage factory workers in movement on the job is implementing a team stretch during the morning huddles. All it takes is for one employee to have a negative attitude to throw off the whole dynamic of the group.

On the contrary, all it takes to change that mentality around is one person! Getting one coworker to stand up and do the stretches in the morning huddle changes the whole culture of the group. That *Let's do this!* attitude is contagious, especially if driven by a leader. If a team leader says and demonstrates that something is important, it becomes a team-building activity that becomes routine. After a while, people won't question it as it soon becomes the norm.

Another use of ground-level employees making a difference in the culture is through informal yet public means. Things like having a bulletin board where people can post healthy recipes they've tried or share fun pictures of activities they've done such as hiking or taking a bike ride are just a couple examples Dr. Marzec explained to me. Even the simple act of having conversations about healthy lifestyles at the workplace can permeate the culture and make a difference. But in order for these things to take root, there must be one or a few employees to begin that shift.

One way to encourage others to share this shift in culture, is surprisingly, through being vulnerable. Brené Brown, Ph.D., MSW, is a research professor at the University of Houston most famous for her work on vulnerability. In her book *Daring Greatly,* she explored how vulnerability, or "uncertainty, risk, and emotional exposure,"[177] can transform the way people lead. Specifically, she believes vulnerability can play a role when seeking to shift a company's culture. "To grow a relationship or raise a family or create an organizational culture or run a school or nurture a faith community, all in a way that is fundamentally opposite to the cultural norms driven by scarcity, it takes awareness, commitment, and work ... every single day" (Brown, 29). She went on to explain that the only way to fight back against the existing pressure hindering you and your ideal culture is by remaining vulnerable and continuing to fight for what you believe in.

Relating Brown's definition of vulnerability to the workplace, I believe teams can express this uncertainty and risk by doing what their peers are not. If people look at someone funny for doing squats in the break room or make comments about a person's lunch box full of whole foods packed at home, it takes a certain type of person, or a normal person being comfortable with the uncomfortable, to continue engaging in those health-conscious efforts despite having an unsupportive environment. Further, swinging the expected norms in a group is not as difficult as it might seem. Sometimes all it takes is asking your friend or coworker to join you.

---

177 Brown, Brené. Daring Greatly: How the Courage to Be Vulnerable Transforms the Way We Live, Love, Parent, and Lead. London: Penguin Life, 2015.

"There's actually some very persuasive leadership research that supports the idea that asking for support is critical, and that vulnerability and courage are contagious," Brown declared (Brown, 54).

As an example, Dr. Marzec compared two worksites she had visited that week. One leader of the ground workers who was frustrated told her, "You know, the guys won't do stretches here. They stay on their phones—they just won't even stand up and participate." The other site she visited did stretches every morning during the team huddle, and it was just part of their daily routine. The leader shared if they didn't do them for a day or two people thought something was wrong.

"It's just an entirely different mindset. All it really takes is a few people being committed to it, having it as their passion, and not being private about it," Dr. Marzec shared with me upon examination of the diametrically opposed morning routines.

Or, as Brown might say, it took a few people being *vulnerable* to shift the norm. Finding ways to seek out individuals who already fully appreciate and practice a healthy lifestyle and encourage them to continue engaging in those behaviors around the workplace would be a good way for managers to shift the communal norms within the workplace.

Many companies have also used this concept of targeting motivated individuals, whom they deem "Wellness Champions," to help shift the culture. A way to incorporate peer-to-peer support, this idea identifies a group leader to spearhead efforts in wellness and keep the group on task.

Friendly competitions is another way companies tap into the support that can be found between coworkers. By targeting camaraderie and peer support, it turns engagement in health behaviors into a friendly competition and challenge. For example, healthy eating challenges, no sugar challenges, physical activity and step challenges are all examples of popular ways employers try to engage their employees.

Targeting people who already partake in wellness behaviors, encouraging conversations on the job, and implementing activities that highlight peer competition and support are all ways to target the existing employees and rely on the powerful presence of *others* to see results.

Individual factors must also be assessed when looking at a community's wellness culture. Looking at the personal level can further point out barriers a company may be facing when trying to implement, or fix, a wellness initiative.

Some questions that are important to ask individual employees are things like *how stressed are you? Do you trust the organization with your information? Is there a sense of community where you work? If not, why do people not seem to be getting along? What do you think could improve a sense of community at your workplace?* All of this must be considered when devising a plan of action to shift the current culture. Very simply, if people dislike each other or there is a lack of communication among workers, you can't find success with peer-led activities. It is necessary to assess all barriers before attempting to change the dynamic within an office.

Only after assessment of the existing culture to make a personalized program can you begin to target engagement with the employees.

"Once you get through the layers and get a program implemented, the magic is who will participate and why," Mary's work at Virgin Pulse has taught her. The next section will show us how to get companies involved in its programs.

What Works

After determining the culture score of a company by examining the different layers of influence from its policies, leaders and managers, and the attitudes of coworkers, Dr. Marzec creates a specific *tailored* profile to determine a plan for each organization.

She first explained the importance of assessing the current culture of a company, followed by examining the resources it already has. "I look at what's there and set expectations appropriately," she established. Only then can she advise the company on how to effectively go about bettering their wellness program through increasing engagement.

For example, a lot of companies Dr. Marzec works with are concerned with the return on investment (ROI) of their wellness programs. Executives complain they've had established programs for three or four years and are not seeing any results. Dr. Marzec comes in and often identifies misalignments in the culture and makes recommendations based on that company's needs.

Often, it is not the actual program that isn't working; rather, she finds the company culture is not compatible with the expected changes. Let's look at a company where communication between employer and employee on their wellness expectations is not the greatest.

Say a large majority of their employees perceive the company's wellness efforts as negative. Feelings such as *My company is watching me. They are using the information from my health assessment to raise my premium. They are going to fire me if I have diabetes because I cost them too much! I need to be healthier so I can work harder so I won't get in trouble,* can be expressed sentiments. Though unfounded, these are thoughts that can run through people's minds when there is a lack of explanation surrounding a wellness program. "If a company is not very intentional about stating its purpose and being clear in its communications and processes, people project their fears onto your intention because you haven't stated it outright," Dr. Marzec depicted.

Companies that see positive outcomes, therefore, are those that communicate clearly about their well-being programs. She concluded, "If trust is really low, ideally you need to do some communications about how you're implementing your programs and more reach in that area before you're going to get lift and behavior change and participation and return on investment and all the other things a company is interested in."

Similar to aligning patient health goals with that of a physician, showing a manager or top-level executive that their company goals of profit, productivity, and engagement are actually influenced by employees' health and well-being is essential. Tying wellness programs in with all of the company's other initiatives to demonstrate that everything is integrated can increase acceptance of such programs. There does not need to be separation of goals; instead, pointing out intersections of priorities will assist in program effectiveness and limit misalignments that disrupt the culture. This can be done through *reflection* on the current landscape of a company, determining both where it has been and where it would like to go.

But what about a company or group of employees that are simply not interested? When a company is not in tune with their wellness efforts or wanting to be involved, Dr. Marzec explained there is a relatively simple fix. "It's the same with a person: you just find out what that stealthy motivator is," she comments.

If a company is not driven by its employees' health, perhaps there is an ongoing safety competition with other manufacturing plant locations in the area. Creating a wellness competition around one that already exists is a great way to ease a company into making wellness efforts.

Another way is to implement wellness in traditions that already exist. If there is a safety breakfast every month to celebrate a plant's safety, finding ways to work health and wellness into that can ease expectations into routines.

"You might not be able to start out with 'Oh, health is every day. Do something every day.' It's going to take a lot longer to infiltrate into weaker cultures because you need to start small," Dr. Marzec emphasized. "You have to be realistic about where the culture is and where the company is, and once people feel like it's not being shoved down their throat, I think you might be surprised at how much more interested in it they are, get them started."

In other words, Dr. Marzec told me that in order to get people engaged in wellness efforts that will last, you must *take things one at a time*. The idea is to help people build the habit after having that initial in-the-door motivator.

Further connecting it to the ROOT model, interventions must meet the company where they are at. Just as I would not tell my patients who couldn't walk longer on the treadmill than three minutes to sign up for a 5k, the key lies in assessing current abilities.

"In my work it's really about helping companies be realistic and relevant about their interventions," Dr. Marzec stated. "That's why it's so important to understand what people's jobs are like day to day." Or, in the case of a personal health promotion program, understand the patient's daily life.

She uses multiple examples to depict this principle.

Say there is a traveling sales employee. Sharing with them how to make use of the wellness resources on the company's campus may not be beneficial if they spend limited time there. Rather, one approach might be teaching them healthy tips on where to get food on the road or techniques for packing a lunch so as to limit eating out at restaurants.

Sometimes there are work situations that are just not optimal but can't be changed. In the case of a shift worker, an approach may be solely focused on how to help maximize sleep during the day. Narrowing in on the primary health concerns of each unique position leads to a more specified and personally relevant solution.

A final example is in the case of a nurse. Hydration is a huge part of wellness that many people overlook. If you keep encouraging a bedside nurse to drink more water, they will get incredible pushback from their manager if they needs to go to the bathroom multiple times a day. Understanding the day-to-day realities of each profession you are working with is critical if your goal is to leave a lasting impact on these employees' lives. Instead of just encouraging drinking more water, perhaps providing a more strategic approach that helps nurses time their self-care is a better approach. Another method of course is to encourage managers to be mindful of these practices and allow wellness to be incorporated into the work routine.

At the end of the day, it really is about playing to all the existing layers that exist around the one target behavior to accomplish the goal.

Mary's job working at a wellness provider calls her to *reflect* on the resources a company already has and find places they aren't utilizing the offered services.

"The more you can integrate and leverage what you're already doing, the more efficient it is," Dr. Marzec pointed out. "I always ask, 'Where can you take what you have and get more out of it?'"

To Dr. Marzec, this is where the field of workplace wellness can be the most fun. Most of the interventions are already established and don't need much tweaking; it is rather in the implementation that companies struggle. Figuring out a strategy to match the needs of the company is where Virgin Pulse delivers progress. A demonstration might be calling in a communications strategist if they are having difficulties spreading the message or bringing in an onsite coordinator for those workplaces where people are not sitting at a desk all day.

It is a better use of resources and limits the amount of time that needs to be spent on these initiatives. She acknowledges there is little time or space to add meetings or committees in. Rather, solutions sometimes need to remain simple and just point out ways they can add little changes into the already existing routine. Take the previous mentioned example of adding stretches at the morning huddle during the safety meeting at manufacturing plants with their utility employers.

Even if companies don't have a budget, Dr. Marzec told me they can still make big changes. "There's so much you can do without spending more money," she stated. She explained that even companies that can't afford to put in a gym can create opportunities for wellness within the daily routine. Two ideas she had incorporated the breath. One was called "square breathing," where you instruct people to bring their shoulders down and keep their back straight and then have them take deep breaths, pausing between the inhale and the exhale and again between the exhale and the inhale.. Another idea she had was "mindful breathing" which called for employees to stop and focus on counting breaths and bringing awareness to the present moment.

Multiple Pillars of Health

As our conversation progressed from identifying places within a workplace that could improve in transparency and coherency on wellness, we began talking about what "health" truly means.

Dr. Marzec emphasized to me that there were far more factors of wellness than diet and exercise that must be considered for a program. Especially within the workplace, other health services must be offered to ensure all aspects of employee well-being are accounted for. Things like financial services, mental and emotional health services, and options for doing community service or practicing mindfulness are all pillars constituting well-being that should be included.

Financial considerations, like budgeting and retirement planning, all feed into wellness because money is one of the biggest stressors in our lives. You can't be focused on your work if you're worried about your electricity getting shut off or how to pay for child care.

Additionally, Dr. Marzec was happy to share that the stigma around seeking services for mental health at the workplace has slowly shifted. She feels in the next few years there will be an increase in companies who want to incorporate mental health as part of their wellness plans. Especially with the rise of technology and apps, there's so much more companies can offer.

To demonstrate the difference from a few years ago, Dr. Marzec talked about employee assistance programs (EAP) today. Whereas before no one would typically join them, today she has seen an EAP worker onsite at a call center and people actually go—they don't feel stigmatized walking down the halls to the office, which is huge. Managers are also grateful because it leaves more room for them to do their job and limits their stress dramatically. When issues or concerns come up, supervisors now have a warm hand-off to a trained professional who can actually offer them resources to help the employees manage the situation.

On top of physical and mental health, there are even increased opportunities for employees to engage with their community through volunteer activities, both allowing the company to give back and offering employees the chance to help out and feel a sense of purpose. This facilitates the complete integration of multiple aspects of a person's health and well-being.

Even within the categories of eating and exercise, further consideration for the complexities of each individual situation must occur.

"We're so tied to calories in and calories out, but our bodies are so much more complicated than that," Dr. Marzec agreed.

So much of our country's health crisis and obesity issue stem from the way our food is processed. The amount of information people have further aggravates an already complex issue. The solution to this must run so much deeper than telling people to exercise more and eat better, which is why more long-lasting, guided solutions should be in place.

Takeaways

While I wish I had more space to delve into the complexities of workplace wellness and explore what currently exists, it serves as a potential solution to the question I posed months ago: *how can we support people in making health behavior changes sustainable, and where can we implement such a program?* Coupled with the ROOT framework uncovered in my research, I believe U.S. companies can, and should, offer the space to help people engage in healthy behaviors for the long term.

Dr. Marzec's work has shown me a very plausible setting to establish ROOTs for effective long-term behavior change.

The workplace offers the time, space, and financial resources to reach an ideal target population of adult Americans. Additionally, the business sector of the United States is always moving at a fast pace and seems to implement changes more quickly than the medical system. If we as a nation hope to reverse the obesity epidemic, we must seek out sustainable solutions. We need to be re-grounded in our roots to ensure nourishment for healthy growth well into our future.

CHAPTER 20

A NOTE ON MINDFULNESS

——

When I first heard about the concept of mindfulness in terms of health behavior management, I was intrigued.

Having read my fair share of books on the matter from Buddhism and attended meditation classes at the University of Michigan in addition to going to a Buddhist temple on Sunday mornings ever since my freshman year of college, I considered myself well-versed on the matter—that is, well-versed in the way only a 21-year-old on a liberal campus can be. But by the second, third, and fourth interview I conducted where mindfulness made its way into the conversation, I began to truly ponder the role present awareness plays in health maintenance.

Surely I could explain to you the ways mindfulness guided the removal of our identity from the conscious stream of narrative constantly playing in our minds or the way it can ground human beings to the present moment at hand and awaken them to the beauty of awareness. I had even learned the many ways it can calm anxiety and reduce stress, but not once had I thought of it in terms of losing weight or changing lifestyle. Perhaps it was simply a trend finding a way to seep into all aspects of our society. Or maybe, instead, there was something there worth noting.

Here we will explore the expansive realm that is mindfulness (in a few words) and how it can, and should, play a role in health behavior interventions.

It's All Mentality

First, before we go any further, I would like to share with you what I mean when I say "mindfulness." Later in this chapter we will look at the medical field's definition; I want to share with you, however, Merriam-Webster's definition, because I feel it best describes the concept: "A mental state achieved by focusing one's awareness on the present moment, while calmly acknowledging and accepting one's feelings, thoughts, and bodily sensations, used as a therapeutic technique."[178]

---

178 "Mindfulness." Merriam-Webster. Accessed June 15, 2019. https://www.merriam-webster.com/dictionary/mindfulness.

I'm a firm believer in the power of thoughts and energies and mindsets. Despite the fact that engaging in poor lifestyles is the result of many confounding factors, often uncontrollable, I feel there exists within all of us the power to change any situation—and that power lies within our mind.

Specifically when it comes to taking on something challenging—let's say a seemingly impossible deadline—no matter how little of a say you feel you have on the matter, there always exists the chance to re-frame the way you are perceiving it. I say this with the caveat understanding that I know there is a vast difference between run-of-the-mill situations people deem "challenging" and ones that are inherently unfair due to a lack of privilege.

Some people call this thinking positive; others deem it optimism or viewing the proverbial glass of water half-full—whatever the name is and however one may feel about it, I believe mentality can completely reverse a situation. For example, as I'm typing this, it is incredibly late and I know I have to set my alarm very early for tomorrow morning. As I'm dreading it now (which I shouldn't be, as there's still an infinite amount of time between now and then and I should truly focus on the task at hand), I am setting the intention that tomorrow morning, though my first thought most probably will be *"Ugh, it's so early, I just want to sleep!"* I will let that pass on through and instead say, *"Good morning! I am so excited for today, and I am so, so awake."* In all honesty, I will most likely proceed with ten jumping jacks and/or ten pushups to confirm and solidify that sentiment with my body (side note: this is not a necessary component should someone face this same situation, though I do highly recommend).

From experience, I know on the inside I will be very tired and fully wishing I could roll back over in bed, but by simply shifting the narrative, I have tricked my mind into thinking I feel alert and ready for the day, all because of a simple change in my thoughts. Re-framing my mind, regardless of whether I actually believe it, gets me to act a certain way. It *changes my behavior.*

In the realm of making health behavior changes, I think the power of mentality can be as simple as pretending to feel confident, even if you feel anything but. It can be as simple as repeating *I am confident, I am confident, I am confident* over and over in your mind throughout the day or more complex, like adopting the mindset of someone you know who is super confident and acting like you are that person as you walk into the gym and face the dreaded mirror you typically can't stand to look in. Changing mentality can be as minute as repeating over and over in your mind *I like vegetables, I like vegetables, I like vegetables,* and I firmly believe you will eat vegetables at some point that day, if only because you begin to question yourself and you want to stop saying the silly mantra. I know this sounds trivial, but I've had success with this technique in the past, and we've also explored the research of Sean Young, who has made similar findings with "neurohacks." I firmly believe shifting the way you think about things, regardless of your actual opinion on the matter, can do wonders so long as you lean into it.

At the end of the day, my view on mentality and the power it can hold in changing action all stems from the practice of mindfulness. It takes a certain level of awareness and the release of control over our thoughts that we so often hold tight to tap into the power of mentality to ultimately guide us to the inertia that will help us overcome our rooted behaviors.

Follow the Feelings

The practice of mindfulness can also serve as a tool to smoothly accept and let go of thoughts that carry a negative energy and prevent us from making positive change. For me, this plays out when I find myself getting trapped in a negative thinking loop, the cycle of endless feelings. Something makes me angry; I become angry that I'm angry; then I begin to wish I wasn't angry, all the while still being angry. It is exhausting. Instead of getting caught in this loop or ignoring that anger you feel when you don't make it to the gym or running away from the fear you feel when you think about drastically changing your diet all at once, I learned from Thich Nhat Hanh's *Peace Is Every Step* to simply notice these negative emotions. He implored us to greet them and say, "Hello stress, how are you today?"[179] Rather than ignoring or shying away from them, which is most people's default, the

---

179 Hạnh, Nhất. Peace Is Every Step. Bantam/AJP, 2013.

simple act of greeting negative emotions can surprisingly be the thing that leaves you less overwhelmed.

Conversely, I used to go full force in the opposite direction. Previously a big proponent of honoring and acknowledging your feelings—I felt it was our duty to go all in and feel every tiny emotion in its entirety to honor it. I felt it wasn't fair to myself if I tried to ignore them and say they didn't matter or had no merit. However, I have since come to learn through experience as well as reading many books that succumbing to these overpowering and crippling emotions of fear, stress, and pain is not the greatest way to go either. By fully identifying with the powerful and negative emotions, we are still allowing them to control us. There is a difference between becoming the strong emotions and then sitting back and allowing them space, observing them from afar, from a place of awareness.

Mindfulness quiets the inner dialogue, silences the thoughts of inadequacy and the words of criticism that plague and clutter our mind and inhibit action. Awareness blissfully, acceptingly lets them float about our consciousness, fully knowing they are merely passing through. Presence of mind allows us to release control, to become a mere observer of our mind's eye so we can in turn be fully engaged in tangible reality, allowing our behaviors and actions to be ROOTed for our highest and best good.

I think the art of mindfulness or the practice of meditation can be found in countless activities. In fact, I bet you have a hobby in your life or an activity that you absolutely love to do—one that transports you to another world, where time does not exist and you feel your sole focus and purpose on this earth is to keep doing whatever you're doing.

For me, I can tap into that source of the infinite when I'm running or writing, my body fully connecting with my spirit, the rational part of my mind completely nonexistent. Ivo, my boyfriend, finds it in gliding across a field, seeing the soccer ball in its totality, hearing nothing but his own breath and the cries of his teammates. For my friend Lily, that state of mind comes when she strums the guitar or glides the bow across her cello, her voice smoothly, perfectly weaving itself into the musical flow. I see it tapped into when my aunt slowly, patiently, cuts up vegetables and fruit in an empty, still house, her mind but a constant hum of being.

We all have the ability to find that inner awareness of the moment at hand. I encourage you to look into your own life and find that moment where things are so still, your mind is but a whisper and your body is merely a vessel. If you can't think of something, don't stress: listen to that tiny voice saying, *Yes, yes I'm here within you too, come and find me.* Seek out activities that you enjoy, the ones that capture your attention, and delve into them, for true immersion into the energy of each moment will be what drives you forward to change.

The closest I've come to living in a continual state of being was the summer after my freshman year of college when

I lived on a farm. Things were so simple. My days were quietly filled with a to-do list left on the counter every morning, reading, running, and journaling. Occasionally I would interact with the guests of the bed and breakfast or get to drive the ten miles into town to make a trip to the post office (which was always an exciting treat, for I got to briefly listen to music). Cell service was almost nonexistent, which offered me the chance to truly disconnect. It was through this simple lifestyle that I most deeply experienced the meaning behind the phrase "live in the moment." Nothing seemed to matter except the task at hand—my mind was silent, seemingly equal parts stunned and immersed in every little thing set in front of me.

It didn't start out this way, however. No, the first week or so was miserable. I constantly questioned what I was doing there, I desperately missed my mom and sisters and friends, and I couldn't seem to do any of the tasks right. I sanded the floors of the barns, painted their walls, weeded and trimmed countless branches, picked hundreds if not thousands of blueberries and raspberries for hours at a time, hopeless and exhausted. And then a peculiar thing happened. Somewhere in between the jam-making and the sheet-washing I realized my mind had gone still. I enjoyed every minute of reaching into the bush, plucking off one blueberry at a time, the sound of dropping them into the wooden pail, *plunk plunk plunk*, the feeling of warmth on my back, listening to the wind. Even the hours I spent at the laundromat washing and folding over twenty sets of sheets and towels, counting coins, rolling baskets to and from the machines, was so incredibly peaceful.

I jokingly refer to my time at Lily Hill Farm as my modern-day Thoreau. Although I somewhat smoothly transitioned back into my old way of life, I carry with me the reminder that true peace can be found in between the moments, that the place of silence and ever-present being can always be tapped into if you just remember to breathe and live slowly, greeting each moment with your removed attention.

In her book *Meditation For the Love of It,* Sally Kempton described slowly learning to identify not with her looks, her personal history, her intelligence, her emotions or opinions, but rather the "subtler part of myself, with that field of spaciousness behind thoughts, with the tender energy in my heart."[180] Upon reading those words, that very source within me seemed to be nodding, agreeing, saying, *Yes, yes, you also know me.* It wasn't until reading this passage that it clicked. I had a flash of deep understanding that the key part is identifying with this feeling, fully letting go of all senses of the ego and truly embodying and becoming this inner source so it may radiate out of each of us and reconnect with its other parts of the world, its brothers and sisters that are everywhere.

---

180 Sally, Kempton. Meditation for the Love of It: Enjoying Your Own Deepest Experience. Place of Publication Not Identified: Readhowyouwant Com, 2012.

The times I have let this inner energy, the driving power behind my being, guide me in my life are the times when things seem to play out so beautifully in my life. My life that is also your life, all our lives, the whole and complete universe. I often refer to this collective energy, this intuition of sorts my soul nudges. Ever do I love following my soul nudges and watching things beautifully fall into place all around. The opportunity to write the words you are reading now being one of those seamless journeys..

I appreciate Kempton's acknowledgement of the balance between still needing to put forth effort and awareness but not forcing these types of experiences with the unknown. Reading that these meditative states arise naturally and spontaneously is reassuring. As long as one is humbly putting forth the energy, things will play out as they may. There needs to be no seeking or searching or figuring as it will come when the time is right and to those who are both earnest and patient, humble and grateful.

One tangible way you can practice this is through mindful eating. There are countless techniques to practice eating mindfully, all relatively simple. The next time you have a meal, try to lengthen it. If you typically finish dinner in less than ten minutes, challenge yourself to make it twenty. If you eat while checking emails or watching TV, if you do it while driving, walking, or standing, simply *sit down*. Eat with no distractions and immerse yourself in the experience that is taste and nourishment of your body. Eat with your loved ones, connect about your days and thoroughly enjoy the act of eating. After every bite of food, I ask you to take a sip of water, slowly and with purpose. If you love numbers, give yourself a target for how many bites it will take to finish your protein, your vegetables, your fruit, and make sure to count every single one. However you choose to do it, I urge you to engage in the full experience of eating, even if only for a couple of minutes to bring your awareness to the present and further support your quest for lasting healthy habits.

These are just a few ways to practice eating mindfully. Aside from following and engaging in the activities that both calm and entrance you, there is another way I love to practice mindfulness. For the sake of simplicity, I shall call this "sensing." It's an incredibly simple game. First, pick one of the senses. Sight, hearing, smell, taste, or touch—whichever seems to be calling you in the moment, go with it. Next, narrow in on one stimuli you are perceiving for that sense. For example, if I am walking across campus and I picked hearing, I will pick a sound I hear and focus solely on that noise while I walk. Every time I find my thoughts beginning to wander, I relocate that bird's cry or the bell tower's ring and intently listen, keeping the sound in my mind's eye.

I don't believe mindfulness is a cure to changing health behaviors, nor do I think its effects are beneficial when standing alone. I do, however, think it plays a critical role in solidifying long-term change. If patients are taught the tools to practice mindfulness in addition to their behavior-specific

ROOT plan, their chances for long-term success will increase. Minimizing stress, helping individuals regain a sense of control over their lives, and simplifying their focus to the task at hand will give patients the power to tackle changing whatever health behavior they are seeking to alter. Mindfulness ties ROOT's efforts together to ensure sustainability.

Mindfulness-Based Stress Reduction

Mindfulness practices are increasingly becoming popular within many sectors of U.S. society. I have consistently seen it across college campuses, in the news, on bookshelves, in businesses, and most relevant to this book, in the medical research and hospital setting.

Using mindfulness as a health intervention was first seen in the 1970s at the University of Massachusetts Medical Center under professor Jon Kabat-Zinn, Ph.D. Coined "mindfulness-based stress reduction" (MBSR), he created an eight-week, evidence-based program that trains patients in mindfulness or, by his definition, teaches them to "pay attention in a particular way: on purpose, in the present moment, and nonjudgmentally." The formal practices within the MBSR program are mindful movement via yoga, a body scan that is a systematic screening to cultivate awareness of the body region by region, and sitting meditation to assist patients with stress, anxiety, depression, and pain.

Following MBSR, Kabat-Zinn founded the Stress Reduction Clinic and, decades later, the Center for Mindfulness in

Medicine, Health Care, and Society at the University of Massachusetts Medical School—both of which helped MBSR get implemented at hospitals across the country. MSBR has been studied across a multitude of health problems, some of which include anxiety and mood disorders, substance abuse, eating disorders, chronic pain, ADHD, insomnia, and oncology; it has sparked the creation of other mindfulness interventions. Kabat-Zinn's work has been incredibly influential in the spread of mindfulness within the current medical system.

MBSR is currently one subset of the general category of mindfulness-based interventions, or MBIs, which are increasingly recognized through writings and teachings within the medical community and beyond. As of 2015, one study found that almost 80 percent of medical schools are reported to offer some element of mindfulness training and have research or education centers dedicated to the field.[181] Further, Margaret Cullen, a licensed marriage and family therapist, certified mindfulness-based stress reduction teacher, and a senior teacher with the Center for Compassion at Stanford, wrote in a research paper that through the exponential growth of evidence-based rationale, MBIs can and should be continually implemented within mainstream settings such as hospitals, schools, prisons, and businesses.[182]

181 Cullen, Margaret. "Mindfulness-Based Interventions: An Emerging Phenomenon." Mindfulness 2, no. 3 (2011): 186-93. doi:10.1007/s12671-011-0058-1.
182 Ibid.

Next we are going to look at some of the MBI research that currently exists on overweight and obesity as well as stress-eating to further explore the effectiveness of including mindfulness practices within a health behavior intervention.

MBIs

It is largely reported that mindfulness and meditation can decrease stress levels.[183] Researchers from Johns Hopkins University in Baltimore conducted a systematic review and found that mindful meditation can help ease psychological stresses like anxiety, depression, and pain.[184] Another study conducted by Brown University medical students looked at the correlation between stress-eating and metabolic-syndrome risk. Their results show that university students who identify as stress eaters gained more weight and had increased nocturnal levels of insulin, cortisol, and blood levels of total/HDL cholesterol ratio during exam periods, typically a time of high stress, when compared to their control levels.[185] Despite only demonstrating short-term con-

183 Buchholz, Laura. "Exploring the Promise of Mindfulness as Medicine." Jama 314, no. 13 (2015): 1327. doi:10.1001/jama.2015.7023.

184 Goyal, Madhav, Sonal Singh, Erica M. S. Sibinga, Neda F. Gould, Anastasia Rowland-Seymour, Ritu Sharma, Zackary Berger, Dana Sleicher, David D. Maron, Hasan M. Shihab, Padmini D. Ranasinghe, Shauna Linn, Shonali Saha, Eric B. Bass, and Jennifer A. Haythornthwaite. "Meditation Programs for Psychological Stress and Well-being." JAMA Internal Medicine 174, no. 3 (2014): 357. doi:10.1001/jamainternmed.2013.13018.

185 Epel, Elissa, Sherlyn Jimenez, Kelly Brownell, Laura Stroud, Catherine Stoney, and Ray Niaura. "Are Stress Eaters at Risk for the

sequences of metabolic health, periods of stress, especially in those who tend to overeat, pose a risk to individuals' health, potentially conferring a greater risk of disease over time, though further studies are called for. This is significant because it highlights the connection between increased levels of stress and both eating behaviors and metabolic markers, regardless of how brief the effects were. Any sort of intervention that can decrease levels of stress, whether physically or perceptually, is noteworthy and should be highly considered for further research and inclusion in treatment.

O'Reilly and colleagues conducted a systematic review to determine the effectiveness of mindfulness-based interventions targeting obesity-related eating behaviors, such as binge-eating, emotional eating, external eating, reactivity to food cravings, restrained eating, mindless eating, and overall unhealthy dietary intake. The interventions used a variety of approaches to carry out mindfulness training, including combined mindfulness and cognitive behavioral therapies, mindfulness-based stress reduction, acceptance-based therapies, mindful eating programs, and combinations of mindfulness exercises. Some examples of these combination practices were mindful breathing, sitting, walking meditations, or mindful yoga stretches.

Out of the twenty-one articles included in the review, eighteen (86 percent) reported

---

Metabolic Syndrome?" Annals of the New York Academy of Sciences 1032, no. 1 (2004): 208-10. doi:10.1196/annals.1314.022.

improvements in the targeted eating behavior. Further, eleven out of the twelve (91.6 percent) studies targeting binge-eating reported improvements in binge-eating frequency and/or severity, five out of the eight studies targeting emotional eating reported improvements, and four out of the six studies that included external eating reported improvements in this eating behavior.[186]

From this data, the authors' conclusions were as follows: "Given the extent of the obesity epidemic, novel approaches to support weight loss are needed. MBIs are poised to complement obesity prevention and treatment efforts. This review concluded that MBIs have growing empirical support as a promising psychoeducational and behavior-based treatment for obesity-related eating behaviors."[187]

Another systematic review that looked strictly at MBIs on weight loss also found that mindfulness techniques reduced weight and improved obesity-related eating behaviors among individuals with overweight and obesity.[188]

These results demonstrate the potential for mindfulness to be an incredibly important piece of a health behavior

---

186 Oreilly, G. A., L. Cook, D. Spruijt-Metz, and D. S. Black. "Mindfulness-based Interventions for Obesity-related Eating Behaviours: A Literature Review." Obesity Reviews 15, no. 6 (2014): 453-61. doi:10.1111/obr.12156.

187 Ibid.

188 Carrière, K., B. Khoury, M. M. Günak, and B. Knäuper. "Mindfulness-based Interventions for Weight Loss: A Systematic Review and Meta-analysis." Obesity Reviews 19, no. 2 (2017): 164-77. doi:10.1111/obr.12623.

intervention for its effects on stress as well as the need to increase mindfulness with eating.

Health Psychology

Developed in the late 1970s, the American Psychological Association defines the field of health psychology as the field of examining how biological, social and psychological factors influence health and illness.[189] Health psychologists use psychological science to promote health, prevent illness, and improve health care systems.

"From the field of health psychology, studies show that perceived vulnerability, meaning the ability to acknowledge our risks and exposures, greatly increases our chances of adhering to some kind of positive health regimen," Brené Brown wrote in her book *Daring Greatly*. "In order to get patients to comply with prevention routines, they must work on perceived vulnerability."[190]

Making true change is scary. People are so comfortable with the known, the certain, the sure, that any and all thoughts of the unknown can be paralyzing. Fears of abandonment, being rejected, or undergoing a great loss are all deeply woven within the human psyche. When presented with even an inkling of reality of those fears, we seek to

189 American Psychological Association. Accessed June 15, 2019. https://www.apa.org/pubs/journals/hea/.

190 Brown, Brené. Daring Greatly: How the Courage to Be Vulnerable Transforms the Way We Live, Love, Parent, and Lead. London: Penguin Life, 2015.

avoid them at all costs. Yet, ironically, and somewhat beautifully, these negatives experiences are all part of the universal
human experience and it is through expressing them that we
will be empowered.

We should strive to acknowledge all of these truths, for
through sharing and relating we can all find a sense of comfort in knowing that we are not alone, that there are others
who share our pain. It is our duty then to call for a health
system that provides us with the space to acknowledge all of
who we are—the pain, the discomfort, our fallibility—so that
we may build up from this and ensure they have the ability
to keep up with programs.

When people are closed off or display a lack of vulnerability—or, in Brown's definition, don't take risks, expose
themselves emotionally, or put themselves in uncertain positions—this can lead to disengagement of behaviors, thus leaving someone unprotected from failure, the very thing they
were trying to avoid.

Specifically, when it comes to topics as personal and
degrading as overweight and obesity, there must be intervention programs in place that leave room for addressing
the stigma. We must, in turn, allow the space for kindness,
compassion, and in Brown's words, vulnerability, to help
individuals overcome the negative barriers and find their
way to well-being. It is critical that interventions acknowledge the difficulties people will face when asked to change
their lifestyle and to embrace them with openness.

Further Thoughts

In addition to focusing on eating well and engaging in more physical activity, I hope that future health programs seek to address all aspects of a patient's wellness. To me, wellness is being surrounded by people who love and support me, no matter what happens. It's remaining connected in body, mind, and spirit to fully acknowledge all parts of my being. It's honoring my body through eating whole foods and engaging in movement every day in some way. It's taking care of my emotional well-being by seeking refuge in my journal or constantly seeking ways to fulfill my sense of purpose in helping others find the same.

Medical interventions first and foremost should be preventative in nature, rather than reactive. In addition to finding ways to support people in changing their lifestyle to more effectively manage their chronic diseases, I feel the medical system needs to lessen the number of prescriptions it offers and in turn focus on ways to fix problems rather than mask them.

Whatever my definition of wellness is, and whatever yours may be, interventions must seek out ways to support every individual across all aspects of their well-being to ensure they have the tools to make the right decisions for them and their health.

Takeaways

The practice of total physical and mental awareness lends nicely to the ROOT framework.

In order for true reflection, you must let go of preconceived notions and learned patterns of behavior for an honest look at where you currently stand.

Taking things one step at a time requires you to pause and assess where you are. It asks you to feel each moment in between your foot leaving the ground and connecting with the path once more, looking not at the long miles of road ahead, but the rocky or flat, grassed or pebbled trail directly beneath you.

To truly embody the spirit of community, to feel the power that stems from connecting with others, you must be entirely and completely present with those around you, open to receiving and humbly sharing to help others, and yourself in the process, reach heights they never knew were possible.

Knowing yourself deeply, firmly having a grasp on your own capabilities and preferences, calls for the essential personal understanding that only comes from presence within.

Some ways to practice mindfulness are as follows:

- Find the hobby that quiets your inner world.
- Practice mindful eating.
- Play "sensing."
- Perform breathing techniques.
- Utilize the MSBR program.

Some additional notes:

- Interventions should incorporate mindfulness techniques in addition to specific problematic behavioral strategies to see results.
- A health promotion program should leave room to help patients express vulnerability so they can overcome mental barriers and in turn grow.

FINAL THOUGHTS

———

"Have you ever had a stress test before?" I turned to Tom and ask.

"No," Tom grunted.

Tom was young, much younger than the average patient we typically saw. He was 5′11″ in height and 47 years old, and he weighed close to 300 pounds.

Skimming his medical records, I saw the typical clinical indications: DM (diabetes mellitus), HLD (hyperlipidemia), CAD (coronary artery disease), PAD (peripheral artery disease), +Smoking, CP (chest pain) and Palps (palpitations).

As Tom got ready for his test with me, I looked up and saw a shirtless, nervous, overweight man being forced to walk on a treadmill until fully exhausted. I smiled at him, attempting to calm his nervous, and asked him to take a deep breath in, pause, and breathe out. He did so and visibly relaxed.

As I began explaining the test, I asked him the health habit screening questions provided to me by the office. Placing the ten electrode stickers on his chest, I determined he is a great candidate for the behavioral health community program. With each clip of hooking him up to the EKG, I told him about the program run by our office's health specialist and asked him if it's something he might be interested in.

Perhaps because he read the flyer of patient testimonials hanging on the wall or maybe because he met someone in the waiting room who was already a member, he decided to sign up for the sessions. After completing the stress test, I informed him that while he was waiting for the doctor to sign off on his stress report he could follow me to my office.

It was here I asked him to fill out a brief survey and worksheet to identify the target behaviors he felt most comfortable working on first, as well as mentioning any support systems or barriers he has that might help or hinder him in this process. Next, I conducted a brief motivational interviewing session to assess where he was at mentally and leave him feeling confident he could take the next steps. As I finished up the session, I asked him to close his eyes and picture a time when he felt truly, deeply proud of himself. As he kept that moment in his mind, I led him through two minutes of a guided breathing. When it was over, I handed him the informational brochure on the program and set up his next appointment, smiling because I knew I would see him next week where we can tackle the changing of his eating patterns and physical activity levels together, as a team.

Recommended Book List:

No Sweat: How the Simple Science of Motivation Can Bring You a Lifetime of Fitness by Michelle Segar

Stick With It: A Scientifically Proven Process for Changing Your Life for Good by Sean Young

Atomic Habits: An Easy & Proven Way to Build Good Habits & Break Bad Ones by James Clear

The Cusp Method: Your Guide to Balanced Portions & a Healthy Life by Jaclyn Digregorio

Eat Move Sleep by Tom Rath

Devoured: How What We Eat Defines Who We Are by Sophie Egan

Mindfulness for Health: A Practical Guide to Relieving Pain, Reducing Stress and Restoring Wellbeing by Danny Penman and Vidyamala Burch

Eating Mindfully: How to End Mindless Eating and Enjoy a Balanced Relationship with Food, Edition 2 by Susan Albers

The Power of Now by Eckhart Tolle

Peace Is Every Step: The Path of Mindfulness in Everyday Life by Thich Nhat Hanh

APPENDIX

———

Introduction

"Adult Obesity Facts | Overweight & Obesity | CDC". 2018. *Cdc.Gov.* https://www.cdc.gov/obesity/data/adult.html.

"Facts & Statistics". 2019. *HHS.Gov.* https://www.hhs.gov/ fitness/resource-center/facts-and-statistics/index.html.

"Fast Food Statistics Infographic". 2019. *Partnersfory-ourhealth.Com.* https://www.partnersforyourhealth.com/ fast-food-statistics#slide0.

"Physical Inactivity In The United States". 2019. *The State Of Obesity.* https://www.stateofobesity.org/physical-inactivity/.

"Portion Sizes And Obesity, News & Events, NHLBI, NIH". 2013. *National Heart, Lung, And Blood Institue.* https:// www.nhlbi.nih.gov/health/educational/wecan/news-events/matte1.htm.

2019. *Cdc.Gov.*
https://www.cdc.gov/physicalactivity/downloads/pa_state_
indicator_report_2014.pdf.

2019. *Cdc.Gov.* https://www.cdc.gov/vitalsigns/pdf/2010-
08-vitalsigns.pdf.

Andreyeva, Tatiana, Joerg Luedicke, and Y. Claire Wang.
2014. "State-Level Estimates Of Obesity-Attributable
Costs Of Absenteeism". *Journal Of Occupational And
Environmental Medicine* 56 (11): 1120-1127. doi:10.1097/
jom.0000000000000298.

Cleveland Clinic. "Obesity is top cause of preventable life-
years lost, study shows." ScienceDaily. www.sciencedaily.
com/releases/2017/04/170422101614.htm (accessed June
12, 2019).

Johnson, S. (2019). *The nation's childhood obesity epidemic:
Health disparities in the making.* [online] https://www.
apa.org. Available at: https://www.apa.org/pi/fami-
lies/resources/newsletter/2012/07/childhood-obesity
[Accessed 13 Jun. 2019].

Kottke, Thomas E., Milo L. Brekke, and Leif I. Solberg.
1993. "Making "Time" For Preventive Services". *Mayo
Clinic Proceedings* 68 (8): 785-791. doi:10.1016/s0025-
6196(12)60638-7.

Writers, Staff. 2019. "Why Are Americans Obese? | Publi-
chealth.Org". *Publichealth.Org.* https://www.publichealth.
org/public-awareness/obesity/.

Yang, Lin, and Graham A. Colditz. 2015. "Prevalence Of Overweight And Obesity In The United States, 2007-2012". *JAMA Internal Medicine* 175 (8): 1412. doi:10.1001/jamainternmed.2015.2405.

Yarnall, Kimberly S. H., Kathryn I. Pollak, Truls Østbye, Katrina M. Krause, and J. Lloyd Michener. 2003. "Primary Care: Is There Enough Time For Prevention?". *American Journal Of Public Health* 93 (4): 635-641. doi:10.2105/ajph.93.4.635.

Foundations

Alageel, Samah, Martin C. Gulliford, Lisa Mcdermott, and Alison J. Wright. "Implementing Multiple Health Behaviour Change Interventions for Cardiovascular Risk Reduction in Primary Care: A Qualitative Study." *BMC Family Practice* 19, no. 1 (2018). doi:10.1186/s12875-018-0860-0.

Final Recommendation Statement: Weight Loss to Prevent Obesity-Related Morbidity and Mortality in Adults: Behavioral Interventions. U.S. Preventive Services Task Force. September 2018. https://www.uspreventiveservicestaskforce.org/Page/Document/RecommendationStatementFinal/obesity-in-adults-interventions1

Kelly, Michael P., and Mary Barker. "Why Is Changing Health-related Behaviour so Difficult?" *Public Health* 136 (2016): 109-16. doi:10.1016/j.puhe.2016.03.030.

Klein, Ezra, and Joe Posner. 2018. *Explained*. DVD. Vox.

Middleton, Kathryn R., Stephen D. Anton, and Michal G. Perri. "Long-Term Adherence to Health Behavior Change." *American Journal of Lifestyle Medicine* 7, no. 6 (2013): 395-404. doi:10.1177/1559827613488867.

Chapter 1

Liao, Sharon. "Safe Weight Loss for Overweight Kids." WebMD. Accessed June 13, 2019. https://www.webmd.com/parenting/raising-fit-kids/weight/features/safe-weight-loss.

Ludwig, David. "Why Calorie Restricted Diets Don't Work." Dr. David Ludwig. February 09, 2017. Accessed June 13, 2019. https://www.drdavidludwig.com/why-calorie-restricted-diets-dont-work/.

Tarman, Vera. "Part I: 12 Steps To Beat The Odds, Abstinent Food Plans." Addictions Unplugged. Accessed June 13, 2019. https://addictionsunplugged.com/2015/10/13/part-i-12-steps-to-beat-the-odds/.

"Why Diets Don't Work...And What Does." Psychology Today. Accessed June 15, 2019. https://www.psychologytoday.com/us/blog/changepower/201010/why-diets-dont-work-and-what-does.

Chapter 2

Segar, Michelle L. *No Sweat: How the Simple Science of Motivation Can Bring You a Lifetime of Fitness*. New York: AMACOM--American Management Association, 2015.

Chapter 3

"Exercise Is Medicine." Exercise Is Medicine. Accessed June 13, 2019. https://www.exerciseismedicine.org/.

Lobelo, Felipe, Mark Stoutenberg, and Adrian Hutber. "The Exercise Is Medicine Global Health Initiative: A 2014 Update." *British Journal of Sports Medicine* 48, no. 22 (2014): 1627-633. doi:10.1136/bjsports-2013-093080.

Sinek, Simon. TED. September 2009. Accessed June 13, 2019. https://www.ted.com/talks/simon_sinek_how_great_leaders_inspire_action?language=en.

Chapter 4

Egan, Sophie. *Devoured: How What We Eat Defines Who We Are.* New York, NY: William Morrow, 2017.

DiGregorio, Jaclyn. "The CUSP Method: Your Guide to Balanced Portions & a Healthy Life EBook: Jaclyn DiGregorio: Kindle Store." Amazon. Accessed June 14, 2019. https://www.amazon.com/CUSP-Method-Balanced-Portions-Healthy-ebook/dp/B06Y5LXN6G.

"How Big Sugar Hid the Dangers of Sugar." Mercola.com. Accessed June 13, 2019. https://articles.mercola.com/sites/articles/archive/2017/12/06/industry-buried-evidence-hiding-sugar-harms.aspx.

"Join the Mealtime Movement." The Mealtime Movement. Accessed June 15, 2019. https://www.mealtimemovement.com/.

"Losing Weight: Getting Started | Healthy Weight | CDC."
Centers for Disease Control and Prevention. Accessed
June 13, 2019. https://www.cdc.gov/healthyweight/los-
ing_weight/getting_started.html.

Pollan, Michael. *The Omnivores Dilemma: A Natural History
of Four Meals.* New York, NY: Penguin Books, 2016.

"Weight Management." Boston Medical Center. September
07, 2017. Accessed June 15, 2019. https://www.bmc.org/
nutrition-and-weight-management/weight-management.

Writers, Staff. "Why Are Americans Obese?" PublicHealth.
org. Accessed June 13, 2019. https://www.publichealth.org/
public-awareness/obesity/.

Chapter 5

Antal, Melissa, and Maria Rivera. "Foublie's Blog: What You
Must Know about Hot Topics in Child & Family Food."
Foublie. Accessed June 14, 2019. http://foublie.com/blog.

"FastStats - Exercise or Physical Activity." Centers for Disease
Control and Prevention. Accessed June 13, 2019. https://
www.cdc.gov/nchs/fastats/exercise.htm.

"Physical Inactivity in the United States." The State of Obesity.
Accessed June 13, 2019. https://www.stateofobesity.org/
physical-inactivity/.

Chapter 6

DeGrassa, Peg. "Delco Woman Recovers from College Eating
Disorder and Launches Unique Wellness Business." Daily

Local News. July 20, 2018. Accessed June 14, 2019. https://
www.dailylocal.com/business/delco-woman-recov-
ers-from-college-eating-disorder-and-launches-unique/
article_266f4037-f5ef-52fb-afcb-dd6f850aecb2.html.

DiGregorio, Jaclyn. "The CUSP Method: Your Guide to Balanced Portions & a Healthy Life EBook: Jaclyn DiGregorio: Kindle Store." Amazon. Accessed June 14, 2019.
https://www.amazon.com/CUSP-Method-Balanced-Por-
tions-Healthy-ebook/dp/B06Y5LXN6G.

Dutton, Gareth R., Michael G. Perri, Melissa Dancer-Brown,
Mary Goble, and Nancy Van Vessem. "Weight Loss Goals
of Patients in a Health Maintenance Organization." Eating Behaviors 11, no. 2 (2010): 74-78. doi:10.1016/j.eat-
beh.2009.09.007.

Goldstein, DJ. "Beneficial health effects of modest weight
loss." International Journal of Obesity Related Metabolic
Disorders. 16, no. 6 (1992): 397-415.

Tate, Deborah F., Robert W. Jeffery, Nancy E. Sherwood,
and Rena R. Wing. "Long-term Weight Losses Associated with Prescription of Higher Physical Activity Goals.
Are Higher Levels of Physical Activity Protective against
Weight Regain?" The American Journal of Clinical Nutrition 85, no. 4 (2007): 954-59. doi:10.1093/ajcn/85.4.954.

Chapter 7

"Diabetes, Heart Disease, and Stroke." National Institute of
Diabetes and Digestive and Kidney Diseases. February 01,

2017. Accessed June 15, 2019. https://www.niddk.nih.gov/
health-information/diabetes/overview/preventing-prob-
lems/heart-disease-stroke.

"How Small Steps Make Big Changes | Jack Canfield." Ameri-
ca's Leading Authority On Creating Success And Personal
Fulfillment - Jack Canfield. January 29, 2019. Accessed
June 14, 2019. https://www.jackcanfield.com/blog/big-
changes/.

"Podcast #329: Stick With It — The Science of Behavior
Change." Interview. *Art of Manliness*(audio blog), August
10, 2017. Accessed June 12, 2019.

Young, Sean. *Stick with It: A Scientifically Proven Process for
Changing Your Life -- for Good.* New York: Harper, 2018.

Chapter 8

Astorino, Dominique Michelle. "Lexi Lost Over 300 Pounds
in 2 Years With These (VERY) Small Changes." POP-
SUGAR Fitness. February 18, 2018. Accessed June 15,
2019. https://www.popsugar.com/fitness/Lexi-Reed-Fat-
GirlFedUp-Weight-Loss-Before-After-44555157.

James Clear. James Clear. September 01, 2018. Accessed June
14, 2019. https://jamesclear.com/behavior-change-par-
adox.

PEOPLE.com. Accessed June 14, 2019. https://people.com/
health/this-couple-dropped-395-lbs-together-we-fell-in-
love-with-taking-care-of-ourselves/.

Staff, Editorial. "From 'Fat Girl Fed Up' to Food-Tracking Pro: How Lexi Reed Lost 312 Pounds and Kept It Off." Woman's World. September 26, 2018. Accessed June 14, 2019. https://www.womansworld.com/posts/fatgirlfedup-myfitnesspal-success-story-166847.

TrimmedandToned. "Lexi Reed 'FatGirlFedUp' Lost 285 Pounds In 18 Months With These 2 Simple Steps!" TrimmedandToned. August 17, 2017. Accessed June 14, 2019. http://www.trimmedandtoned.com/lexi-reed-fatgirlfedup-lost-285-pounds-18-months-2-simple-steps/

TODAY. YouTube. May 24, 2018. Accessed June 14, 2019. https://www.youtube.com/watch?v=_qgtwz77hZM.

Chapter 9

"Financing Weight Loss Surgery." WebMD. Accessed June 14, 2019. https://www.webmd.com/diet/obesity/financing-weight-loss-surgery#1.

"Why Only 1% of Eligible Patients Choose Bariatric Surgery." Advanced Surgical and Bariatrics of NJ, PA. June 21, 2018. Accessed June 14, 2019. https://www.bariatricsurgerynew-jersey.com/why-only-1-percent-patients-choose-bariatric-surgery/.

Aschbrenner, Kelly A., John A. Naslund, and Stephen J. Bartels. "A Mixed Methods Study of Peer-to-peer Support in a Group-based Lifestyle Intervention for Adults with Serious Mental Illness." *Psychiatric Rehabilitation Journal* 39, no. 4 (2016): 328-34. doi:10.1037/prj0000219.

Belluz, Julia. "We're Barely Using the Best Tool We Have to Fight Obesity." Vox. May 16, 2019. Accessed June 14, 2019. https://www.vox.com/science-and-health/2017/12/7/16587316/bariatric-surgery-weight-loss-lap-band.

Gray, Cindy M., Kate Hunt, Nanette Mutrie, Annie S. Anderson, Jim Leishman, Lindsay Dalgarno, and Sally Wyke. "Football Fans in Training: The Development and Optimization of an Intervention Delivered through Professional Sports Clubs to Help Men Lose Weight, Become More Active and Adopt Healthier Eating Habits." *BMC Public Health* 13, no. 1 (2013). doi:10.1186/1471-2458-13-232.

Imanaka, Mie, Masahiko Ando, Tetsuhisa Kitamura, and Takashi Kawamura. "Effectiveness of Web-Based Self-Disclosure Peer-to-Peer Support for Weight Loss: Randomized Controlled Trial." *Journal of Medical Internet Research* 15, no. 7 (2013). doi:10.2196/jmir.2405.

Leahey, Tricia M., and Rena R. Wing. "A Randomized Controlled Pilot Study Testing Three Types of Health Coaches for Obesity Treatment: Professional, Peer, and Mentor." *Obesity* 21, no. 5 (2013): 928-34. doi:10.1002/oby.20271.

Lemstra, Mark, Yelena Bird, Chijioke Nwankwo, Marla Rogers, and John Moraros. "Weight Loss Intervention Adherence and Factors Promoting Adherence: A Meta-analysis." Patient Preference and Adherence. August 12, 2016. Accessed June 14, 2019. https://www.ncbi.nlm.nih.gov/pmc/articles/PMC4990387/.

Chapter 10

"Access to Healthier Food Retailers - United States, 2011."
Centers for Disease Control and Prevention. November 22,
2013. Accessed June 14, 2019. https://www.cdc.gov/mmwr/
preview/mmwrhtml/su6203a4.htm?s_cid=su6203a4_x.

"Oklahoma City Mayor Puts City on a Diet." NBCNews.com.
January 04, 2008. Accessed June 15, 2019. http://www.nbc-
news.com/id/22503467/ns/health-diet_and_nutrition/t/
oklahoma-city-mayor-puts-city-diet/.

Center for Disease Control and Prevention. National HIV
Behavioral Surveillance
System in Men Who Have Sex with Men– Round 4: Forma-
tive Research Manual.
December 20, 2013

Cornett, Mick. TED. Accessed June 14, 2019. https://www.ted.
com/talks/mick_cornett_how_an_obese_town_lost_a_
million_pounds/transcript?language=en.

Daumann, Frank, Robin Heinze, Benedikt Römmelt, and
Anne Wunderlich. "An Active City Approach for Urban
Development." Journal of Urban Health : Bulletin of the
New York Academy of Medicine. April 2015. Accessed
June 14, 2019. https://www.ncbi.nlm.nih.gov/pmc/articles/
PMC4411321/.

Galvin, Gaby. "Designing Health Communities Requires
Collaboration." U.S. News & World Report. November
1, 2017. Accessed June 14, 2019. https://www.usnews.com/

news/healthiest-communities/articles/2017-11-01/how-urban-design-affects-community-health.

Gittelsohn, Joel, Allan Steckler, Carolyn C. Johnson, Charlotte Pratt, Mira Grieser, Julie Pickrel, Elaine J. Stone, Terry Conway, Derek Coombs, and Lisa K. Staten. "Formative Research in School and Community-based Health Programs and Studies: "state of the Art" and the TAAG Approach." Health Education & Behavior : The Official Publication of the Society for Public Health Education. February 2006. Accessed June 14, 2019. https://www.ncbi. nlm.nih.gov/pmc/articles/PMC2475675/.

Yang, Jennifer. "Oklahoma Mayor Put His City on a Million-pound Diet. Did It Work?" Thestar.com. November 16, 2015. Accessed June 15, 2019. https://www.thestar.com/ news/insight/2015/11/16/oklahoma-mayor-put-his-city-on-a-million-pound-diet-did-it-work.html.

Sallis, James F., Ester Cerin, Terry L. Conway, Marc A. Adams, Lawrence D. Frank, Michael Pratt, Deborah Salvo, Jasper Schipperijn, Graham Smith, Kelli L. Cain, Rachel Davey, Jacqueline Kerr, Poh-Chin Lai, Josef Mitáš, Rodrigo Reis, Olga L. Sarmiento, Grant Schofield, Jens Troelsen, Delfien Van Dyck, Ilse De Bourdeaudhuij, and Neville Owen. "Physical Activity in Relation to Urban Environments in 14 Cities Worldwide: A Cross-sectional Study." The Lancet387, no. 10034 (2016): 2207-217. doi:10.1016/s0140-6736(15)01284-2.

Chapter 11

"National Center for Chronic Disease Prevention and Health Promotion | CDC." Centers for Disease Control and Prevention. Accessed June 14, 2019. https://www.cdc.gov/chronicdisease/index.htm.

Robertson, Michelle. "The Move from SF to Oakland: What's It Really like across the Bay?" SFGate. July 24, 2018. Accessed June 14, 2019. https://www.sfgate.com/expensive-san-francisco/article/moving-from-sf-to-oakland-what-its-like-gig-13089623.php.

Chapter 12

"Chronic Loneliness Is a Modern-Day Epidemic." Fortune. Accessed June 14, 2019. http://fortune.com/2016/06/22/loneliness-is-a-modern-day-epidemic/.

"Cortisol." You and Your Hormones. Accessed June 14, 2019. http://www.yourhormones.info/hormones/cortisol/.

"The Cost of Loneliness Project." The Cost of Loneliness Project. Accessed June 14, 2019. https://www.thecostofloneliness.org/.

Anderson, G. Oscar. "Loneliness Among Older Adults: A National Survey of Adults 45." AARP. September 01, 2010. Accessed June 14, 2019. https://www.aarp.org/research/topics/life/info-2014/loneliness_2010.html.

Chao, Ariana M., Ania M. Jastreboff, Marney A. White, Carlos M. Grilo, and Rajita Sinha. "Stress, Cortisol, and Other Appetite-related Hormones: Prospective Predic-

tion of 6-month Changes in Food Cravings and Weight."
*Obesity*25, no. 4 (2017): 713-20. doi:10.1002/oby.21790.

Kim, Leland. "Loneliness Linked to Serious Health Problems
and Death Among Elderly." Loneliness Linked to Serious
Health Problems and Death Among Elderly | UC San
Francisco. June 18, 2012. Accessed June 14, 2019. https://
www.ucsf.edu/news/2012/06/98644/loneliness-linked-se-
rious-health-problems-and-death-among-elderly.

Chapter 13

Lisa Quast, "6 Ways To Empower Others To Succeed," Forbes,
August 21, 2012, , accessed June 15, 2019, https://www.
forbes.com/sites/lisaquast/2011/02/28/6-ways-to-empow-
er-others-to-succeed/#487498275c62.

Young, Sean. *Stick with It: A Scientifically Proven Process for
Changing Your Life -- for Good.* New York: Harper, 2018.

Part 4

"Evolution of Medical Ethics." The Hippocratic Oath.
Accessed June 15, 2019. https://owlspace-ccm.rice.edu/
access/content/user/ecy1/Nazi Human Experimentation/
Pages/Hippocratic Oath-modern.html.

Chapter 14

"The Rudd Center for Food Policy and Obesity Www ..."
Accessed June 14, 2019. http://www.uconnruddcenter.org/
files/Pdfs/MI Example scripts.pdf.

Agerwala, Suneel M., and Elinore F. Mccance-Katz. "Integrating Screening, Brief Intervention, and Referral to Treatment (SBIRT) into Clinical Practice Settings: A Brief Review." *Journal of Psychoactive Drugs* 44, no. 4 (2012): 307-17. doi:10.1080/02791072.2012.720169.

Miller, William Richard., and Stephen Rollnick. *Motivational Interviewing: Helping People Change.* New York: Guilford Press, 2013.

Sjöling, Mats, Kristina Lundberg, Erling Englund, Anton Westman, and Miek C. Jong. "Effectiveness of Motivational Interviewing and Physical Activity on Prescription on Leisure Exercise Time in Subjects Suffering from Mild to Moderate Hypertension." *BMC Research Notes* 4, no. 1 (2011). doi:10.1186/1756-0500-4-352.

Soderstrom, Carl A., Carlo C. Diclemente, Patricia C. Dischinger, J. Richard Hebel, David R. Mcduff, Kimberly Mitchell Auman, and Joseph A. Kufera. "A Controlled Trial of Brief Intervention Versus Brief Advice for At-Risk Drinking Trauma Center Patients." The Journal of Trauma: Injury, Infection, and Critical Care 62, no. 5 (2007): 1102-112. doi:10.1097/ta.0b013e31804bdb26.

Chapter 15

"Tips for Showing Empathy When Providing Healthcare." Ameritech College of Healthcare. April 12, 2018. Accessed June 15, 2019. https://www.ameritech.edu/blog/empathy-when-providing-care/.

American Academy of Orthopaedic Surgeons. "Physician empathy a key driver of patient satisfaction: New study supports enhanced physician-patient communication training." ScienceDaily. www.sciencedaily.com/releases/2016/03/160301114118.htm (accessed June 12, 2019).

Iafolla, Teresa. "Improve Physician Empathy in 7 Simple Steps." Improve Physician Empathy in 7 Simple Steps. Accessed June 15, 2019. https://blog.evisit.com/improve-physician-empathy-in-7-simple-steps.

Rocque, Rhea, and Yvan Leanza. "A Systematic Review of Patients' Experiences in Communicating with Primary Care Physicians: Intercultural Encounters and a Balance between Vulnerability and Integrity." *Plos One*10, no. 10 (2015). doi:10.1371/journal.pone.0139577.

Chapter 16

"Chapter 3 Everyone Has a Role in Supporting Healthy Eating Patterns." Chapter 3 Introduction - 2015-2020 Dietary Guidelines. Accessed June 15, 2019. https://health.gov/dietaryguidelines/2015/guidelines/chapter-3/.

"Rural Health Information Hub." Social Determinants of Health for Rural People Introduction. Accessed June 15, 2019. https://www.ruralhealthinfo.org/topics/social-determinants-of-health.

Emmons, Karen M., Elizabeth M. Barbeau, Caitlin Gutheil, Jo Ellen Stryker, and Anne M. Stoddard. "Social Influences, Social Context, and Health Behav-

iors Among Working-Class, Multi-Ethnic Adults."
*Health Education & Behavior*34, no. 2 (2006): 315-34.
doi:10.1177/1090198106288011.

Golden, Shelley D., and Jo Anne L. Earp. "Social Ecological Approaches to Individuals and Their Contexts."
*Health Education & Behavior*39, no. 3 (2012): 364-72.
doi:10.1177/1090198111418634.

Kreuter, Marshall W., Nicole A. Lezin, and Laura A. Young. "Evaluating Community-Based Collaborative Mechanisms: Implications for Practitioners."
Health Promotion Practice 1, no. 1 (2000): 49-63.
doi:10.1177/152483990000100109.

Mclean, N., S. Griffin, K. Toney, and W. Hardeman. "Family Involvement in Weight Control, Weight Maintenance and Weight-loss Interventions: A Systematic Review of Randomised Trials." *International Journal of Obesity*27, no. 9 (2003): 987-1005. doi:10.1038/sj.ijo.0802383.

Robinson, Tanya. "Applying the Socio-ecological Model to Improving Fruit and Vegetable Intake Among Low-Income African Americans." *Journal of Community Health*33, no. 6 (2008): 395-406. doi:10.1007/s10900-008-9109-5.

Stokols, Daniel, Judd Allen, and Richard L. Bellingham. "The Social Ecology of Health Promotion: Implications for Research and Practice." *American Journal of Health Promotion*10, no. 4 (1996): 247-51. doi:10.4278/0890-1171-10.4.247.

"The Effects of Toxic Stress on Children | Henry Ford." Live-Well. February 21, 2019. Accessed June 15, 2019. https://henryfordlivewell.com/child-experiencing-toxic-stress/.

Valente, Thomas W., and Patchareeya Pumpuang. "Identifying Opinion Leaders to Promote Behavior Change." *Health Education & Behavior*34, no. 6 (2006): 881-96. doi:10.1177/1090198106297855.

Valente, T. W., and R. L. Davis. "Accelerating the Diffusion of Innovations Using Opinion Leaders." *The ANNALS of the American Academy of Political and Social Science*566, no. 1 (1999): 55-67. doi:10.1177/000271629956600105.

Chapter 17

"Podcast #329: Stick With It — The Science of Behavior Change." Interview. *Art of Manliness*(audio blog), August 10, 2017. Accessed June 12, 2019.

"Sean Young | Changing Your Life for Good with SCIENCE." Interview. *Www.jordanharbinger.com*(audio blog). Accessed June 12, 2019.

Fox, Jesse, and Jeremy N. Bailenson. "Virtual Self-Modeling: The Effects of Vicarious Reinforcement and Identification on Exercise Behaviors." *Media Psychology*12, no. 1 (2009): 1-25. doi:10.1080/15213260802669474.

Hershfield, Hal E., Daniel G. Goldstein, William F. Sharpe, Jesse Fox, Leo Yeykelis, Laura L. Carstensen, and Jeremy N. Bailenson. "Increasing Saving Behavior Through Age-Progressed Renderings of the Future Self." *Journal of*

*Marketing Research*48, no. SPL (2011). doi:10.1509/jmkr.48. spl.s23.

Houston, Jack. "A Psychologist Explains How Trader Joe's Gets You to Spend More Money." Business Insider. February 19, 2019. Accessed June 15, 2019. https://www. businessinsider.com/trader-joes-how-gets-you-spend-money-psychologist-2019-1.

Macrae, C. Neil, Jason P. Mitchell, Kirsten A. Tait, Diana L. Mcnamara, Marius Golubickis, Pavlos P. Topalidis, and Brittany M. Christian. "Turning I into Me: Imagining Your Future Self." *Consciousness and Cognition*37 (2015): 207-13. doi:10.1016/j.concog.2015.09.009.

Macrae, C. Neil, Jason P. Mitchell, Marius Golubickis, Nerissa S. P. Ho, Rain Sherlock, Raffaella Parlongo, Olivia C. M. Simpson, and Brittany M. Christian. "Saving for Your Future Self: The Role of Imaginary Experiences." Self and Identity 16, no. 4 (2016): 384-98. doi:10.1080/15298868.20 16.1264465.

Mitchell, Jason P., Jessica Schirmer, Daniel L. Ames, and Daniel T. Gilbert. "Medial Prefrontal Cortex Predicts Intertemporal Choice." *Journal of Cognitive Neuroscience*23, no. 4 (2011): 857-66. doi:10.1162/jocn.2010.21479.

Schultz, Colin. "Some People See Their Future-Selves as Strangers." Smithsonian.com. October 29, 2012. Accessed June 15, 2019. https://www.smithsonianmag.com/smart-news/some-people-see-their-future-selves-as-strangers-98378412/.

Schwartz, Barry. TED. Accessed June 15, 2019. https://www.
ted.com/talks/barry_schwartz_on_the_paradox_of_
choice?language=en.

Young, Sean. *Stick with It: A Scientifically Proven Process for
Changing Your Life -- for Good.* New York: Harper, 2018.

Chapter 18

"Health and Behavior Assessment and Intervention (HBAI)
Services Coverage of Chronic Disease Self-Management
Education Medicare and Medicare Advantage." National
Council on Aging. Accessed June 12, 2019.

"Managing Your Health in the Age of Wi-Fi." Mayo Clinic.
August 16, 2017. Accessed June 15, 2019. https://www.may-
oclinic.org/healthy-lifestyle/consumer-health/in-depth/
telehealth/art-20044878.

"Remarks by the President on Fiscal Policy." National
Archives and Records Administration. Accessed June 15,
2019. https://obamawhitehouse.archives.gov/the-press-
office/2011/04/13/remarks-president-fiscal-policy.

"3 Weight Loss Services Your Plan May Cover." WebMD.
Accessed June 15, 2019. https://blogs.webmd.com/public-
health/20150519/3-weight-loss-services-your-plan-may-
cover.

Gawande, Atul, and Atul Gawande. "The Cost Conundrum." The New Yorker. June 19, 2017. Accessed June 15,
2019. https://www.newyorker.com/magazine/2009/06/01/
the-cost-conundrum.

Goozner, Merrill. "Editorial: The Paradigm Is Shifting." Modern Healthcare. March 09, 2019. Accessed June 15, 2019. https://www.modernhealthcare.com/opinion-editorial/editorial-paradigm-shifting.

Norris, Louise. "What Do I Need to Know About Health Insurance Changes for 2019?" Verywell Health. December 25, 2018. Accessed June 15, 2019. https://www.verywellhealth.com/health-insurance-changes-facts-before-enrollment-4151694.

Chapter 19

"Corporate Wellness Market Worth $90.7 Billion By 2026 | CAGR 6.8%." Market Research Reports & Consulting. Accessed June 15, 2019. https://www.grandviewresearch.com/press-release/global-corporate-wellness-market.

"FastStats - Overweight Prevalence." Centers for Disease Control and Prevention. Accessed June 15, 2019. https://www.cdc.gov/nchs/fastats/obesity-overweight.htm.

"Industry Market Research, Reports, and Statistics." IBISWorld. Accessed June 15, 2019. https://www.ibisworld.com/industry-trends/specialized-market-research-reports/life-sciences/wellness-services/corporate-wellness-services.html.

"U.S.: Number of Full-time Workers in April 2019." Statista. Accessed June 15, 2019. https://www.statista.com/statistics/192361/unadjusted-monthly-number-of-full-time-employees-in-the-us/.

Badham, Peter FudaRichard. "Fire, Snowball, Mask, Movie: How Leaders Spark and Sustain Change." Harvard Business Review. August 01, 2014. Accessed June 15, 2019. https://hbr.org/2011/11/fire-snowball-mask-movie-how-leaders-spark-and-sustain-change.

Brown, Brené. *Daring Greatly: How the Courage to Be Vulnerable Transforms the Way We Live, Love, Parent, and Lead.* London: Penguin Life, 2015.

Forwardist. "A Brief History of the 8-hour Workday, Which Changed How Americans Work." CNBC. May 05, 2017. Accessed June 15, 2019. https://www.cnbc.com/2017/05/03/how-the-8-hour-workday-changed-how-americans-work.html.

Gallup, Inc. "In U.S., 40% Get Less Than Recommended Amount of Sleep." Gallup.com. Accessed June 15, 2019. https://news.gallup.com/poll/166553/less-recommended-amount-sleep.aspx.

Chapter 20

American Psychological Association. Accessed June 15, 2019. https://www.apa.org/pubs/journals/hea/.

Carrière, K., B. Khoury, M. M. Günak, and B. Knäuper. "Mindfulness-based Interventions for Weight Loss: A Systematic Review and Meta-analysis." *Obesity Reviews* 19, no. 2 (2017): 164-77. doi:10.1111/obr.12623.

Cullen, Margaret. "Mindfulness-Based Interventions: An Emerging Phenomenon." *Mindfulness*2, no. 3 (2011): 186-93. doi:10.1007/s12671-011-0058-1.

Epel, Elissa, Sherlyn Jimenez, Kelly Brownell, Laura Stroud, Catherine Stoney, and Ray Niaura. "Are Stress Eaters at Risk for the Metabolic Syndrome?" *Annals of the New York Academy of Sciences*1032, no. 1 (2004): 208-10. doi:10.1196/annals.1314.022.

Goyal, Madhav, Sonal Singh, Erica M. S. Sibinga, Neda F. Gould, Anastasia Rowland-Seymour, Ritu Sharma, Zackary Berger, Dana Sleicher, David D. Maron, Hasan M. Shihab, Padmini D. Ranasinghe, Shauna Linn, Shonali Saha, Eric B. Bass, and Jennifer A. Haythornthwaite. "Meditation Programs for Psychological Stress and Well-being." *JAMA Internal Medicine*174, no. 3 (2014): 357. doi:10.1001/jamainternmed.2013.13018.

Hạnh, Nhất. *Peace Is Every Step*. Bantam/AJP, 2013.

"Mindfulness." Merriam-Webster. Accessed June 15, 2019. https://www.merriam-webster.com/dictionary/mindfulness.

Oreilly, G. A., L. Cook, D. Spruijt-Metz, and D. S. Black. "Mindfulness-based Interventions for Obesity-related Eating Behaviours: A Literature Review." *Obesity Reviews*15, no. 6 (2014): 453-61. doi:10.1111/obr.12156.

Sally, Kempton. *Meditation for the Love of It: Enjoying Your Own Deepest Experience*. Place of Publication Not Identified: Readhowyouwant Com, 2012.

ACKNOWLEDGMENTS

It was not apparent to me that a life goal of mine was to write a book until a) I stumbled across the secret wish hidden amongst the words of early diary and journal entries and b) I physically started writing it. The book you are holding would not have been possible without the help of many others that I was lucky to have stumbled across on this journey we call life.

First and foremost, I'd like to thank my family. To my dad and sisters, Caroline and Meredith, thank you for your endless love and support while I traversed the throes of wavering confidence and questioning my sense of purpose- your words were exactly what I needed to hear in each moment. To all my loving grandparents, aunts, uncles, and cousins, I appreciate your excitement for my life and this venture. It was through you I was reaffirmed in my work.

Thank you to all my interviewees- without you, this book would not exist. I learned an incredible deal from each and every one of you and will carry forward the knowledge you instilled as I venture to form my own niche within the world of health and wellness.

To both my Michigan and high school friends, thank you for allowing me to share with you the ups and downs of the writing process. A special thank you to Kaela Theut- it was an incredible honor to write alongside you and soak up your beautiful flow of the English language- and Ivo Cerda-your intelligent mind constantly pushing me to refine my ideas and trust in myself.

To all my pre-ordered readers out there- you are incredible! Thank you for your dedication and support to helping make this book a reality. I hope with all my being you uncover something in these pages that can help you in your life.

I'd like to especially thank the people who invested more in my publishing and pre-ordered multiple copies of my book.

With special thanks to:

Crawford Robertson

Gretchen Hartwig

Jim Owens

Brian Sipotz

Susan and Tom Krisch

Garrett Sutton

Thad Wilhelm

Carole Oestreich

Dave Janks

Audrey Janks

Alex Janks

Greg and Susan Janks

Michelle Janks

Randy Dean

Thank you to everyone. Your financial support allowed me to transform countless pages of notes and interviews into the book you are about to read.

Lastly, a HUGE thank you to Eric Koester, Brian Bies, Stephanie McKibbon, NeKisha Wilkins, Mateusz Cichosz, and the rest of the team at New Degree Press. Your consistent motivation and support, coupled with the behind the scenes work of writing and publishing a book will never be forgotten.

www.ingramcontent.com/pod-product-compliance
Lightning Source LLC
Chambersburg PA
CBHW071520180526
45171CB00002B/318